Future Law, Ethics, and Smart Technologies

Value Inquiry Book Series

Founding Editor

Robert Ginsberg

Editor-in-Chief

J.D. Mininger

VOLUME 393

Philosophy and Human Rights

Series Editor

John-Stewart Gordon (*International Center for Ethics in the Sciences and Humanities, University of Tübingen, Germany*)

Editorial Board

The titles published in this series are listed at *brill.com/vibs* and *brill.com/phur*

Future Law, Ethics, and Smart Technologies

The Future of Legal Education

Edited by

John-Stewart Gordon

BRILL

LEIDEN | BOSTON

Cover illustration: Photo by John-Stewart Gordon.

The Library of Congress Cataloging-in-Publication Data is available online at https://catalog.loc.gov
LC record available at https://lccn.loc.gov/2023039366

Typeface for the Latin, Greek, and Cyrillic scripts: "Brill". See and download: brill.com/brill-typeface.

ISSN 2542-5153
ISBN 978-90-04-68291-7 (hardback)
ISBN 978-90-04-68290-0 (e-book)
DOI 10.1163/9789004682900

This book is printed on acid-free paper and produced in a sustainable manner.

Contents

Acknowledgements

The current textbook, *Future Law, Ethics, and Smart Technologies*, offers an extensive exploration of intricate topics bridging law, ethics, and smart technologies, specifically designed for students, with a focus on those studying law. It features contributions from an array of established experts and emerging scholars, hailing from diverse academic origins, including Lithuania, Germany, and Australia.

The contributors, in alphabetical order, are as follows: Darius Amilevičius (Vytautas Magnus University), Paulius Astromskis (Viliusis & Partners), Tomas Berkmanas (VMU), Paulius Čerka (VMU), Vladislav V. Fomin (Vilnius University), John-Stewart Gordon (Lithuanian University of Health Science), Edita Gruodytė (VMU), Julija Kiršienė (VMU), Deividas Kiršys (Mykolas Romeris University), Karolis Kubilevičius (VMU), Giedrė Kvedaravičienė (VMU), Kęstutis Mosakas (VMU), Sven Nyholm (Ludwig Maximilian University of Munich), Aušrinė Pasvenskienė (VMU), Adam Poulsen (University of Sydney), Milda Žaliauskaitė (VMU). I am very thankful to all these authors for their great work and their willingness to contribute an article to this volume. This research was part of the "Integration study of future law, ethics and intelligent technologies" project (No. 09.3.3-LMT-K-712-01-0173), being executed at Vytautas Magnus University. The research was funded by the European Social Fund under Measure No. 09.3.3-LMT-K-712, "Improvement of the qualification of researchers through high-level R&D projects."

I am grateful to Brill for expressing interest in including this book in the Philosophy and Human Rights subseries of the Value Inquiry Book Series and appreciate the exceptional support provided by the team at Brill during the final stages of the volume's development. Additionally, I extend my heartfelt thanks to the project members and my former PhD student, Kęstutis Mosakas, whose exceptional editorial assistance was invaluable to the project's success; without his help, I would have undoubtedly struggled with the finer details.

John-Stewart Gordon
International Center for Ethics in the Sciences and Humanities, University of Tübingen, Germany
Previously a professor at Vytautas Magnus University
May 2023

Figures and Tables

Figures

Tables

Notes on Contributors

Darius Amilevičius
is an associate professor at the Department of Informatics of Vytautas Magnus University and the head and chief researcher of the Machine Learning for Language research group at the Institute of Digital Resources and Interdisciplinary Research of Vytautas Magnus University. With over 20 years of experience in research and teaching, he is a member-supporter of Confederation of Laboratories for Artificial Intelligence research in Europe (CLAIRE), an expert of the Research Council of Lithuania, and a member of European AI Alliance and CLARIN ERIC. From 2017–2020, he served as an expert on the AI Think-Tank of the Ministry of Economics of Lithuania. His research interests cover artificial intelligence technologies and natural language technologies. He has extensive experience in developing and managing collaborative projects, including those funded by European Structural Funds, and has authored or co-authored over 25 scientific publications over the past 10 years.

Paulius Astromskis
is a technology lawyer, academic, and presenter with expertise in delivering legal solutions for clients across multiple tech sectors. He specializes in addressing corporate and compliance concerns for FinTech companies. His current research focuses on exploring technological solutions to legal challenges, regulating artificial intelligence, and examining the future of legal education.

Tomas Berkmanas
is an associate professor at the Faculty of Law of Vytautas Magnus University in Kaunas, Lithuania. His areas of specialization include legal philosophy and theory, constitutional law, professional ethics, and legal education. He served as the head of the Department of Private Law from 2008 until 2011, as the Vice-Dean for Research from 2011 until 2015, and as the dean of the Faculty of Law from 2015 until 2020. Tomas Berkmanas is the founder and Senior Editor of the Baltic Journal of Law & Politics, an expert of the Lithuanian Research Council, and a participant in various research and infrastructural projects. He is also an author of numerous journal and book articles and conference presentations.

Paulius Čerka
is a licensed attorney at law in Lithuania with a master's degree in law (2001) and a doctoral degree in social sciences (2004) from Vytautas Magnus University,

Lithuania. He is also an experienced lecturer, leading several courses at the Law School and Faculty of Economics and Management of Vytautas Magnus University. Additionally, he is an active participant in various business seminars on current topics for professional societies and the Lithuanian Auditors Association. Paulius Čerka regularly visits the Pegaso University of Naples and has been appointed by the Lithuanian government as a mediator in ICSID (2022), the world's leading institution devoted to international investment dispute settlement. His main areas of expertise include commercial litigation, mediation, international investment disputes, and taxation. He is fluent in both English and Russian.

Vladislav V. Fomin
is a Distinguished Professor at the Kaunas Faculty of Vilnius University and a visiting professor at the Faculty of Computing of the University of Latvia. Since earning his PhD degree in 2001 from the University of Jyväskylä in Finland, Vladislav Fomin has held academic positions at the University of Michigan in Ann Arbor, Copenhagen Business School, Delft University of Technology, Montpellier Business School, Rotterdam School of Management, and Vytautas Magnus University in Lithuania. In 2021, Vladislav was Fulbright Research Scholar at the Weatherhead School of Management, Case Western Reserve University in Cleveland, OH. Prof. Fomin has authored over 100 scientific publications in journals, conferences, and as book chapters, including *Information Systems Research*, *Academy of Management Proceedings*, *Technology Forecasting and Social Change*, *Journal of Strategic Information Systems*, *Communications of the Association for Information Systems*, *International Journal of IT Standards & Standardization Research*, *Telecommunications Policy*, *Knowledge, Technology & Policy*. His conference publications and presentations include Academy of Management, The International Conference on Information Systems, European Conference on Information systems, Hawaii International Conference on System Sciences, and others.

John-Stewart Gordon
is an adjunct professor at LSMU in Kaunas, Lithuania (since 2022). Before, he was a full professor of philosophy (2015–2022), chief researcher at the Faculty of Law (2018–2022), founder and head of the Research Cluster for Applied Ethics (2016–2022), and principal investigator of the EU-funded research project "Integration Study on Future Law, Ethics, and Smart Technologies" (2017–2022) at Vytautas Magnus University in Kaunas, Lithuania. Furthermore, he is an associate editor at *AI & Society* (since 2020), a member of the editorial boards of *Bioethics* (since 2007), *AI & Society* (since 2018), the *Baltic Journal of*

Law & Politics (2018–2022), and he has been an area-editor and board member of the Internet Encyclopedia of Philosophy (2007–2014). Furthermore, he is the general editor of the book series *Philosophy and Human Rights* at Brill. John spent extended research stays at the universities of Queen's, Oxford (multiple times), Toronto, Maynooth, Tallinn (multiple times), the Karolinska Institut in Stockholm, and the Academy of International Affairs NRW in Bonn. He has written and edited numerous books in the context of practical philosophy and published many peer-reviewed articles and special issues in leading international journals and encyclopedias.

Edita Gruodytė
is a tenured professor and Vice-Dean for Research at the Faculty of Law in Vytautas Magnus University. She has also worked as an attorney at law for 15 years. With over 20 years of experience in participating in various national and international projects, scientific activities, and research, she has been a member of several public bodies, including the Permanent Commission for the Assessment of Activities of Judges, prosecutors' ethical commission, ECLAN (European Criminal Law Academic Network), and prosecutors' attestation committee. She is also an editor of the Scopus journal *Baltic Journal of Law and Politics* and the chief editor of the legal journal *Law Review/Teisės apžvalga*. Professor Gruodytė is the author or co-author of various books and scientific articles and has successful experience in supervising PhD students. Her research interests include national and European criminal law and procedure, human rights, legal ethics and professionalism, and law and technologies.

Julija Kiršienė
is the Vice-Rector for Research at Vytautas Magnus University. She is also a professor in the Department of Private Law. She has served as a member of several public bodies, including the Judicial Court of Honor at National Courts Administration of Lithuania, Management Board of European Union Fundamental Rights Agency (FRA), and as the chairperson of the board of Kaunas Science and Technology Park. She is the author and co-author of more than 50 scientific articles and books. Her research interests include contract law, tort law, law and technologies, legal ethics and professionalism, and human rights.

Deividas Kiršys
is a PhD candidate at Mykolas Romeris University. His scientific interests are related to the contemporary and future influence of innovations on law, ethics,

society, and policymaking. He is currently researching the legal impact of drones on private law.

Karolis Kubilevičius
is a PhD candidate at the Faculty of Law at Vytautas Magnus University in Kaunas, Lithuania. His research interests include constitutional law, human right law, technology law, and European Union law. As a legal practitioner, he also specializes in civil law. Karolis has authored and co-authored various scientific articles and has experience as a lecturer and participant of various research initiatives.

Giedrė Kvedaravičienė
EMBA, is a health innovation expert with an interest in economic and applied ethics research and advocacy. She is an alumna of the USA government funded IVLP program (2008), a Fulbright grantee (2022) at the Johns Hopkins University, and a PhD candidate in economics at Vytautas Magnus University. With extensive professional experience in healthcare, Ms. Kvedaravičienė has held top-level management positions in private healthcare and has worked in public affairs and government relations. She has represented the global medical device industry as Digital Health Director at COCIR in EU-level policy making. Ms. Kvedaravičienė has also served as a board member and vice-chair of the American Chamber of Commerce in Lithuania from 2008 to 2022, leading the Life Sciences and Health Committee at AmCham Lithuania. She continues to support young professionals as a mentor in the Enterprise Lithuania and MITA (Agency for Science, Innovation and Technology) programs in Lithuania.

Kęstutis Mosakas
is a junior researcher at the Faculty of Law of Vytautas Magnus University. He also worked as a junior researcher in the EU-funded research project "Integration study on Future Law, Ethics, and Smart Technologies" (2018–2022), was the research assistant of the Research Cluster for Applied Ethics (VMU, 2017–2023), and taught classes on applied ethics and philosophy of technology (VMU). Since 2023, he has been an associate editorial board member for the journal *AI & Society*. Kęstutis holds a bachelor's degree in English philology (2013, VMU), master's degree in practical philosophy (2017, VMU), and a PhD in philosophy (2023, VMU). His main fields of research are applied ethics and ethics of technology (moral status and rights of robots in particular), with his secondary areas of interest being meta-ethics, philosophy of mind, and philosophy of religion.

Sven Nyholm
is Professor of the Ethics of Artificial Intelligence at the Ludwig Maximilian University of Munich. He is also an associate editor of the journal *Science and Engineering Ethics*. Before taking up his current position in Germany, Nyholm worked for several years in the Netherlands. He was born in Sweden in 1981, studied philosophy and musicology at Lund University, and then completed his PhD at the University of Michigan in the USA. Nyholm's research covers a wide range of topics within ethics and applied ethics. His articles have appeared in general philosophy journals, bioethics journals, and technology ethics journals. He is the author of three books: *Revisiting Kant's Universal Law and Humanity Formulas* (De Gruyter, 2015), *Humans and Robots: Ethics, Agency, and Anthropomorphism* (Rowman & Littlefield, 2020), and *This is Technology Ethics: An Introduction* (Wiley-Blackwell, 2023).

Aušrinė Pasvenskienė
is the vice-dean of the Faculty of Law at Vytautas Magnus University (VMU). She is an associate professor and researcher at the VMU Faculty of Law and Education Academy and an expert at the European Association of Education Law and Policy (Antwerp, Belgium). Her research interests include law and technologies, fintech, education technologies, education law, and human rights in education.

Adam Poulsen
is a research fellow and computer scientist at the University of Sydney in New South Wales, Australia. His research covers human-computer interaction, co-design, diversity and inclusion, vulnerable communities, applied ethics, and healthcare and social technologies. At present, Adam primarily focuses on exploring the co-design of technologies to support education and socio-emotional and cognitive development in culturally diverse low-and middle-income countries. Previously, through his research, Adam developed a novel value sensitive design approach, values in motion design, to model social robots for members of the older LGBTIQ+ community experiencing loneliness. He has conducted extensive research addressing the disability community and the older population, including those living with dementia, to advance equity in healthcare technology design and social service provision. Adam holds a PhD from Charles Sturt University, Australia.

Milda Žaliauskaitė
is a PhD student at Vytautas Magnus University, Faculty of Law, who is preparing a dissertation on "The Concept of Advance Will in Private Law: Balancing

between Public and Private Interests." Milda Žaliauskaitė has a master's degree in law and a master's degree in business and management. She has also studied at Michigan State University (MSU) College of Law and received an MSU Certificate in Transnational Law. Her scientific interests include private law, particularly contract law, health law, including mental health and disability law, technology law, and other related fields. Milda Žaliauskaitė has authored various publications on advance will, the right to autonomy, the rights of persons with special needs, and other related topics. Additionally, Milda Žaliauskaitė is an actively practicing lawyer, mainly in the field of private law. She is currently the head of the Legal Department, a lecturer at Vytautas Magnus University, and a lawyer in private practice. Milda Žaliauskaitė periodically participates in various scientific and management national and international projects.

CHAPTER 1

General Introduction

John-Stewart Gordon

1.1 The Future of Legal Education

The edited volume *Future Law, Ethics, and Smart Technologies* is a comprehensive textbook for students, particularly law students, who want to become familiar with the complex issues at the intersection of law, ethics, and smart technologies. The impact of artificial intelligence (AI) on law is substantial given that it thoroughly permeates human life. The ever-increasing technological developments in the context of AI, computer science, and robotics have not only profoundly shaped our societies but have also posed substantial challenges to our national and international legal systems (Gordon 2020a). Some of the better-known examples are autonomous systems (transportation, weapons), machine bias in law, electronic personhood, the so-called black box problem, the problem of transparency, and the demands for explainability. The mentioned examples are a great concern and a significant challenge for the legal field (Gordon 2021b; Kurki 2019).

Only recently have people working in the legal profession as academics, practitioners (lawyers, attorneys, and judges), and policymakers fully realized the significant impact of AI on law (Gordon 2021b; Nissan 2017; McGinnis and Pearce 2014; Surden 2014). To deal with the new situation, it is necessary to revise the existing legal curricula and promote the professional development of people currently working in the legal sector (Pasvenskiene and Astromskis 2020). To underestimate the impact of AI on law or to think that one could continue to practice law without a proper understanding of the new technologies endangers human lives and undermines the very nature of law itself.

This textbook serves as a solid introduction to the issues mentioned above, with contributions by colleagues from different disciplines (e.g., law, philosophy/ethics, economy, and computer science) whose common interest concerns AI and its impact on legal and ethical issues. The book provides, first, a general overview of the effects of AI on major disciplines such as ethics, law, economy, political science, and healthcare. Second, it offers a comprehensive analysis of major key issues concerning law: (a) AI decision making, (b) rights, status, and responsibility, (c) regulation and standardization, and (d) education. Third, it contains three different guidelines: (a) Guidelines for the

 | DOI:10.1163/9789004682900_002

regulation of information technologies (IT), (b) Guidelines for the regulation of robotics (ethics), and (c) Guidelines for the improvement of the lawyers' qualification (law).

This general introduction reflects, at least to some extent, the approach of this edited volume by providing a brief overview of AI's impact on law on one hand and, on the other hand, offering some general remarks on how to adjust current legal education to respond to the significant challenges presented by AI.

1.2 AI's Impact on Law

The following four issues can be seen as the most persisting AI problems in the legal context. There is no easy solution concerning these very fundamental problems. In the following discussion, I will only offer a very brief overview of the four examples, since they will be sufficiently analyzed in the textbook. However, it is important to mention them at the outset to prepare the readers for the main topic of this book, namely how to revise legal education given the far-reaching impact of AI on the law.

1.2.1 *Autonomous Systems: Moral and Legal Responsibility*

Autonomous systems are not only built into self-driving cars, buses, trucks, public trains and even planes but are also used in the military (e.g., drones, underwater vehicles, and at some future point robot soldiers), in sex robots, as vacuum cleaners, and as a supporting tool for decision making in law in the US. The widespread implementation of autonomous systems in our work world and private life causes substantial ethical and legal problems regarding moral and legal responsibility in cases of harm caused by these systems. Who is responsible in such cases? The autonomous machine, the user, the programmer, or the company that sells the machines? Or do all parties share responsibility in these cases?

Of course, not all autonomous machines have the same capabilities. Therefore, ethical and legal responsibility differs from case to case, particularly concerning the fields of application. An autonomous vacuum cleaner usually cannot cause any severe harm to other human beings (though insects might be killed in the operating process). In contrast, malfunctioning self-driving cars can become a deadly weapon threatening passengers and other traffic participants. Therefore, the technical requirements and safety precautions concerning their proper functioning are incredibly high. But what is if a self-driving car causes property damage or harm to other people? Who is morally and legally responsible? And who must pay for damages or injury done to other traffic participants in cases where the autonomous system fails (Nyholm and Smids 2016)?

Many autonomous machines operate unsupervised after successful programming and training. However, in numerous cases, particularly highly complex situations (e.g., driving a car or military operations), some people argue that one should adhere to the human-in-the-loop approach that requires human interaction for final decisions. This would solve the problem of moral and legal responsibility, given that a human being is responsible for the final decision. Still, it also contradicts the very idea of using fully autonomous systems in the first place. They are built to take on human tasks that either are burdensome because they are dull and monotonous, or are quite dangerous (e.g., warfare), or make life easier for millions of users (e.g., self-driving cars). Hence, the human-in-the-loop approach would undermine the very goal of using such systems in the first place, at least to some extent.

It has been suggested, however, to either (a) provide the most sophisticated autonomous systems with legal personhood to solve the issue of legal liability in cases of damages or harms done (e.g., in the context of self-driving cars), or (b) to offer special insurance for autonomous machines that covers any damages caused by such systems. Both approaches seem reasonable, but they depend on the technological sophistication of the particular autonomous machine. At this moment, it seems rather far-fetched to provide autonomous systems with legal personhood, since they currently lack the relevant cognitive capabilities (Gordon 2020b). Therefore, offering special insurance for autonomous systems might be the best option at this time.

1.2.2 *Machine Bias*[1]

Many people believe that smart technologies would end human bias because of machines' supposed "neutrality." However, we have realized that machines may maintain and even substantiate human bias toward women, different ethnicities, the elderly, people with medical impairments, or other groups (Kraemer et al. 2011; Mittelstadt et al. 2016). Consequently, one of the most urgent questions in the context of machine learning is how to avoid machine bias (Daniels et al. 2019). The idea of using AI systems to support human decision making is, in general, an excellent objective given AI's "increased efficiency, accuracy, scale and speed in making decisions and finding the best answers" (World Economic Forum 2018, 6). However, machine bias can undermine this

1 This section is slightly revised from my Encyclopedia entry (Gordon and Nyholm 2021).

seemingly positive situation in various ways. Some striking cases of machine bias are as follows:

1. Gender bias in hiring (Dastin 2018)
2. Racial bias in that certain racial groups are offered only particular types of jobs (Sweeney 2013)
3. Racial bias in decisions on the creditworthiness of loan applicants (Ludwig 2015)
4. Racial bias in decisions whether to release prisoners on parole (Angwin et al. 2016)
5. Racial bias in predicting criminal activities in urban areas (O'Neil 2016)
6. Sexual bias when identifying a person's sexual orientation (Wang and Kosinski 2018)
7. Racial bias in facial recognition systems that prefer lighter skin colors (Buolamwini and Gebru 2018)
8. Racial and social bias in using the geographic location of a person's residence as a proxy for ethnicity or socio-economic status (Veale and Binns 2017)

We can recognize at least three reasons for machine bias: (a) data bias, (b) computational or algorithmic bias, and (c) outcome bias (Springer et al. 2018, 451). First, a machine learning system trained using data that contain implicit or explicit imbalances reinforces the distortion in the data concerning any future decision making, thereby making the bias systematic. Second, a program may suffer from algorithmic bias due to the developer's implicit or explicit biases. The design of a program relies on the developer's understanding of the normative and non-normative values of other people, including the users and stakeholders affected by it (Dobbe et al. 2018). Third, outcome bias could be based on historical records, for example, to predict criminal activities in certain particular urban areas; the system may allocate more police to a specific location, resulting in an increase in reported cases that would have been unnoticed before. This logic would substantiate the AI system's decision to allocate the police to this area, even though other urban areas may have similar or even greater numbers of crimes, more of which would go unreported due to the lack of policing (O'Neil 2016).

Most AI researchers, programmers, and developers, as well as scholars working in the field of technology, believe that we will never be able to design a fully unbiased system. Therefore, the focus is on reducing machine bias and minimizing its detrimental effects on human beings. Nevertheless, various questions remain. What type of bias cannot be filtered out, and when should we be satisfied with the remaining bias? What does it mean for a person in court to be subject to human bias and machine bias, with both forms of injustice potentially helping to determine their sentence? Is one type of bias not enough? Should we not rather aim to eliminate human bias instead of introducing a new type?

1.2.3 *Electronic Personhood*

Electronic or artificial personhood is the idea that artificial machines may, at some point, become so intelligent and autonomous that they would be considered morally and legally responsible for their actions. The European Parliament's Resolution on Civil Law Rules on Robotics (CLRR) and its recommendation to the European Commission (2017) substantiate that the ideas of (a) providing legal status to robots and (b) granting the most sophisticated robots "electronic personhood" are already under serious consideration by policymakers (Gordon 2021a, sec. 1). In §59 f. of the CLRR, the European Parliament suggests the following legal invention:

> Creating a specific legal status for robots in the long run, so that at least the most sophisticated autonomous robots could be established as having the status of electronic persons responsible for making good any damage they may cause, and possibly applying electronic personality to cases where robots make autonomous decisions or otherwise interact with third parties independently.

Various experts have substantially questioned this initiative. In particular, "a group of AI and robotics experts, industry leaders, and specialists from the fields of law, medicine, and ethics drafted" the *Open Letter to the European Commission: Artificial Intelligence and Robotics*[2] in response to the CLRR. They claimed that the idea of granting machines electronic personhood was based on misleading ethical, legal, and technological assumptions about the true capabilities of current machines (Gordon 2021a, sec. 2). Although it is undoubtedly true that existing machines are not persons, it is correct to think about these issues properly in advance to be prepared for and avoid any problems once we see the advent of such highly sophisticated machines. The idea of artificial moral and legal personhood has been discussed in detail by, for example, Gordon (2021a).

2 The Open Letter can be found at http://www.robotics-openletter.eu/.

In October 2017, the humanoid robot Sophia developed by Hanson Robotics officially became a Saudi Arabian honorary citizen. Though supporters claim this is justified given her extraordinary autonomous nature and human-like capabilities, most experts believe her capabilities are immensely overrated and that Saudi Arabia's motivation for granting Sophia honorary citizenship was nothing more than a publicity campaign for the country.[3]

But is there anything like *electronic* personhood? What are the necessary criteria for moral and legal personhood? Does electronic or artificial personhood require consciousness? And if so, will it ever be possible to build conscious machines that could be held responsible for their actions (Mosakas 2021)? In moral philosophy, there is a long-standing debate about the concept of personhood and its relation to the question of moral status (Clarke et al. 2021; Warren 1997; concerning AI, see Gordon and Gunkel 2022). According to the standard view, a being has full moral status and hence enjoys moral and legal protection if it is *sapient*. Sapience refers to a set of cognitive abilities that a being should have in order to be regarded as a person; for example, such a being should be rational, intelligent, autonomous, self-aware, and conscious. The typical adult human being is a person. Whether human beings with severe cognitive impairments, infants, or the great apes should be considered persons is a matter of serious debate in philosophy (Singer 2009). According to this view, a robot could become a person if it meets the above-mentioned relevant criteria (Gordon 2020b). Whether this is technologically possible is again a matter of debate among experts.

In addition, some experts argue that it is possible to regard even current robots as legal persons depending on the legal requirement[4] for personhood (Darling 2016). For example, corporations are commonly considered legal persons, which could be seen, according to some scholars, as a possible starting point to think about legal personhood for robots too. The problem with this view is that corporations are eventually run by real people and do not exist independently of human beings. They are created by human beings, run by human beings, and can be shut down by human beings. This is different for

---

3 There is a difference between honorary citizenship and ordinary citizenship. The first does not replicate the rights and privileges of the latter. In other words, Sophia—unless stated in the national laws of the particular country—does not have, e.g., a Saudi Arabian passport, the right to reside in the country, or to enjoy the rights, protections and freedoms related to ordinary Saudi Arabian citizenship. Usually, honorary citizenship is symbolic and granted because of admiration for something worthy of a particular distinction.

4 For example, some scholars may base their legal reasoning on Bryant Smith's (1928) view that everything can become a legal person, which "facilitates regulation".

highly sophisticated robots that match or supersede human-like capabilities in the mid-term or long-term future (Kurzweil 2005; Bostrom 2014). If they meet the relevant criteria for moral personhood, then they are automatically entitled to the related legal rights that come with it (Gordon 2020b). These and related issues are discussed in several chapters of this book.

1.2.4 *AI and Legal Decision Making*

Not only do law firms implement AI in the process of their work, but AI applications have also become quite common in support of judges' decisions, particularly in the US, regarding whether to release prisoners on parole (see above). Some people believe that, at some future point, we will even see the advent of artificial judges, attorneys, and lawyers. This belief is not unjustified. For example, autonomous transportation started with support systems intended to guide people in driving their car—that is, to make driving safer. Now we are nearing the advent of fully autonomous driving.

Analogously, one could claim, the legal profession will introduce AI to receive support with various levels of legal decision making and eventually the legal profession will see the advent of fully autonomous artificial lawyers and judges who sentence human beings, at least sometime in the future (this is no science fiction anymore). Many people believe that AI is the savior for most of our problems, particularly in the law regarding fair and objective decision making. Human beings (including judges) have biases that might undermine fair legal judgments. To avoid this, it is argued that one should aim to replace human judges with artificial ones. Is that a good idea? Should we, in general, strive to implement AI in law without hesitation?

We have already seen in the previous section on machine bias (sec. 1.2.2) that AI is prone to bias and may reinforce or even exacerbate the situation of biased decision making. If such a system is widely used in law, everything becomes worse, not better. Unless we are not sure about machine bias in law, we are morally obligated to have the human-in-the-loop to avoid worse outcomes. Furthermore, machine learning, neural networks, and quantum computing often surprise us with unforeseen (and often positive) results in many areas of their application (e.g., Big Data). However, most cases cannot be adequately explained, since current AI systems have become "black boxes." This is a problem concerning legal decision making. Legal decisions must be transparent and clear, in particular when it comes to judging. How did the AI system arrive at its legal recommendation? This is an important issue that must be resolved sufficiently before one can use AI in judging, or in any legal decision making for that matter. Law requires a trustworthy AI.

Moreover, when judging, the human judge's most significant advantages are his general knowledge about human nature and his common-sense knowledge, which often play an essential part in judging. Current AI systems are still (and most probably will remain for the next few decades) unable to come to grips with both issues. Whether current AI systems in law can show mercy against the background of extenuating circumstances might be reasonably called into question. Understanding a particular situation often requires knowledge about human nature and common-sense knowledge. A good judge has both of these; a poor judge only follows the strictness of law independently of any extenuating circumstances. In his main ethical writing, the *Nicomachean Ethics*, Aristotle once claimed that going to the judge is tantamount to going to justice itself. Whether this is also true for an AI judge remains an open question.

1.2.5 *The Upshot*

The implementation of AI in law will substantially impact how the legal profession develops, and not only concerning the significant changes in legal education and how legal decisions are made on the job. Of course, there are many advantages when using AI in law, particularly regarding the rather tedious work that requires only some legal expertise. On the other hand, there are quite a few problems with implementing AI in law, as seen in the previous sections. The trick is that we should always be aware of such systems' current capabilities and pitfalls. The final say should remain with human beings—at least, for now. The next part will introduce some ideas on how one could prepare the legal profession to better adapt to the significant changes that AI systems present for our societies and the law.

1.3 Remarks on Adjusting Legal Education to AI's Challenges

Experts widely agree that AI poses significant challenges to the law in general and to the legal profession in particular. Therefore, it is of utmost importance to revise existing forms of legal education to help members of the legal profession (a) to properly understand the complex issues caused by the widespread implementation of AI in our living world and (b) to empower them to deal with the new situation accordingly. There are, at least, two main ways to put this into practice: first, one must change the existing legal curricula, and second, one should offer (compulsory) advanced training for members of the legal profession. Both strategies help to secure the continued existence of fair and just lawyering and judging in the legal profession. Below, I will provide some brief remarks on addressing these issues in practice.

1.3.1 *Revising the Legal Curriculum*

There are at least three different starting points to change the existing legal curricula, which will be briefly mentioned below.

1.3.1.1 Introducing Obligatory Courses on Smart Technologies and AI

1.3.1.1.1 *The Interdisciplinarity of Law*

It is of great significance to revise the study of law so that legal studies become interdisciplinary. By introducing computer science, robotics, and ethics into the legal curriculum, it is possible to raise the appropriate awareness of problems caused by AI. The goal, however, is not to turn lawyers into computer scientists or ethicists but, instead, to provide students with sufficient knowledge to understand and appreciate the important issues that arise as we implement AI in society.

1.3.1.1.2 *Tech Skills or Expertise as a Duty*

Law students should be required to have a sufficient understanding of technological contexts concerning AI and law. To achieve this, students should attend introductory courses in the relevant disciplines such as computer science, informatics, and ethics to gain enough knowledge to become better lawyers in the future.

1.3.1.1.3 *The Nature of AI*

The compulsory courses on smart technologies should provide law students with the ability to understand the challenges and pitfalls of AI in general (Gordon 2020c) and how they impact the legal profession in particular. Only if one understands the nature of AI, at least to some extent, can one adequately see the underlying problems caused by the widespread implementation of AI in society, which will provide the basis for fair and just lawyering and judging.

1.3.1.2 Raising Awareness and Understanding of Ethical Issues Concerning AI and Law

Of course, it is not the goal to turn law students into professional ethicists. Still, it is essential to empower them to determine the relevant ethical issues at the intersection of AI and law (e.g., machine bias, racial profiling). This is not an easy task. To accomplish this goal, it is not sufficient for students to just attend one introductory course on ethics; instead, analogously to the education of professional clinical ethics consultants, substantial training is needed that undergirds the competence of the involved person in legal decision making. The future lawyer is an *interdisciplinary* lawyer whose competence and skills go far beyond her legal profession.

The application of law requires lawyers to understand the world around them properly. A technologically advanced society is fundamentally different from a rural society whose members are not directly threatened by the impact of AI. The more complex a society is, the higher the stakes are for fair and just lawyering and judging. A rural society without cars does not have to be competent in the complexities of autonomous transportation, legal responsibilities, different insurance schemes, and adequate laws to govern all the aforementioned issues.

To meet this ethical challenge and become proficient in ethical issues caused by AI, law students should attend regular classes on ethics, AI, and computer science that are tailored to meet their educational needs so that they can become better lawyers, attorneys, and judges.

1.3.1.3 Legal Explainability

Current members of the legal profession—and even more so future lawyers—should be aware of the problems involved in introducing AI in the context of legal decision making (e.g., machine bias). Advanced AI systems are like black boxes that do not provide the user with an explanation of a given outcome or a history of steps in decision making. However, the process is different in legal decision making so as to uphold trustworthiness in the legal system. For example, a person has the right to understand *why* he is sentenced or denied a loan from the bank. In other words, members of the legal profession must know when to trust and not to trust AI support systems in the context of legal decision making. Otherwise, members of the legal profession will be playing with the lives of their fellow citizens without paying proper respect to the issues raised by AI.

1.3.2 *Obligatory Advanced Training for Lawyers, Attorneys, and Judges*

What should members of the legal profession do if they already work in their field of expertise but lack additional training concerning AI and law? It is of utmost importance for all members of the legal profession who have responsibilities in society, particularly the practitioners of law such as judges and attorneys, to attend compulsory advanced training courses to avoid participating in unfair and unjust rulings. To meet their special educational needs, one must prepare adequate interdisciplinary courses—including online options—to help them properly understand the complexities regarding AI and law. One cannot judge correctly in modern, highly technologically advanced societies with the means and standards of yesterday.

For example, suppose that a judge cannot understand the problems caused by AI concerning law and legal decision making. In that case, he will become more and more incapable of judging correctly and his work will be undermined, with resulting injustices analogous to machine bias in law. Ultimately, society should be prepared to replace such members of the legal profession when they endanger their fellow citizens' lives by their lack of expertise and understanding, which could eventually cause severe harm to others.

1.4 Conclusions

This textbook helps law students and members of the legal profession to understand and appreciate the problems in the context of AI and law. The legal profession must change to adapt to the impact of AI on modern society in general and on law in particular. Soon, we will see a new type of lawyer emerge: the *interdisciplinary lawyer*. We hope that the chapters in this book will contribute to this greatly needed transition.

References

Angwin, J., J. Larson, S. Mattu, and L. Kirchner. 2016. "Machine Bias." *ProPublica*. https://www.propublica.org/article/machine-bias-risk-assessments-in-criminal-sentencing.

Bostrom, N. 2014. *Superintelligence: Paths, Dangers, Strategies*. Oxford University Press.

Buolamwini, J., and T. Gebru. 2018. "Gender Shades: Intersectional Accuracy Disparities in Commercial Gender Classification." *Proceedings of the 1st Conference on Fairness, Accountability, and Transparency*, PMLR 81, 77–91.

Clarke, S., H. Zohny and J. Savulescu. 2021. *Rethinking Moral Status*. Oxford University Press.

Daniels, J., M. Nkonde, and D. Mir. 2019. *Advancing Racial Literacy in Tech*. https://datasociety.net/output/advancing-racial-literacy-in-tech/.

Darling, K. 2016. "Extending Legal Protection to Social Robots: the Effects of Anthropomorphism, Empathy, and Violent Behavior towards Robotic Objects." In *Robot Law*, edited by R. Calo, A. M. Froomkin, and I. Kerr, 213–34. Edward Elgar.

Dastin, J. 2018. "Amazon Scraps Secret AI Recruiting Tool That Showed Bias Against Women." Reuters, October 10. https://www.reuters.com/article/us-amazon-com-jobs-automation-insight/amazon-scraps-secret-ai-recruiting-tool-that-showed-bias-against-women-idUSKCN1MK08G.

Dobbe, R., S. Dean, T. Gilbert, and N. Kohli. 2018. "A Broader View on Bias in Automated Decision-Making: Reflecting on Epistemology and Dynamics." *2018 Workshop*

on Fairness, Accountability and Transparency in Machine Learning during ICML, Stockholm, Sweden (July 18 version). https://arxiv.org/abs/1807.00553.
Gordon, J.-S., and D. Gunkel. 2022. "Moral Status and Intelligent Robots." The *Southern Journal of Philosophy* 60(1): 88–117.
Gordon, J.-S., and S. Nyholm. 2021. "The Ethics of Artificial Intelligence." *Internet Encyclopedia of Philosophy*. https://iep.utm.edu/ethics-of-artificial-intelligence/.
Gordon, J.-S. 2021a. "Artificial Moral and Legal Personhood." *AI & Society* 36: 457–71.
Gordon, J.-S. 2021b. "AI and Law: Ethical, Legal, and Socio-political Implications." *AI & Society* 36(2): 403–668. (special issue).
Gordon, J.-S. 2020c. "Building Moral Machines: Ethical Pitfalls and Challenges." *Science and Engineering Ethics* 26: 141–57.
Gordon, J.-S. 2020b. "What Do We Owe to Intelligent Robots?" *AI & Society* 35: 209–23.
Gordon, J.-S. 2020a. *Smart Technologies and Fundamental Rights*. Brill and Rodopi.
Kraemer, F., K. Van Overveld, and M. Peterson. 2011. "Is There an Ethics of Algorithms?" *Ethics and Information Technology* 13: 251–60.
Kurki, V. 2019. *A Theory of Legal Personhood*. Oxford University Press.
Kurzweil, R. 2005. *The Singularity Is Near*. Penguin Books.
Ludwig, S. 2015. "Credit Scores in America Perpetuate Racial Injustice: Here's How." *The Guardian*, October 13. https://www.theguardian.com/commentisfree/2015/oct/13/your-credit-score-is-racist-heres-why.
Mittelstadt, B., P. Allo, M. Taddeo, S. Wachter, and L. Floridi. 2016. "The Ethics of Algorithms: Mapping the Debate." *Big Data and Society* 3(2).
Mosakas, K. 2021. "On the Moral Status of Social Robots: Considering the Consciousness Criterion." *AI & Society* 36(2): 429–43.
Nissan, E. 2017. "Digital Technologies and Artificial Intelligence's Present and Foreseeable Impact on Lawyering, Judging, Policing and Law Enforcement." *AI & Society* 32(3): 441–64.
Nyholm, S., and J. Smids. 2016. "The Ethics of Accident-Algorithms for Self-Driving Cars: an Applied Trolley Problem?" *Ethical Theory and Moral Practice* 19(5): 1275–89.
O'Neil, C. 2016. *Weapons of Math Destruction*. Allen Lane.
Pasvenskiene, A., and P. Astromskis. 2020. "The Future of Legal Education: Do Law Schools have the Right to be Conservative?" *Baltic Journal of Law & Politics* 13(1): 191–217.
Pearce, R., and J. Mcginnis. 2014. "The Great Disruption: How Machine Intelligence Will Transform the Role of Lawyers in the Delivery of Legal Services." *Fordham Law Review* 82(6): 3041–3066.
Singer, P. 2009. "Speciesism and Moral Status." *Metaphilosophy* 40(3–4): 567–81.
Smith, B. 1928. "Legal Personality." *Yale Law Journal* 37(3): 283–99.
Sweeney, L. 2013. "Discrimination in Online Ad Delivery." *Acmqueue* 11(3): 1–19.

Springer, A., J. Garcia-Gathright, and H. Cramer. 2018. "Assessing and Addressing Algorithmic Bias—But Before We Get There." *2018 AAAI Spring Symposium Series*, 450–54. https://www.aaai.org/ocs/index.php/SSS/SSS18/paper/viewPaper/17542.

Surden, H. 2014. "Machine Learning and Law." *Washington Law Review* 89(1): 87–115.

Wang, Y., and M. Kosinski. 2018. "Deep Neural Networks Are More Accurate Than Humans at Detecting Sexual Orientation from Facial Images." *Journal of Personality and Social Psychology* 114(2): 246–57.

Warren, M. A. 1997. *Moral Status: Obligations to Persons and Other Living Things*. Clarendon Press.

Veale, M., and R. Binns. 2017. "Fairer Machine Learning in the Real World: Mitigating Discrimination without Collecting Sensitive Data." *Big Data and Society* 4(2).

World Economic Forum and Global Future Council on Human Rights. 2018. *How to Prevent Discriminatory Outcomes in Machine Learning* (white paper). http://www3.weforum.org/docs/WEF_40065_White_Paper_How_to_Prevent_Discriminatory_Outcomes_in_Machine_Learning.pdf.

PART 1

The Impact of AI on Major Disciplines

Introduction to Part 1

It would be difficult to overstate the impact AI is making (and continues to make) on some of the most important domains of human life. Human capabilities such as reason, perception, planning, communication, and complex decision making, are now effectively simulated by machines (both physical and virtual ones),[1] whereas the broad scope of application of these capacities, generally subsumed by the catch-all term "intelligence," is what makes AI so universal. Moreover, AI is ubiquitous—pieces of software can be copied and duplicated, whereas physically embodied AI-based machines that we commonly refer to as "robots" can be mass-produced in factories. And with computing power becoming ever so cheap and so plentiful—and still dramatically growing in efficiency and availability[2]—we have every reason to believe that the future of humanity will be inseparable from and will be significantly shaped by AI.

The goal of this part is to outline the impact AI has had on some of the major areas of interest—namely, ethics, law, economy, political sciences, and healthcare—and present some likely expectations for the future. The part first covers ethics, a philosophical enterprise concerned with the fundamental value questions (e.g., what is the good life, the right action, justice). The ethics of AI is a sub-branch of ethics that attempts to ensure that the development and utilization of AI systems occur in line with our fundamental values and principles. Chapter 2 covers some of the main ethical challenges brought by AI, such as privacy, machine bias, ethical programming, artificial moral agency, robot rights, and the possibility of technological singularity. It also touches on the need to rethink some of our current ethical approaches and paradigms to make them fit better in a world of AI.

Then, in chapter 3, the main issues concerning the legal regulation of AI and related technological innovations are presented. This chapter provides a comprehensive outline of the main legal challenges in the context of AI, such as autonomous decision making, the internet of things, big data, blockchain technologies, cyber-physical systems and sensitive data, digital assets and property rights, sharing economy and shared assets, and, finally, challenges related to the use of drones and airspace. The chapter also identifies the main fields of law that AI will impact most strongly—namely, privacy, liability, and property.

---

1 https://www.stateofai2019.com/chapter-2-why-is-ai-important/.

2 https://siliconangle.com/2021/04/10/new-era-innovation-moores-law-not-dead-ai-ready-explode/.

 | DOI:10.1163/9789004682900_003

Chapter 4 covers AI's impact on the economy. Without any doubt, the use and development of AI systems will continue to contribute greatly to the global economy and to reshape the job market, potentially automating most if not all jobs in the process. The chapter outlines the future potential of AI in relation to economic growth, relates it to previous technological revolutions, and then discusses some structural changes that AI creates in the job market. Lastly, the chapter covers the digitization of the economy and the applications of AI in financial markets.

Chapter 5 turns to AI's impact on political sciences, as well as the political field in a more general sense. This impact concerns first and foremost the use of AI in administrative procedures, such as online government services, e-petitions, and voting, as well as the use of AI in political decision making, which would effectively replace government officials. The chapter covers some of the key definitions in this context (e.g., "e-governance" and "e-democracy") and states the main principles regarding the use of AI in political processes (i.e., transparency, explainability, fairness, and human-centricity). Then, it proceeds by outlining the current technological possibilities with respect to the use of AI in political science, the safety requirements, and the main risks involved.

Finally, chapter 6 concerns the impact of AI on healthcare. Both scholars and practitioners generally agree that AI can greatly enhance progress in healthcare by providing new tools to diagnose diseases and discover new drugs, processing and managing medical data, health monitoring, caregiving, and even partaking in surgeries.[3] The chapter first provides the context of accommodating AI-enabled innovations in healthcare and then moves on to discuss the ethical and social challenges involved in the implementation of AI in healthcare, as well as certain practical challenges such as patient data security, privacy, and risk management. The chapter is rounded off with the implications of the COVID-19 pandemic and some concluding remarks on the main priorities of AI development in healthcare.

---

3 https://www.wwt.com/article/5-benefits-of-using-ai-in-healthcare.

CHAPTER 2

Ethics

John-Stewart Gordon and Kęstutis Mosakas

2.1 Artificial Intelligence and Ethics

The technological developments in artificial intelligence (AI), robotics, computer science, and related disciplines have had a deep and far-reaching sociopolitical impact on human society and how it will be organized in the future. The deep impact concerns all areas of human life, but the following areas will most likely face the greatest impact: ethics, law, political sciences, healthcare, and the economy. This development is substantiated by the fact that more and more human responsibilities have been taken over by autonomous machines, in the so-called fourth industrial revolution. This important shift of responsibilities from human beings to machines *necessarily requires* that the autonomous machines know the difference between morally good and bad decisions, in particular in areas of utmost importance, such as the field of law (to counteract machine bias in law). In other words, one must "put ethics into the machine" (Anderson and Anderson 2011; Wallach and Allen 2009). But what is AI?

According to a recent definition, AI is

> the ability of a digital computer or computer-controlled robot to perform tasks commonly associated with intelligent beings. The term is frequently applied to the project of developing systems endowed with the intellectual processes characteristic of humans, such as the ability to reason, discover meaning, generalize, or learn from past experience.
>
> COPELAND 2020

Or, to put it more simply, AI provides machines with the means to do things that usually require human intelligence. It is common to distinguish at least two forms of AI: strong or general AI and weak AI. There is no current intelligent machine that is equipped with general AI, which is considered the Holy Grail in research with respect to AI systems. Only general AI is comparable to human intelligence and would provide machines that either match or surpass human capabilities. The possibility of the advent of such machines has been critically discussed among experts and laypeople alike. The well-known

 | DOI:10.1163/9789004682900_004

futurist and Google's director of engineering, Ray Kurzweil, predicts that we will have such AI systems by the year 2045 (Kurzweil 2005). The famous Oxford philosopher Nick Bostrom (2014) and the late well-known astrophysicist Stephen Hawking expressed warnings about the dangers of general AI, which are related to the view that humanity should be careful to develop machines that either match or surpass human beings (called technological singularity) because they may turn against their creators. On the other hand, weak AI systems, which are currently universally applied, usually fulfil one particular task, such as playing chess or the Chinese game Go or driving our cars (i.e., autonomous transportation).

A number of substantial problems with respect to AI systems and their application in different contexts require careful ethical analysis (Gordon and Nyholm 2021). For example, some machines reveal a significant bias against ethnic minorities in law, in the context of applying for credit loans, and on the job market. Furthermore, some self-learning AI systems have become sexist in their interaction with users or have exhibited a substantial gender bias. In addition, it is widely discussed whether machines will ever become conscious and hence entitled to moral and legal status and even to moral and legal rights—or whether consciousness is even required for the ascription of status and rights (Gunkel 2012). Yet another issue concerns the so-called black box problem, which deals with the issue of machine decisions that cannot be predicted based on their particular algorithms (the problem of opacity). Other debates concern the future of work (mass unemployment), the human-machine relationship in the context of sex and partnerships, the nature of human capabilities if most tasks are done by intelligent machines (de-skilling), and the future of political governance (AI Governance).

These and related issues will deeply influence the way our societies work. Without a doubt, the impact of AI on ethics is substantial and will become of utmost significance for existential questions related to how we should live and what is a good life in a world that is more and more determined by autonomous and intelligent machines. The next section will provide a more detailed description of some of the main problems in the context of AI and ethics.

2.2 Ethical Challenges

The ethical issues pertaining to AI are vast and numerous (see Müller 2020). Their vastness is tied to the fact that the ability to simulate intelligent behaviour has extremely varied domains of use, ranging from rather mundane tasks (e.g., vacuum cleaning, playing games) to vitally important ones (e.g., healthcare, warfare, transportation, data collection and processing). In addition, the expansion of AI—both in terms of its scope of application and capabilities—is greatly desirable for the simple reason that it allows humans to achieve more of their goals and to do so more effectively than they could otherwise. Indeed, it is by virtue of their intelligence that humans managed to dominate the planet as they did in the first place. It is, therefore, no wonder that researchers and futurists view AI as the key to human progress—assuming that we would be able to control it and align it with our goals and values, of course. At present, however, AI is also the source of unprecedented ethical challenges. This holds true for both AI systems that exist today and those that will exist in the future. Additionally, because of the very diverse and transformative impacts of AI on human society, it is imperative to re-examine our conceptions of the good life against the background of AI so as to find answers to the many important ethical challenges involved.

2.2.1 *Privacy*

One such challenge has to do with people's right to privacy. This concerns online data collection based on the trail left by any individual user, as well as real-world AI surveillance systems equipped with high-resolution cameras and facial recognition. Notably, online data collection has become a profitable venue that allows companies to adjust their behavior toward the user or to simply sell the data. Indeed, the knowledge of one's sensitive data, such as one's financial or medical history, can easily allow companies to deny somebody a credit loan or insurance. What makes this even more worrisome is the fact that users can be manipulated online with relative ease. For example, companies can nudge the user into accepting certain privacy settings on a website through annoying pop-up windows or shape the user's behavior through data analytic techniques (Yeung 2017). Moreover, aside from being useful to companies, personal data can also be used by governments to serve their own purposes, such as tracking their citizens (i.e., mass surveillance). This raises important questions regarding the right to one's own data and to what extent companies and governments alike should be allowed to use personal data (Véliz 2020). Another related issue is that of public video surveillance, which can be done through smart-city cameras or drones, which are becoming smaller in size and yet more capable. Although surveillance technologies can be indispensable in securing the public order, they can also infringe on people's privacy—especially if they are equipped with facial recognition systems—and even be used to track people. This is particularly concerning in countries run by authoritarian regimes.

2.2.2 *Machine Bias*

Then there is the problem of machine bias. This concerns not so much the ethics of how AI systems are used by humans but a problem inherent to the design of certain systems. In particular, it concerns machine learning, including so-called "deep learning," which has come to prominence due to its great flexibility and effectiveness. The fact that an AI system can pick up a bias—either due to faulty algorithms or, more commonly, due to skewed data that it learns from—raises ethical concerns regarding the use of such systems. To give a couple of examples, Amazon was forced to scrap a recruitment tool in 2017 because it was unjustifiably penalizing women's resumes (Dastin 2018), whereas the software developed by Northpointe for predicting likely recidivists was exhibiting racial bias against black people (Angwin et al. 2016). Even though it seems uncontroversial to describe the use of such biased software as wrong, avoiding or resolving machine bias itself is by no means a straightforward task. For example, AI systems based on deep neural networks are "opaque" in the sense that it is unclear, even to the experts, exactly how such systems arrive at the decisions they make. For this reason, many have insisted that explainability should be one of the top priorities when it comes to AI systems (Floridi et al. 2018)—although it remains to be seen whether this goal can be attained without sacrificing their effectiveness.

2.2.3 *Putting Ethics into the Machine*

Another issue of utmost importance has to do with the ethical decision making of autonomous AI systems. Because systems of this sort will be operating in the world without any external human input, it seems necessary to provide them with some way of making ethical decisions. This is especially true for systems that are more likely to become involved in ethically complex situations in which people's lives or well-being is at stake, such as autonomous vehicles (e.g., cars, trains, buses, planes) and autonomous military weapons. Although autonomous vehicles are expected to increase traffic safety and be more environment-friendly, they too will get involved in accidents, which raises questions related to both responsibility attribution and the ethical programming of such vehicles (Nyholm 2018). Similar concerns arise for autonomous military weapons and drones that are equipped with lethal weapons and thus have the power to take lives. Although there is considerable resistance to the development of such weapons (see Lin et al. 2008), it should be clear that they should only be used—if at all—once the risk of their potential ethical repercussions has been minimized, as a single mistake could prove to be very costly.

2.2.4 *Artificial Moral Agents*

Similarly, the idea of ethical programming should be taken very seriously with respect to future forms of AI with broader capacities. This relates to the question of building so-called artificial moral agents (AMAS), or AI systems that are capable of moral reasoning and decision making. However, it remains unclear what kind of ethics such machines should follow. Some insist that they should follow one of the major ethical theories "top-down," such as utilitarianism or Kantian deontology; others think that the machine should construct its own ethics "bottom-up" by learning from certain paradigmatic cases, while still others hold that a hybrid approach or something completely new should be considered instead (Gordon 2020). Moreover, it remains contested whether AMAS should be built in the first place. While some have argued that bringing such artificial beings into existence is socially disruptive and unnecessary, others insist that AMAS may help us learn more about ethics in addition to being useful for certain practical purposes, such as decision making in the context of medical ethics.

2.2.5 *Robot Rights*

Some of the resistance to building AMAS stems from the fact that if AMAS were to exist, we may be morally obligated to provide them with certain rights, which is another important point of contention regarding the ethics of AI. At present, it is simply not clear that artificially intelligent robots will always be at the disposal of human beings to be used as humans please. Indeed, the current trajectory of technological development has convinced numerous AI researchers that by the end of the present century machines will come close to—if not exceed—human intelligence (Müller and Bostrom 2014). And once that happens, it is far from obvious whether such beings should be treated as mere tools. A common view is that in order to have moral status and corresponding rights, machines would need to have conscious minds—similar to those of human beings and some non-human animals. This raises all kinds of problematic issues pertaining to the nature of mentality and how we can detect it in other entities—especially if these entities are so vastly different from us as robots are.

In an attempt to circumvent these problems, certain authors, such as Gunkel (2018), have proposed radically relational approaches to moral consideration, according to which a being should be treated morally if it stands in social relations. This approach seems particularly important for the coming decades, because that is when we can expect the gradual integration of robots into society to start. For example, artificial beings such as robotic companions, pets, and caregivers already exist today and will likely become increasingly sophisticated in the coming years and decades. Moreover, even if moral consideration is not entirely a matter of social relations, there may be other reasons to consider extending legal protection to social robots, given their intimate involvement in human affairs.

2.2.6 *Singularity*

Finally, there are certain long-term AI-related challenges, such as the existential threats posed by general AI (Bostrom 2014). This first and foremost has to do with the so-called (technological) singularity scenario, also known as the intelligence explosion. According to this scenario, the emergence of the first machines with general intelligence will, shortly after, be followed by something like "machine superintelligence," given that the early general AI will be more capable of building other intelligent machines than humans are. And once even more intelligent machines take this task up, machine intelligence is expected to explode, leaving human intelligence far behind.

Some scholars, like Ray Kurzweil (2005), believe that the growth in intelligence initiated by the first general AI will become exponential, while others expect it to be more linear. Whatever the case, the potential existence of beings so vastly superior to humans in their intelligence is bound to raise serious existential concerns. Perhaps eradicating humanity will not be among the goals of superintelligent AI. However, many have noticed that even if that were the case, that does not guarantee that such artificially intelligent beings will behave ethically towards humans in the long run. For this reason, various proposals have been made as to how humans could ensure that such AI remains "friendly" towards them, including different ways of motivational control and control through restraints. At present, however, it is unclear how exactly superintelligent AI could be controlled—or how it may be aligned with our fundamental values.

2.3 AI's Possible Impact on Ethics and Moral Philosophy

Technologically sophisticated machines might have, at some point, general AI and might eventually match or surpass human capabilities. This possibility gives rise to a number of substantial socio-political and legal consequences which concern how we think about our ethical key terms and moral theories. At least five main issues are of utmost significance and will be briefly described below (see Gordon and Gunkel 2022).

2.3.1 *Expanding the Moral Circle*

The history of ethics is to some degree the history of who belongs to the moral community and hence who is entitled to moral and legal protection. Women, ethnic minorities, members of the LGBTQ+ community, animals, and even the environment have gained consideration for inclusion in the moral community, and perhaps intelligent machines will have their turn in the future. If intelligent robots will, at some point, belong to our moral community, then this development will have a deep and far-reaching impact on human society. Membership in the moral community comes with moral and legal rights. In other words, intelligent machines can no longer be forced to do something they do not want to do; for example, sex robots may become reluctant to offer sex to their "owners" and killer robots may refuse to fight our wars. In addition, and most importantly, a being that either matches or surpasses human capabilities should not be "owned" in the first place, since this is tantamount to slavery. Furthermore, such robots could enter into legal contracts or vote. In sum, human beings would create a new artificial species that would be entitled to the same (or similar) rights that humans have.

2.3.2 *On Moral and Legal Personhood*

The concept of personhood is one of the most important key notions in moral and legal philosophy, because it determines whether an entity is entitled to either moral and legal status or moral and legal rights (based on its particular status). The typical adult human being is considered the prime example of a being that has full moral and legal status as well as being entitled to the full list of moral and legal rights. In contrast, for example, a fish has no moral and legal status and therefore is not entitled to any moral and legal rights, given its lack of personhood.

Usually, the concept of personhood is fleshed out by further criteria that must be met for an entity to claim personhood. The well-known philosopher Frances Kamm has suggested that sentience (i.e., the ability to feel, perceive, or experience subjectively) and consciousness (i.e., the ability to think) are each sufficient to determine whether a being has moral status. In other words, "An entity has moral status when, in its own rights and for its own sake, it can give us reason to do things such as not destroy it or help it" (Kamm 2007, 229). If intelligent machines meet one of the suggested criteria, then humanity would be forced to accept them as beings entitled to moral protection. They would give us reason, according to Kamm, not to destroy them but to welcome them in the moral and legal community.

2.3.3 *The Moral Relevance of the Dichotomy of Moral Agency and Patiency*

A moral agent is a being who has full moral status and can act rationally according to his reasons. Moral agency logically includes moral patiency, but not vice versa. A moral patient can be considered morally without necessarily having the capabilities of sentience and consciousness. For example, the Grand Canyon in Arizona can be considered morally without having a moral status. Its moral consideration could be fully based on its unique formation and beauty that invoke in us an awe-inspiring sensation. In this context, the Grand Canyon would be a moral patient.

What about intelligent machines? Some philosophers such as David Gunkel (2012) claim that one should replace the classical dichotomy with the concept of "thinking otherwise," which states that morality is based on social relations between different beings including robots. Others try to integrate intelligent robots in the classical dichotomy. In the end, it must be clear that there should be only one criterion to evaluate all entities, independently of their species membership. This, however, has substantial consequences for human society.

2.3.4 *Is Being "Alive" Morally Relevant?*

Traditionally, the ascription of moral status and rights concerned only living beings such as human beings and higher animals and not dead or inanimate matter such as stones. *Being alive* should not be confused with "having a soul" because this would exclude *all* animals, which—according to Western religious tradition—do not have a soul. Rather, "being alive" refers to the particular substratum of what the entity is made of and whether the entity is powered by biological processes instead of, for example, a battery. In this case, can an intelligent and autonomous robot that either matches or surpasses human capabilities ever be considered "alive"? Or is the category of being powered by biological processes morally irrelevant? These and related questions are discussed in research. For example, proponents of the computationalist point of view, such as David Chalmers (1996, Chapter 9), claim that consciousness is not necessarily rooted in carbon-based beings such as humans but could also emerge in silicon-based environments. Numerous experts at the intersection of AI, robotics, and computer science take this view for granted. It remains to be seen which position is correct.

2.3.5 *Is (Human) Embodiment Morally Relevant?*

The idea that only embodied beings are morally relevant has been widely accepted among experts and laypeople alike. The reason is that we simply have not encountered any other non-embodied intelligent beings before. Whether such beings must also be human-like with respect to their particular bodies can be reasonably questioned, given the case of animal embodiment. Many animals matter morally to us regarding our decision making. In recent times, however, we have also come to consider the environment morally important, by virtue of either its *intrinsic* value—i.e., it matters for its own sake—or its *instrumental* value for human beings.

What about intelligent robots? Robots are artificial beings with an artificial body; therefore, they are embodied entities. Admittedly, their bodies obviously differ from human bodies (unless we are talking about cyborgs, which are part human and part machine), but as we have seen in the cases of the environment and animal embodiment, *human* embodiment seems to be morally irrelevant. The idea that only humans deserve moral significance amounts to speciesism, i.e., racism at the species level (Singer 2009). Therefore, human embodiment is neither a sufficient nor necessary criterion for moral consideration as such.

2.4 Conclusion

This essay had three main goals. First, it provided some brief remarks on the relation between AI and ethics in general terms, to show the significance of AI for our ethical reasoning and decision making. This has been further substantiated in the second part, which briefly introduced some ethical challenges in the context of AI and its application. Here, the main goal was to make the reader more familiar with the current and future ethical problems related to AI. Third, the essay has considered the ethical impact of AI on our moral key terms and approaches. AI is not only just another fancy, smart tool; it is the very architecture of all future tools and has the potential to influence how we think about ethics and moral philosophy in quite significant ways. Traditional beliefs, which are unable to solve the complex issues in the context of AI, will be replaced by convictions that pay more proper consideration to the particularities and specifics of AI and the human-machine relation. This has great significance for law and legal sciences, as can be seen in later chapters of this textbook.

Study Questions

1. What is AI? Why is it so important?
2. How does the advance of AI threaten people's privacy?
3. How can machines become biased, and why is this a relevant factor?
4. What is technological singularity and what are the related risks?

5. Why is machine consciousness considered relevant in ethics?
6. What is the potential impact of AI on the field of ethics as a whole?

References

Anderson, M., and S. L. Anderson, eds. 2011. *Machine Ethics*. Cambridge University Press.

Angwin, J., et al. 2016. "Machine Bias." *ProPublica,* May 23, 2016. https://www.propublica.org/article/machine-bias-risk-assessments-in-criminal-sentencing.

Bostrom, N. 2014. *Superintelligence: Paths, Dangers, Strategies*. Oxford University Press.

Chalmers, D. 1996. *The Conscious Mind: In Search of a Fundamental Theory*. Oxford University Press.

Copeland, B. J. 2020. "Artificial Intelligence." *Britannica.com*. https://www.britannica.com/technology/artificial-intelligence.

Dastin, J. 2018. "Amazon Scraps Secret AI Recruiting Tool That Showed Bias Against Women." Reuters, October 11, 2018. https://www.reuters.com/article/us-amazon-com-jobs-automation-insight/amazon-scraps-secret-ai-recruiting-tool-that-showed-bias-against-women-idUSKCN1MK08G.

Floridi, L., et al. 2018. "AI4People—An Ethical Framework for a Good AI Society: Opportunities, Risks, Principles, and Recommendations." *Minds and Machines* 28(4): 689–707.

Gordon, J.-S. 2020. "Building Moral Machines: Ethical Pitfalls and Challenges." *Science and Engineering Ethics* 26(93): 141–57.

Gordon, J.-S., and D. Gunkel. 2022. "Moral Status and Intelligent Robots." The *Southern Journal of Philosophy* 60(1): 88–117.

Gordon, J.-S., and S. Nyholm. 2021. "The Ethics of Artificial Intelligence." *Internet Encyclopedia of Philosophy*. https://iep.utm.edu/ethics-of-artificial-intelligence/.

Gunkel, D. 2012. *The Machine Question. Critical Perspectives on AI, Robots, and Ethics*. MIT Press.

Gunkel, D. 2018. *Robot Rights*. MIT Press.

Kamm, F. 2007. *Intricate Ethics: Rights, Responsibilities, and Permissible Harm*. Oxford University Press.

Kurzweil, R. 2005. *The Singularity Is Near*. Penguin Books.

Lin, P., G. A. Bekey, and K. Abney. 2008. *Autonomous Military Robotics: Risk, Ethics, and Design. ONR Report*. California Polytechnic State University, San Luis Obispo, December 20, 2008. http://ethics.calpoly.edu/ONR_report.pdf.

Müller, V. C. 2020. "Ethics of Artificial Intelligence and Robotics." *Stanford Encyclopedia of Philosophy*. https://plato.stanford.edu/entries/ethics-ai/.

Müller, V. C., and N. Bostrom. 2014. "Future Progress in Artificial Intelligence: a Poll Among Experts." *Journal of Experimental and Theoretical Artificial Intelligence.* Special Issue: Impacts and Risks of Artificial General Intelligence.

Nyholm, S. 2018. "The Ethics of Crashes with Self-Driving Cars: a Roadmap, I." *Philosophy Compass* 13(7): e12507.

Singer, P. 2009. "Speciesism and Moral Status." *Metaphilosophy* 40(3–4): 567–81.

Véliz, C. 2020. *Privacy is Power: Why and How You Should Take Back Control of Your Data.* Penguin Books.

Wallach, W., and C. Allen. 2009. *Moral Machines. Teaching Robots Right from Wrong.* Oxford University Press.

Yeung, K. 2017. "Hypernudge: Big Data as a Mode of Regulation by Design." *Information, Communication & Society* 20(1): 118–36.

Further Reading

Bartneck, C., et al. 2021. *An Introduction to Ethics in Robotics in AI.* Springer.

Bostrom, N., and E. Yudkowsky. 2014. "The Ethics of Artificial Intelligence." In *Cambridge Handbook of Artificial Intelligence*, edited by W. Ramsey and K. Frankish, 316–34. Cambridge University Press.

Coeckelbergh, M. 2020. *AI Ethics.* MIT Press.

Lin, P., K. Abney, and G. A. Bekey, eds. 2014. *Robot Ethics: the Ethical and Social Implications of Robotics: Intelligent Robotics and Autonomous Agents.* MIT Press.

CHAPTER 3

Transformative Smart Technologies: Mapping Challenges of Private Law

Julija Kiršienė, Edita Gruodytė and Deividas Kiršys

It is obvious that such technologies as the internet, artificial intelligence (AI), robots, blockchain, autonomous cars, drones, and gene editing are blurring the lines between human and technological capabilities, as well as changing the world profoundly and irrevocably.[1] Transformative innovations may lead our lives into chaos, if we fail to find adequate measures to frame them. One of these framing measures is legal regulation.

For example, AI might drastically improve every smart device that we use in our day-to-day lives, enabling robotic vacuum cleaners, personal assistants, smart thermostats, driverless cars, personal drones, and many others to learn and function on their own. It might be used to process, classify, and interpret huge amounts of information, or combined with medical software and equipment to monitor, diagnose, and even cure patients. Drones can be paired with a variety of onboard components such as data receivers and transmitters, video cameras, thermal sensors, and facial recognition software. They can be tools for collecting large amounts of information as well as functioning in groups or swarms that learn and think collectively. The decentralized, immutable, and secure nature of blockchain technology also enables it to converge with other technologies because it has the potential to make every centralized process fully autonomous; it can be used to protect self-driving cars or to secure the internet of the future.

As transformative technologies become more and more embedded in our daily routine, we begin to notice that they are not just neutral objects or tools, but rather mediators (Hildebrandt 2015), which indeed shape, interpret, transform, and make meaning of human lives. The potential of transformative innovations, however, comes along with a set of tensions and risks, which can ultimately work against the well-being of humankind.

This chapter of the book will briefly present a case analysis of technological innovations such as artificial intelligence, robots, blockchain, the internet of

1 This chapter of the book is based on Kiršienė et al. (2019).

 | DOI:10.1163/9789004682900_005

things, cryptocurrencies, digital assets, the sharing economy, cyber-physical systems, self-driving transportation, and drones, so as to uncover a majority of the underlying legal issues to which many emerging innovations might contribute.

3.1 Transformative Innovations

3.1.1 *Artificial Intelligence and the Challenge of Autonomous Decision Making*

Transformative innovations are increasingly based on AI technology, with human-like skills such as learning, speech recognition, automated reasoning, sensing, interaction, problem solving, and creativity. Where human involvement in AI decision making is obvious, there is no need to re-examine legal regulation, because the companies that currently manufacture devices with AI (such as toys, cars, or kitchen appliances) are already subject to a well-developed doctrine of product liability. However, researchers argue that the already existing product liability legal framework is likely to become inadequate as commercially available AI machines become more sophisticated and autonomous, eventually blurring the lines between the responsibilities of manufacturers and of users. Therefore, a distinction between devices with deterministic and cognitive AI is important.

Both deterministic and cognitive devices perform their tasks through algorithms; however, the difference between the two types is that the first type does not have the ability to learn and is predictable, whereas the latter devices have learning capabilities that make their behavior stochastic or random (United Nations Educational, Scientific and Cultural Organization 2017). AI technology uses cognitive algorithms that are programmed not merely to perform specific tasks, but also to learn and further develop themselves in interaction with their environment. Given the complexity of the design, construction, and programming of AI devices, a central legal issue will be the ability to track the reasons for all past actions (and omissions).

More about the characteristics of AI, epistemic opacity in AI decision making, and the vague legal status of electronic personhood and the legal status of AI is presented in part 3 of this book.

3.1.2 *Robots and the Challenge of Defining Smart Technologies*

> Many ways in which robotics technologies are combined with other technologies and are applied in the creation and allocation of services and

> products, as well as the many ways in which the term robot is used by experts and laypeople, make it difficult to provide a generally acceptable definition of what robot is.
>
> LEENES ET AL. 2017, 3

A traditional definition defines a robot as "a mechanical device that works automatically or by computer control" (Cambridge Business English Dictionary), i.e., some physical thing (machine) with certain defined features created for specific automation purposes, usually without the need for human control. Such examples may be found in industry, where there are dangerous and repetitive functions such as stamping or packing where no intelligence is needed, and where certain specific functions are implemented with robot help. Also, they have become more popular in households for such automated functions as moving the lawn or cleaning the house. With the development of AI, the concept of robots is changing radically as they combine control software with mechanical or electronic components (DeBruyne and Vanleenhove 2021, 16) and could gain certain features such as deep learning inherent to AI. For example, self-driving vehicles integrate such features as monitoring, control, data collection and exchange, and making certain decisions. Such robots (hereafter referred to as smart robots), as shown in Figure 3.1, are part of AI.

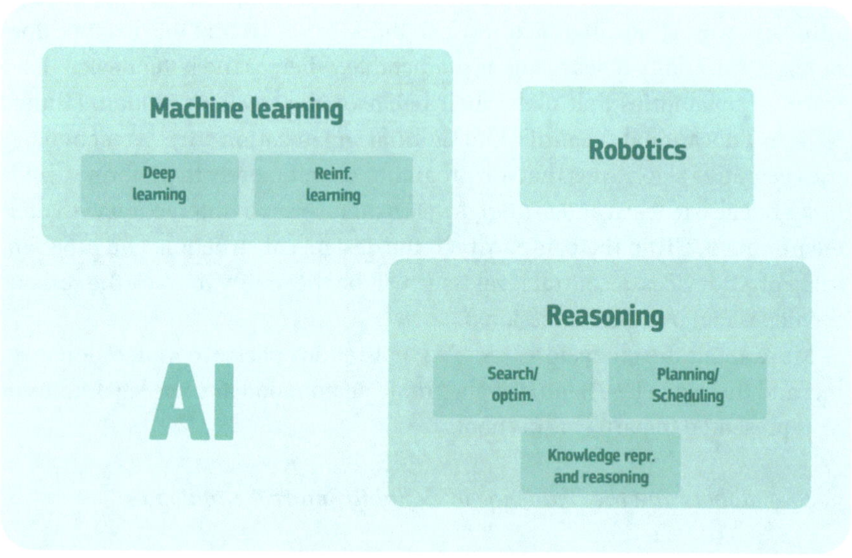

FIGURE 3.1 A simplified overview of AI's subdisciplines and their relationship to each other
SOURCE: EC HIGH-LEVEL EXPERT GROUP ON AI (2019, 5)

A definition provided by EU experts covers features of smart robots, describing them as "AI in action in the physical world (also called embodied AI)" (EC High-Level Expert Group on AI 2019, 4) and endowed with such qualities as perception, reasoning, action, and learning, as well as interaction capabilities with other systems (EC High-Level Expert Group on AI 2019, 4). Examples of such robots include self-driving cars, flying taxis, robotic vacuum cleaners, humanoid robots, nanorobots etc. This new conception of robots requires certain interaction between humans and robots and offers some level of autonomy in robot functioning. This could raise the same legal issues as noted above and discussed in the chapter on AI and electronic personhood.

3.1.3 *The Internet of Things and the Challenge of Big Data*

The internet of things (IoT) is considered a set of revolutionary complex technologies that combines several categories. Human beings, physical objects and the internet provide huge new opportunities to communicate, collect and share data, and create new forms of communication. The IoT is "perceived as a far-reaching vision with technological and societal implications" (International Telecommunication Union, Recommendation 2012, 5). One of the distinct features of IoT-interdependent connectivity is that it connects various technologies and data such as hardware, software, telecommunications networks, and data distribution, yielding three possible categories of connectivity: automatic interconnectivity between machines (e.g., smartphones and smart refrigerators); data analysis between technologies and humans (e.g., obtaining data from computers and sensors); and collaboration connectivity between people (e.g., video calls, Viber). The IoT covers both physical (electric and electronic equipment) and virtual (application software) items and is characterized by such features as interconnectivity, heterogeneity, dynamic changes, enormous scale and thing-related services (International Telecommunication Union, Recommendation 2012, 2). The main features and capacities are indicated in Figure 3.2, which stresses the new dimension of "any thing communication" introduced by the IoT.

The IoT provides far-reaching opportunities for interconnecting physical and virtual objects using various sensor technologies, big data, machine learning, artificial intelligence, various wireless sensor networks, and broad forms of connectivity technologies such as WiFi, Bluetooth, 4G, and 5G.

One of the IoT's distinct features is the collection and use of huge amounts of data. "Every two years data is doubling in size and is expected to reach 44 zettabytes in the next four years" (Farhan et al. 2018, 3). This causes both technical (such as storage, velocity, veracity, etc.) and legal (data protection, privacy, security, data inaccuracy, etc.) issues that need to be addressed. As is

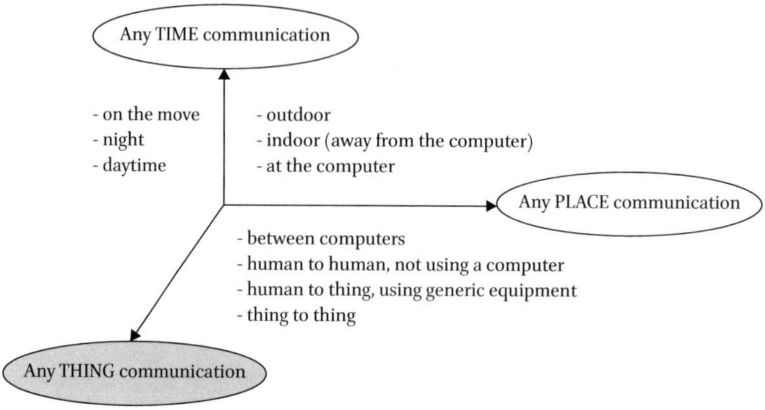

FIGURE 3.2 The new dimension introduced in the IoT
SOURCE: INTERNATIONAL TELECOMMUNICATION UNION, RECOMMENDATION (2012, 3)

evident from Figure 3.3, each of the mentioned technical issues related to the management of big data also raises certain legal issues such as trustworthiness and safety of data.

For example, if someone breaks into smart technologies, he may get various highly intimate details about one's private life: private pictures, eating, traveling habits, information about activities, when the person is not at home, health issues, age, fingerprint, voice, etc. The problem is intensified by the fact that usually these data are shared across several devices, which means easier access to and use of these data to personalize advertisements, sell personal data to other subjects, commit identity thefts, or take control of one's house or computer. If such systems as smart country electricity or traffic regulation systems, social security, and tax databases are hacked, threats to such values as human life, health, public security, state stability, and the economy can arise, requiring effective preventive measures. From a legal point of view, the main difficulty in setting up and using a privacy standard is related to existing laws, which are different in every nation (and even in different states and provinces within those nations; Fabiano 2017, 212), and virtual reality does not have boundaries. Liability issues are involved as many actors could be blamed. Suppose that someone, after hacking into one's smart home security system (which is controlled by a smartphone), breaks into the house and steals valuables. Who is liable for the theft? The manufacturer of the smartphone, the installer of the smart home, or the creator of the app? Sometimes it may be tricky for the consumer to find a guilty person or even prove fault, due to the complexity and interconnectedness of technologies and black box problems.

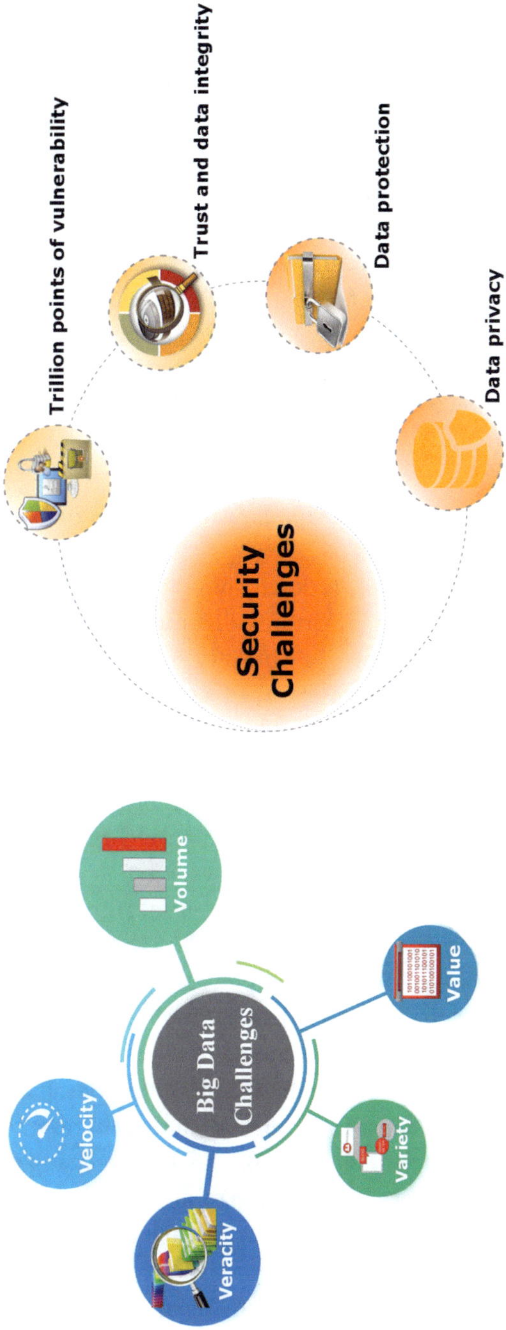

FIGURE 3.3 Big data technical and security challenges
SOURCE: FARHAN ET AL. (2018, 3)

These legal issues require international regulation and standardization. Such states as the UK, USA, and Australia have enacted certain national policies, but they are not effective in virtual space as offenders are using complex technologies covering many states. The EU is actively involved in creating a general policy for the IoT. For example, security issues are addressed in the EU's Cybersecurity Strategy for the Digital Decade (European Commission 2020), indicating that new rules should be introduced and existing legal regimes should be revised and adapted to deal with new challenges. With regard to the IoT, the EU aims to provide regulation to ensure an Internet of Secure Things, but currently there is no unified and clear regulation. Also, the enactment of regulations at the EU level does not provide protection at the international level. Therefore, close cooperation between involved actors (e.g., businesses, information technology experts, and lawyers) both at regional and international levels is needed.

3.1.4 *Blockchains and the Challenge of Immutability and Decentralization of Data*

Blockchain technology is not revolutionary or ground-breaking by itself and is more like an integral or updated part of a distributed peer-to-peer system. It serves as a tool to solve a core problem of software systems, which have struggled to achieve and maintain the integrity of a purely distributed peer-to-peer system that has unknown reliability and trustworthiness (Drescher 2017, 31). This has been particularly hard to achieve because for a distributed peer-to-peer network to work without a centralized authority, it must have consensus upon every message transmitted. Before blockchain, however, a scattered group of random individuals did not have a way to confirm that a particular event had occurred if it was not verified by a central authority.

Technically speaking, blockchain is simply a data structure where each block is linked to another block. The network timestamps transactions by hashing them into an ongoing chain of hash-based proof-of-work, forming a record that cannot be changed without redoing the proof-of-work. This arrangement suggests that data stored in blockchain are immutable, because to access data from the oldest block, one must go through all the blocks from the newest one until the first block is reached. Performing this task to change any data contained in the blocks becomes almost impossible, because all stored data are encrypted using cryptography techniques, and each time a new node is added, it has to download the entire ledger and synchronize with the network.

Software developers have already realized the potential of blockchain technology and have started to use it to create digital currencies, self-executing smart contracts, and cryptographic tokens that can represent property or ownership interest in emerging services. Due to their vast applicability, various types of blockchains constantly arise: payment processing and currency, supply chain management, asset protection, identification, personal record systems and passwords.

Two central features of blockchain technology make it distinctive: the system can be completely decentralized and, as noted above, the data contained in blocks can become immutable. These features also represent the greatest challenge in terms of data protection under the EU's General Data Protection Regulation (GDPR). The fundamental idea behind GDPR is to provide data subjects with the ability to control their personal data, allowing them to freely access and erase any unwanted records. Exercising these rights relies entirely on central authorities who are controllers of data. Public blockchain technology, on the other hand, may store data in its databases perpetually, which means that once data are placed in a distributed ledger system, they cannot be deleted.

Currently, neither the European Union nor the United States has legislation or clear guidelines ensuring data protection regarding blockchain. This lack of legislation creates not only legal uncertainties, but also a privacy risk regarding personal data. The present situation is similar to the emergence of the internet: it took approximately two decades for people and regulators to understand that putting a vast amount of personal data (in most cases, without any particular reason) out for everybody to see, without a mechanism to properly control or regulate the situation, can induce serious negative effects on our daily lives, as the Cambridge Analytica scandal has shown.

Another noteworthy implication that emerges through blockchain is Decentralized Autonomous Organizations (DAOs). A DAO is an organization that functions through rules encoded as computer programs called "smart contracts" (Chohan 2017, 1). Instead of a traditional organizational structure managed by a set of humans interacting in person and controlling property via the legal system, in DAOs, management and control are automated according to protocols specified in code and enforced on the blockchain. In other words, DAOs are based on self-governing software that lives on the internet and exists autonomously (humans are not involved), providing the benefits of but without the inflexibility of formal corporate structures. Instead of concentrating on decision making at the executive level, for instance shareholders of DAOs can participate in decision making by decentralized voting. By removing centralized management, DAOs could eliminate the errors and corruption introduced by humans and bring new forms of democratic collective action, transforming top-down governance approaches that are criticized for their inflexibility, opacity, slowness, and democratic deficit (Boucher et al. 2017, 20–21).

Just like regular legal entities, DAOs could engage in commerce; therefore not only could legal problems with damages and/or losses occur (who should be responsible if the organization is operated autonomously?), but also traditional notions of legal personality could be challenged. As opposed to traditional corporations or organizations, DAOs are neither owned nor controlled by any single corporate or governmental agency, nor any individual person. Yet they can interact with the public in a way that might give rise to specific rights and obligations. DAOs can thus have a significant effect on third parties and might even be at the source of certain torts or wrongdoings. Some believe that the aforementioned problems could be mitigated by adopting the nearest person principle, but only if the creators of DAOs are known. However, if DAOs are created by other DAOs or by anonymous persons, this principle would not suffice. Either way, creating functionally working DAOs is no easy task. Therefore, close cooperation between businesses, lawyers, and programmers will be inevitable.

3.1.5 *Cyber-Physical Systems and the Challenge of Sensitive Data*

Cyber-physical systems are a high-tech innovation that has been increasingly used in the field of healthcare. The key legal issue concerning the application of these systems in practice is the protection of privacy. Cyber-physical systems integrate intelligent technologies, combining sensors, medical equipment and software, and physical systems. These systems, developed by the science of robotics, are currently widely used in medicine as surgically or otherwise medically implanted medical intelligent technologies that can monitor, analyze, and treat patients, enhance the mobility and integration of people with disabilities and elderly people, and perform other vital functions. Smart medical technologies such as insulin pumps, hearing aids, brain stimulators, and heart pacemakers have improved the quality of life for millions of people. On the other hand, it is obvious that their applications are not limited to medicine. For example, microchips inserted under the skin are currently being actively discussed and experimented with for identification, mutual settlement, prevention of kidnappings, and other purposes.

These devices usually measure, store and, by using feedback, process a large amount of human health data. Therefore, smart cyber-physical and cyber-biophysical systems can be the target of potential thieves of this information and other individuals with malicious intent. In the event of a cyber attack, one or more of the information security attributes, also known in the literature as the information cyber security triad (i.e., confidentiality, integrity, and availability) may be violated.

It is evident that the more information is collected, stored, and processed through these innovations, the more attractive it is to potential villains, which consequently leads to potential harm to consumers. In Lithuania, a scandal recently occurred when the data of thousands of clients were stolen from a plastic surgery clinic called "Grožio chirurgija," i.e., not only the names of the patients but also their complaints, procedures performed, intimate photographs, and other highly sensitive data. Criminals later blackmailed clients of the clinic, demanding money. Clearly, the importance of protecting sensitive information from cyber attacks has become apparent.

3.1.6 *Digital Assets and Property Rights*

With the advent of computers, the internet, social networks, and smart devices, virtual space has fundamentally changed people's lives, taking up an increasing share of social life and posing new challenges of legal regulation not only in terms of privacy and data protection, but also in terms of property rights. As people become more involved in virtual spaces on their smartphones, computers, and databases, they create and store an increasing amount of digital data that may have personal or property value, referred to as electronic or *digital assets*. McCarthy defines digital assets as digital information stored on a computer, smartphone, hard drive, third-party server, or other computer-related technology. Thus, digital assets include (but are not limited to) music, movies, video games, and software, i.e., objects related to intellectual property. Digital assets can also include data, texts, images, codes, computer programs, databases, software email accounts, avatars on game servers, accounts on social networks, digital photographs, or virtual currency such as Bitcoin, to which a person has a right and an interest; however, these assets do not include money in bank accounts, even though they can be managed through electronic access. The following types of digital assets may be distinguished: (1) personal digital assets, such as photographs, documents, letters, and audio and video recordings; (2) accounts on social networks, such as Facebook or Twitter; (3) financial accounts, such as electronic banking, PayPal and other accounts; and (4) digital assets related to commercial or business activities (McCarthy 2015). In addition to these types of digital assets, the content of electronic communication is also considered a digital asset.

The main legal issues related to the regulation of digital assets include their definition, the implementation of property rights (rights of ownership, use, disposal), participation in civil circulation, and the protection of privacy. For example, in the case *In re Facebook Ireland Ltd* (Dominicé and Haux 2020, 251), the Court ordered Facebook to give the deceased girl's parents access to her Facebook account and the records it contains. Regarding the protection of individual privacy, Facebook had not granted access to the parents. The court reasoned its decision on the grounds that the contract between the user and Facebook was no different from other agreements binding the parties, so the rights and obligations arising from the contract could be transferred to the user's heirs. In response to Facebook's argument that allowing parents to join their daughter's Facebook account would violate the privacy of third parties, the court stated that parents are heirs under the law with a right to know what their minor daughter was doing online. In addition, the court noted that heirs may read the confidential letters of the deceased without infringing on the rights of a third party, which means that, by analogy, this practice may also apply to electronic correspondence and other forms of personal communication.

3.1.7 *The Sharing Economy and the Challenge of Shared Assets*

Gaps in legal regulation arise not only from the penetration of technological innovations into everyday life, but also from social innovations that are changing the paradigm of the provision of goods and services and the satisfaction of needs. For example, the phenomenon of the sharing economy is based not only on digitalization but also on public involvement or participation in commercial activities.

In the literature, the sharing economy is described in different ways, e.g., as a collaborative economy platform, mesh, human to human (H2H) or peer to peer (P2P), on demand, digital, app, or community marketplace. These descriptions partly reflect the essential characteristics of this phenomenon. The Communication from the European Commission on this topic defines the sharing economy as business models that operate through digital collaboration platforms used by private individuals to provide goods and services for temporary use on the open market (European Commission to the European Parliament 2016).

In addition to the well-known accommodation sharing platform Airbnb and transport sharing platforms such as Uber and Lyft, there is a growing number of peer-to-peer lending platforms, e.g., SoFi, Lending Club, Savy.lt, Fin Bee, and NEOfinance; human resource sharing platforms, e.g., TaskRabbit, Zaarly, oDesk, and Mechanical Turk; platforms for sharing things, e.g., Car2Go, Zipcar, Turo, Getaround, Dalinuosi.lt, and other multifaceted platforms, such as Wag (dog-walking platform), Postmates (platform for delivery of goods within an hour), Washio (laundry service platform), and Luxe (car parking platform). According to the model of activity, sharing platforms differ from, for example, e-commerce or from short-term car or bicycle rent and loan platforms in that the goods or services offered do not belong to the platform owner but to private individuals, not necessarily natural persons, for whom the sharing activity is an additional source of income or is even carried out altruistically. A. Sundararajan highlights the following key features of the sharing economy: crowd-based networks as well as blurred boundaries between personal and professional activities, employee and independent service providers, work and leisure, private and public interests, goods and services (Sundararajan 2016).

The Communication from the European Commission (2016) emphasizes that the sharing economy promotes competition and consumption, reduces the cost and quality of the goods and services concerned, and enables a wide range of people to earn extra money on their own by planning their own time. The participation economy builds trust between independent suppliers and consumers of goods and services. The reason why sharing platforms can offer services at a lower price is that they have to pay, for the most part, only fixed costs such as salaries, taxes, rents, utility costs, insurance and the like, but as they increase supply, they have almost no marginal costs that increase with growing production.[2] In addition, service providers operating through sharing platforms, as a rule, pay less tax to the state than traditional companies do, as one of the goals of the sharing economy is to enable individuals to earn more without burdening them with taxes. Business models of the sharing economy promote innovation and transparency and create conditions for competitiveness and economic growth.

On the other hand, sharing platforms often operate under uncertain and obscure legal regulation, particularly in the areas of consumer and employee rights, protection, privacy, promotion of equal opportunities and fair competition, non-discrimination, and environmental protection. The legal regulation of the sharing economy is in a so-called gray area, as it usually does not fall within the typical classification of legal relations into public and private, business and personal, labor and professional, producers/sellers and consumers, commercial property and personal property. For example, most sharing platforms do not take responsibility for the activities and quality of services provided by service providers registered on these platforms; therefore, for instance, apartments offered for short-term rent may not meet safety and hygiene requirements. The Communication from the European Commission states that while the EU should actively support the opportunities for innovation, competitiveness, and growth offered by economic progress, constraints on legal regulation are also possible. They must be reasonable, proportionate, and as mild as possible, taking into account the specificities of the business

2 For more information, see Balionytė (2021).

model and relevant innovative services, without favoring any single business model and with a view to ensuring public interest.

3.1.8 *Drones and the Challenge of Airspace Availability for Everyone*

The emergence and surprising popularity of drones have triggered not only major investment by companies but also discussions among academics and public authorities regarding their legal implications. Drones may have negative effects on public safety, individual privacy, and property rights that could eventually lead to socio-economic problems.

According to the European Aviation Safety Agency (EASA) (2018), the two main threats drones pose to public safety are air risks (collision with a manned aircraft or other drones) and ground risks (collision with persons or critical infrastructure). Dangers to public safety can also derive from poor reliability of internal components of the drone. As drone technology becomes cheaper, more drones may be used by unexperienced pilots and fewer safety-related features may be included. Harm may also occur because of user error. Piloting a drone from the ground may involve long periods of boredom, interruptions, and lapses in concentration, which may cause the drone to accidentally crash into obstacles. User error could be avoided entirely through fully autonomous drone operation; however, increasing levels of autonomy might create other safety issues, such as more errors in mission planning.

Another major concern is privacy. Most drones carry on-board video cameras that can capture images of superior quality. Some are equipped with sensors that can help the drones avoid obstacles, while others can autonomously follow a person around; the higher-end drones even have advanced facial recognition capabilities. With such extensive technological surveillance capabilities and the relative invisibility and silent flight of drones, it is no surprise that individuals might feel as if they are constantly under surveillance.

Different dimensions of privacy might be infringed by drone use. For example, drone impacts on behavioral privacy may alter how individuals behave in society. As more and more drones with surveillance capabilities take to the skies, everyone can expect to be constantly watched, regardless of whether they behave suspiciously or not. This, in turn, may result in a form of self-discipline called the "chilling effect" (Clarke 2014). Privacy can also be infringed upon by using drones to transmit images of people's activities within homes or enclosed back yards, or to track the movement of private vehicles. Privacy of association may be undermined by using drones to gather and analyze information about groups of individuals. Combining drone-gathered information with facial recognition software would allow drones to identify people's affiliation with certain groups or organizations, or to predict meeting locations and schedules.

Property is another basic human right directly infringed upon by drone use. Drones usually operate just above the surface of the earth. This area is quite ambiguous since it is governed by both aviation law and property law. Aviation law regulates lower altitude airspace from above, whereas property law regulates it from below. Aviation law is grounded in the fundamental right of safety, while property law is a fundamental right in and of itself. The most sensitive part of lower altitude airspace, where drone use can be most intrusive, is in the closest reaches of the earth, which are governed by property law. Until now, property disputes in the lower altitude airspace have been resolved on an *ad hoc* basis, which means that in every case the court would have to determine whether the intrusion was "so immediate and direct as to subtract from the owner's full enjoyment of the property and to limit his exploitation of it" (*United States v. Causby*, 328 U.S. 256 1946). This might have been a viable approach when lower altitude airspace was practically empty, but it will gradually become too arduous to employ as our skies become congested with drones and more disputes emerge. Clearly, a new system to govern property relations in the lower altitude airspace is required. To date, some technological solutions to this property dilemma have emerged, one of which is geo-fencing technology. However, this cannot be sufficient to protect property rights until a clear regulatory framework for lower altitude airspace is established. Sadly, lack of proper regulation and enforcement remains one of the two major limitations delaying the rapid adoption of drones, the second limitation being short battery life (Rao et al. 2016).

Although first steps in the right direction have already been taken (some jurisdictions in the EU and US have already published drone-specific regulations), they are very small relative to the current growth rate of the drone industry. Current legislation may address issues surrounding drone use to some extent, but it is probably only a temporary solution. It is safe to say that current developments in drone legislation are lagging behind the economic and technological developments in the industry.

3.2 Conclusions and a Call for Value-Based Legal Regulation

An analysis of technological innovations from the regulatory perspective shows that transformative innovations create a non-exhaustive list of interdependent challenges, which are summarized in Figure 3.4. From the case analysis, we can distinguish at least three fields of law that will suffer the strongest impact: privacy, liability, and property.

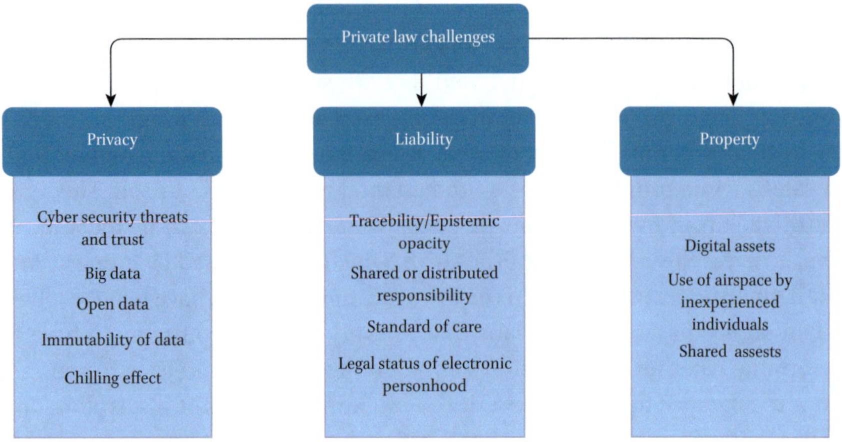

FIGURE 3.4 Transformative innovations and private law

Although the mapped challenges are based on the analysis of some innovative technologies, most of them would be applicable to other technologies as well. It is likely that the vast majority of emerging innovations will have at least some properties inherent to artificial intelligence, the internet of things, blockchains, digital assets, or drones; therefore, the analysis seemingly addresses many of the legal implications that other technologies might introduce.

This short analysis of technologies shows some of the factors underlying the emerging legal implications. First, anticipating that every smart device will eventually be able to exhibit at least some degree of autonomy because of advancements in AI technology, one of the most evident reasons is the growing level of "consciousness" and autonomy of emerging technologies. Some of the identified challenges related to this factor could be epistemic opacity in AI decision making, the vague legal status of electronic personhood, the ability to aggregate significant amounts of data in ways that reveal the private behavior of individuals, and property legislation that is no longer up to date and cannot properly regulate the use of digital assets.

A second factor could be the growing availability of transformative innovations to the broader public and the development of participatory models in the economy and other social spheres, including law. Social networks (Facebook, Twitter, Instagram), the sharing economy (Uber, Airbnb, Task Rabbit), and cryptocurrencies (Bitcoin, Ethereum) are just a few examples of this phenomenon. In terms of the analyzed technologies, the mapped challenges that reflect this tendency are airspace ownership, regulation of air traffic in the lower airspace as it becomes congested with unlicensed users, immutability of data in public blockchains, fair distribution of value in co-created ownership (the sharing economy), and distributing machine responsibility among stakeholders.

A third reason is the tendency for transformative innovations to function in regulatory uncertainty. In the system of legal rules, there is a very common division of categories into certain binary systems: public versus private, business versus personal, labor versus professional, manufacturer versus consumer, commercial property versus personal property. However, in the context of transformative innovations, these regulatory schemes often do not correspond to reality, as quasi-professional, quasi-commercial, quasi-public legal relationships emerge the regulation of which lies in the so-called "gray zone." Some argue that most current legal instruments are too slow and ineffective to regulate transformative innovations. According to Prof. Mireille Hildebrandt (2015), modern law grew up in a print culture and remains firmly wedded to the medium of text. Thus, legal concepts and instruments developed in print culture may be ineffective in the internet age. Therefore, traditional hierarchical regulatory models should be replaced by decentralized, soft, inclusive governance tools as well as foresight instruments.

In a future where all devices will be interconnected, intelligent, and able to learn from past experiences, and where every technology will be able to monitor, interpret, and predict human behavior, the values we embed in their design during the early stages of their development become crucial to ensure a good life for human beings. Waiting until technology is fully developed and only then trying to understand their social, economic, and political impact would be too difficult, if not impossible.

Values-based legal regulation should align with the principles and values enshrined in the Treaty on European Union and the Charter of Fundamental Rights, i.e., the principles of beneficence, non-maleficence, autonomy and justice, human safety, health and security, freedom, privacy, integrity and dignity, self-determination and non-discrimination, equality, justice and equity, informed consent, private and family life, and personal data protection (European Parliament 2017), as well as with other underlying principles and values of the Union law, such as "non-stigmatization, transparency, autonomy, individual responsibility and social responsibility" (European Parliament 2017).

Study Questions

1. What are the main regulatory challenges posed by smart technologies?
2. How would you define AI and robots?

3. What are the main implications and challenges of data usage for smart technologies?
4. What is the IoT? What are its main features and what legal challenges does it present?
5. What are the main implications of drone use?

References

Balionytė, E. 2021. *Ar dalijimosi ekonomika nepažeidžia sąžiningos konkurencijos?* [*Does the sharing economy violate fair competition*?]. Master thesis. https://eltalpykla.vdu.lt/handle/1/34584.

Boucher, P., et al. 2017. *How Blockchain Technology Could Change Our Lives: In-Depth Analysis*. European Parliament, Directorate-General for Parliamentary Research Services. http://bookshop.europa.eu/uri?target=EUB:NOTICE:QA0217043:EN:HTML.

Chohan, U. W. 2017. "The Decentralized Autonomous Organization and Governance Issues." *Discussion Paper Series: Notes on the 21st Century, How Blockchain Could Change Our Lives: In-Depth Analysis*.

Communication from the European Commission to the European Parliament. 2016. The European Economic and Social Committee and the Committee of the Regions. *A European Agenda for the Collaborative Economy*. http://ec.europa.eu/transparency/regdoc/rep/1/2016/LT/COM-2016-356-F1-LT-MAIN-PART-1.PDF.

DeBruyne, J., and C. Vanleenhove. 2021. *Artificial Intelligence and the Law*. Intersentia.

Dominicé, A. M., and D. H. Haux. 2020. "The Decision of the German Federal Court of Justice against Facebook: Opportunity to Define Digital Heritage?" *Santander Art & Culture Law Review* 2(6): 251–60.

Drescher, D. 2017. *Blockchain Basics. a Non-Technical Introduction in 25 Steps*. Apress.

European Commission. 2020. *The EU's Cybersecurity Strategy for the Digital Decade*. Joint communication to the European parliament and the Council. JOIN/2020/18 final, Brussels, 16.12.2020 https://eur-lex.europa.eu/legal-content/EN/TXT/PDF/?uri=CELEX:52020JC0018&from=EN.

EASA. 2018. "Introduction of a regulatory framework for the operation of unmanned aircraft systems in the 'open' and 'specific' categories." Technical opinion. European Aviation Safety Agency, 01/2018. file:///C:/Users/28718/Downloads/Opinion%20No%2001-2018.pdf.

EC High-Level Expert Group on AI. 2019. *A Definition of AI: Main Capabilities and Scientific Disciplines*. https://www.aepd.es/sites/default/files/2019-12/ai-definition.pdf.

European Parliament. 2017. *Resolution of 16 February 2017 with Recommendations to the Commission on Civil Law Rules on Robotics (2015/2103(INL))*. https://eur-lex.europa.eu/legal-content/EN/TXT/?uri=CELEX%3A52017IP0051.

Fabiano, N. 2017. "Internet of Things and the Legal Issues Related to the Data Protection Law according to the New European General Data Protection Regulation." *Athens Journal of Law* 3(3): 201–14.

Farhan, L., et al. 2018. "A Concise Review on Internet of Things (IoT): Problems, Challenges and Opportunities." 2018 11th International Symposium on Communication Systems, Networks & Digital Signal Processing (CSNDSP).

Hildebrandt, M. 2015. *Smart Technologies and the End(s) of Law*. Edward Elgar.

International Telecommunication Union. 2012. Recommendation ITU-T Y.2060, *Overview of the Internet of Things*. http://handle.itu.int/11.1002/1000/11559.

Leenes, R., et al. 2017. "Regulatory Challenges of Robotics: Some Guidelines for Addressing Legal and Ethical Issues." *Law, Innovation and Technology* 9(1): 1–44.

McCarthy, L. 2015. "Digital Assets and Intestacy." *BUJ Science and Technology Law* 21: 385.

Rao, B., et al. 2016. "The Societal Impact of Commercial Drones." *Technology in Society* 45: 83–90. https://doi.org/10.1016/j.techsoc.2016.02.009.

Sundararajan, A. 2016. *The Sharing Economy: the End of Employment and the Rise of Crowd-Based Capitalism*. MIT Press.

United Nations Educational, Scientific and Cultural Organization. 2017. *Robotic Ethics*.

Further Reading

Clarke, R. 2014. "The Regulation of Civilian Drones' Impacts on Behavioural Privacy." *Computer Law & Security Review* 30(3): 286–305.

Holder, C., et al. 2016. "Robotics and Law: Key Legal and Regulatory Implications of the Robotics Age (Part I of II)." *Computer Law & Security Review* 32(3): 383–402.

Holder, C., et al. 2016. "Robotics and Law: Key Legal and Regulatory Implications of the Robotics Age (Part II of II)." *Computer Law & Security Review* 32(4): 557–76.

Hong-Ning Dai, et al. 2020. "Big Data Analytics for Manufacturing Internet of Things: Opportunities, Challenges and Enabling Technologies." *Enterprise Information Systems* 14: 9–10.

Kiršienė, J., et al. 2019. "Rethinking the Implications of Transformative Economic Innovations: Mapping Challenges of Private Law." *Baltic Journal of Law & Politics* 12(2): 47–77.

Księżak, P., and S. Wojtczak. 2020. "AI Versus Robot: in Search of a Domain for the New European Civil Law." *Law, Innovation and Technology* 12(2): 297–317.

Rule, T. A. 2015. "Airspace in an Age of Drones." *Boston University Law Review* 95: 155–208.

CHAPTER 4

The Economy

Paulius Čerka

4.1 The Importance of Technology to Economic Development

4.1.1 *AI's Potential to Contribute to Global Economic Activity*

> The world we have created today as a result of our thinking thus has problems which cannot be solved by thinking the way we thought when we created them.
>
> ALBERT EINSTEIN

AI has great potential to contribute to global economic activity (McKinsey Global Institute 2018). AI is bringing dramatic changes to the economy. Clearly, AI has the potential to become one of the main contributors to global economic growth. According to the "Artificial Intelligence Is the Future of Growth" report by Accenture, AI can help double annual economic growth rates, boost labor productivity, and shorten the timeline to growth with various degrees of effectiveness for most countries. Global economies are looking to capitalize on this potential growth.

Countries looking to become forerunners in new technology have developed national strategies aimed at promoting the growth of AI. The European Union is taking the initiative with a coordinated AI plan that was released in December 2018. The main goal of the plan is "for Europe to become the world-leading region for developing and deploying cutting-edge, ethical and secure AI, promoting a human-centric approach in the global context."[1] The broadly cited research done by McKinsey Global Institute in September 2018 focused on modeling AI's potential impact on the economy. Scientists applied a simulation-based approach to determine that "AI has the potential to deliver additional economic output of around $13 trillion or 16% to global output by 2030 thereby boosting global GDP by about 1.2 percent a year." The same study states, "An early average simulation indicates that by 2030, 70% of

1 Lietuvos Ekonomikos ir inovacijų ministerija ir ekspertų grupė: https://eimin.lrv.lt/uploads/eimin/documents/files/DI_strategija_ENG(1).pdf.

 | DOI:10.1163/9789004682900_006

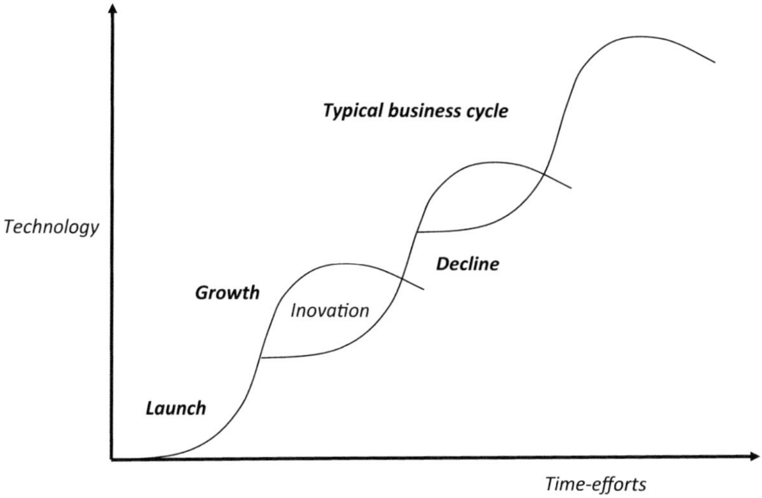

FIGURE 4.1 Time-efforts/technology performance

companies will adopt any one type of available AI technologies" (McKinsey Global Institute 2018). So basically, we already know the global economy will experience an increase, but we still need a more specific picture of whether developed and developing countries will be affected in a similar manner, how AI will affect unemployment rates in specific countries and globally, and how this impact will continue over time. Our concerns are based on the same study's indication that AI impact will "typically follow an S-shaped curve justified by a slow start" (see Figure 4.1) and "realization of full economic impact of AI deployment can be gradually observed over a period of 5 years" (McKinsey Global Institute 2018).

A November 2017 report from McKinsey on the effects of automation on jobs, skills, and wages for the period ending in 2030 estimates that fully 50% of current work activities are automatable by technologies that have already been tested and found effective. The report predicts that in 60% of occupations, at least one-third of activities could be automated. The report expects that 400 million to 800 million people could be displaced by automation in the next 12 years, creating a challenge potentially greater than past historic shifts, at least in the modern era (see also Figure 4.2).

Most experts agree that AI's impact on the economy most likely will be large as the effects of technological and industrial revolutions in the past. But an overall positive effect does not mean good news for everyone in the economy. Those who will embrace technology will benefit most, and those who fail to flexibly adopt their businesses or professional skills will experience losses. "The

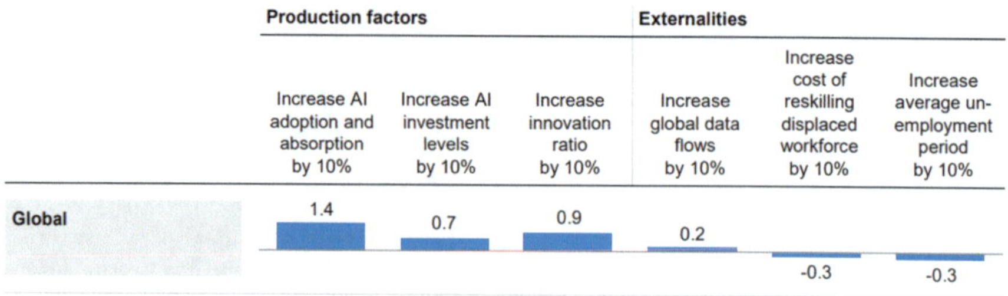

FIGURE 4.2 Effects of AI on the labor market
SOURCE: BLOOMBERG (2018)

benefits of AI are likely to be distributed unequally, and if the development and deployment of these technologies are not handled effectively, inequality could deepen, fueling conflict within societies. This research is our attempt to simulate how the transition to AI might unfold. We will continue to refine our analysis as new data become available and as we learn more about how the shift to AI is progressing on the ground. Our hope is that this research can help inform the ongoing discussion about AI and its potential impact on the global economy" (McKinsey Global Institute 2018).

Normally it is held that technological inventions shift the isoquant of production down, but technological process could be neutral, labor-saving, or capital-saving (see Figure 4.3).

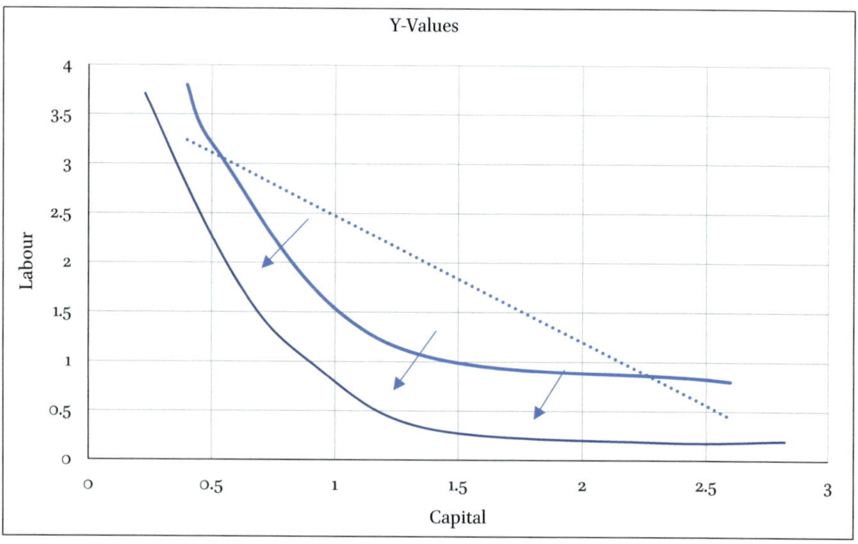

FIGURE 4.3 Isoquant of production

4.2 Lessons from Past Technological Revolutions' Impacts for the Economy

In seeking answers to our question, we will apply the analogy of technology effects in past history to derive lessons for our present and future challenges. Hence, before analyzing AI's impact on the economy, we have to evaluate more basically the influence of technology on the economy, since AI is part of technology development or, in some cases, particular examples of technology itself. Since the impact of technology is so heavily analyzed and there are centuries of historical experience regarding how the economy changes due to new technologies, it would be reasonable to state principles that describe the correlation between technology and economy and then apply these principles to AI's impact.

In some sense, human history is the history of knowledge, and it is accepted by most scholars that technology and productivity are the main engines of economic growth, since technology determines the competitiveness of economic actors in the market.

Since in every economic change caused by technology there is some resistance, we can expect the same with AI technologies. Such opposition is typically referred to as a "Luddite movement" with its paradoxes: "Luddite invents machine to destroy technology more quickly." "The Luddites were a secret oath-based organization" (Byrne 2013) of textile workers who protested against manufacturers who used machines in the 19th century in Britain. Basically, they saw the implementation of automation as a dishonest behavior by businesses "to get around standard labour practices" (Conniff 2011), since "time spent learning the skills of employees craft would go to waste, as machines would replace their role in the industry."[2] Luddites justified their cause by the fact that "it was very hard to find jobs because producing things in factories required fewer workers than producing those same things in a workshop. This left many people unemployed and angry." So "Luddite" became a general term for opposition to automation and new technologies in general.[3]

Most of society, even if objecting to technological dominance, continues to increase its consumption of AI: "College students take out their earbuds to discuss how technology dominates their lives. But when a class ends, Loyola University of Chicago professor Steven E. Jones notes, their cellphones all come to life, screens glowing in front of their faces, and they migrate across the lawns

2 "Who Were the Luddites?" History.com. Retrieved December 12, 2016.

3 "Luddite," *Compact Oxford English Dictionary* at AskOxford.com. Accessed February 22, 2010.

like giant schools of cyborg jellyfish" (Conniff 2011). It is evident that there is no turning back now. It is true that not all effects of technology are positive, but our focus should be on policies that respond to changes in the structure of the workforce or business organization resulting from new technologies.

In late 2000, intensive automation was happening in the industrial economy, which led to product improvements and process efficiencies. As a result, we now have about 90% less human presence in factories and their former tasks are done by robots, who perform the work of thousands of former laborers. If machines do everything, is there a place left for humans? This is not only a question for writers of science fiction and fantasy. How will this trend affect the middle-knowledge jobs that usually support society's functioning? First, we are lucky that we can take lessons from our history.

> People have been worried about "new machines" and their effect on the human condition for centuries. Only the machine has changed; the concerns remain the same. Back in the early 1800s, during the First Industrial Revolution, the Luddites in northwestern England responded to the introduction of power looms by smashing them. They recognized that their textile jobs were at risk. It turned out that they were right; the machines did take over their jobs. Then the same thing happened in agriculture. At the beginning of the 19th century—when the Luddites were smashing looms—80% of the U.S. labor force was working the land. Today, less than 2% of U.S. workers are in agriculture.
>
> FRANK ET AL. 2017

Similarly, "Electrification of US industry in the early 20th century benefited from a flexible educational system that gave people entering the labor force the skills needed to switch from farm work as well as training opportunities for existing workers to develop new skills. In the same way, education and training should give today's workers the wherewithal to thrive in a new economy in which repetitive cognitive tasks—from driving a truck to analyzing a medical scan—are replaced by new skills such as web engineering and protecting cyber security. More generally, future jobs will probably emphasize human empathy and originality: the professionals deemed least likely to become obsolete include nursery school teachers, clergy, and artists" (Mühleisen 2018). What do these facts mean? Basically, technology will change our human labor structure and distribution of employment across economic sectors, but on the other hand, new workplaces will be created with high demand for a human labor force.

The changes our society is experiencing now, we can also see in the past. History can teach us a lot. On one hand, new technology is driving growth and increasing productivity and economic wealth, but on the other hand it dramatically changes the distribution of labor functions. Also, all technological revolutions brought a bubble along with them. "Despite the complex effects of automation on labor, there is ample evidence that, historically, automation fosters productivity growth. For example, Crafts (2004) documents the effects of steam engine technology on productivity in the UK in the 19th century" (Furman and Seamans 2018). "But every technological revolution has brought two types of prosperity. The first type is turbulent and exciting like the bubbles of the 1990s and 2000s and like the Roaring Twenties, the railway mania, and the canal mania before. They all ended in a bubble collapse. Yet, after the recession, there came the second type: the Victorian boom, the Belle Époque, the Post War Golden Age and … the one that we could have ahead now. Bubble prosperities polarize incomes; Golden Ages tend to reverse the process" (Perez 2013).

The changes we experience are not new; our forefathers went through them in so-called industrial revolutions. For example, "When the steam engine enabled mechanization during the Second Industrial Revolution, experts openly worried that the substitution of machinery for human labor might render the population redundant" (*The Economist*, June 25, 2016). The initial reaction was fear of rising unemployment, warned against by most economists "due to our discovery of means of economizing the use of labor outrunning the pace at which we can find new uses for labor" (quoted in Schwab 2016). Yes, unemployment is certainly coming to present workplaces, as stated in an Oxford University study indicating that about 50% of total U.S. job tasks will probably be transferred to new machines during the next decade or so (Benedikt and Osborne 2016).

"We also review recent research in this area that suggests that AI and robotics have the potential to increase productivity growth but may have mixed effects on labor, particularly in the short run. In particular, some occupations and industries may do well while others experience labor market upheaval. We then consider current and potential policies around AI that may help to boost productivity growth while also mitigating any labor market downsides, including evaluating the pros and cons of an AI specific regulator, expanded antitrust enforcement, and alternative strategies for dealing with the labor market impacts of AI, including universal basic income and guaranteed employment" (Furman and Seamans 2019).

4.3 Structural Changes in Employment because of AI

Changes in employment demand and talent requirements in the AI era have been more evident in developed countries and leading companies. Taking the United States as an example, the technological changes over the past few decades—particularly the rapid growth of computer processing speed and capabilities and the automation of everyday tasks—have resulted in a decrease in the time spent on manual and cognitive tasks, especially by production line and operations workers and office clerks. At the same time, demand has continued to grow for professional service talent, with an emphasis on communications, logic and creation, and technical talent dealing with computer technologies.

In China, we have also observed similar changes in employment demand and talent requirements. In this wave of technological progress, positions relying on creativity and communications will continue to grow. At present, AI technology in China is still at an introductory stage, so changes in employment demand in the AI field are limited and are mainly reflected in a demand for basic technical talent. From a recruitment perspective, companies are placing greater emphasis on technical skills, particularly ability in basic AI (He 2018).

> From a theoretical perspective, innovation has four effects on labor markets. The first is that automation can directly displace labor in the affected sector. The second is that automation can create new jobs in new areas. ... Third, higher incomes increase demand for jobs throughout the economy, including in ways that are not directly linked to technology. ... Finally, technology may replace specific tasks rather than entire jobs—leaving substantial room for human employment in jobs that will be changed by workers having a new tool at their disposal.
>
> FURMAN AND SEAMANS 2018

In summary, we may state that AI as new technology will lead to changing patterns of business and labor activity and not a decrease in overall employment. Therefore, AI will not wipe off jobs and will, in fact, have a neutral or only minimally negative impact on long-term overall employment. But AI will affect the present picture of business and labor tasks and functions. We already see some traditional firms going out of business and some structural unemployment, which contributes to increased inequality in society. AI technology is likely to disrupt labor markets, increasing the demand for certain skills and potentially increasing wage gaps (see Table 4.1).

TABLE 4.1 Impact on jobs in various sectors

Employment categories	2015	2016	2017	2018	2019	2020	2021	2022
Management, business, and financial	9%	19%	29%	40%	51%	64%	77%	92%
Professional and related	8%	17%	27%	37%	48%	60%	73%	87%
Protective service	6%	12%	19%	26%	35%	44%	54%	66%
Nor-protective	6%	12%	19%	27%	35%	44%	55%	67%
Sales and related	7%	14%	23%	32%	41%	52%	63%	76%
Office and admin support	7%	15%	23%	32%	42%	52%	64%	76%
Farming, fishing, forestry	6%	11%	18%	24%	32%	40%	50%	62%
Construction and extraction	6%	11%	18%	24%	31%	40%	49%	60%
Installation, maintenance, and repair	6%	11%	17%	24%	31%	39%	49%	60%
Production	6%	11%	18%	24%	32%	40%	50%	61%
Transportation and material moving	6%	11%	18%	25%	32%	41%	51%	62%

4.4 Digitization of the Economy

After we have analyzed technology's impact on the economy, we should also learn some insights from the digitalization of the economy, since AI is not only new technology but also a product of a broader digitization process. We already mentioned that AI as new technology will change the structure of the labor force. AI, as a part of the digitization process, will change the face of business models too. Usually, the digital economy is understood as an economic activity that uses digital technologies to provide goods and services. Such digital communication technologies are part of our everyday lives as the internet, e-mail, digital payments, and social media. These digitization elements change the face of business models, since digital communication has opened up cheap and instantaneous communication, digital payment systems (credit cards, bitcoin, and other systems), enabled cashless operations and digital automation done by computer and more and more by AI, and made it possible to use massive amounts of various data almost instantaneously. Factories, street shops, newspaper ads, and check cashing centers have been replaced by data centers, internet websites, social media, and e-payment systems. Today, some digital services do not provide physical goods at all (for example, Netflix and Spotify). Huge business provide services almost exclusively in a digital manner, such as Airbnb (booking accommodations online), Amazon and eBay (online marketplaces), or Netflix (marketing films online).

It is not hard to notice the advantages of the digital economy. It has increased access to information for consumers, making it easier for consumers to make comparisons and choose the best products. Digitization helps consumers save time in obtaining services or purchasing items. Therefore, we can see reduced service provision costs for businesses. Digitization has also increased the possibilities for greater personalization of products related to consumers. Again, lower costs mean lower barriers to market entry. New businesses may be started with less capital investment; as a result, more people can start businesses or even work from home.

On the other hand, we can expect some negative effects too. Digitization opened up possibilities to increase monopoly power for some actors (such as Amazon, Google, Facebook), by opening up global markets to them without high entry costs. Also, we can notice a decrease of community, since there is decrease in physical meeting places for people. Again, digitization has created greater risks regarding privacy issues, since private data are now more easily collected. Digitization was expected to solve environmental issues, but actually digital data centers contribute to increased use of all types of energy and to our so-called throw-away culture, in which, thanks to rapid changes in digital technology, items are dumped for new ones more and more intensively, leading to greater use of raw materials. "AI's impact on consumer-oriented businesses is one of the most substantial among the plethora of industries it has revolutionized, and this trend is likely to continue. Amazon is one of the latest to embrace this trend, opening its first cashierless grocery store called "Amazon Go"—a prominent innovation in redefining consumers' shopping experience" (Baral 2018).

AI's impact has not been fully evaluated yet. Stephen Hawking shared this warning: "Success in creating effective AI could be the biggest event in the history of our civilization. Or the worst. So we cannot know if we will be infinitely helped by AI or ignored by it and sidelined, or conceivably destroyed by it" (quoted in Hruska 2017). We must acknowledge not only positive effects but also risks related to AI:

> Although AI clearly augments efficiency for both producers and consumers, there is significant speculation in the American media concerning AI taking over jobs and throwing millions into poverty. A Bruegel analysis shows that "54% of EU jobs [are] at risk of computerization," arguing that job losses are very likely to be significant. This point is further substantiated by a report submitted by McKinsey, one of the leading management consulting firms, which speculates that "in 60 percent of occupations, at least one-third of activities could be automated" by 2030. The report also expects between 400 and 800 million people to be displaced by automation technology in the next 12 years—hardly a prediction to be excited about.
>
> BARAL 2018

In summary, most scholars hold the view that AI has great potential to change the economy, increase productivity growth, and create major labor disruptions. Scientific research is still assessing these issues.

4.5 AI Applications in the Financial Markets

Some economic sectors are more sensitive to AI technology innovation than others. We could forecast that financial markets will be strongly affected by AI innovation, primarily because data analysis is fundamental for financial markets and data analysis problems are a sphere where AI outweighs human cognitive abilities. Since financial markets are fast-moving, complex networks with numerous participants, AI will affect markets in such spheres as trading processes, risk management, assessment and control, resource optimization, and control and compliance processes (e.g., identity protection, anti-money laundering standards). AI already is greatly implemented into solving those problems. AI algorithms will mitigate human error factors and AI automation will optimize unnecessary processes. AI innovation in financial markets will not only change possibilities for customers and businesses, but also for government agencies. AI systems should be able to detect manipulation, fraud, or other kinds of illicit activity by applicant patterns on vast data, whereas humans were unable to spot such actions. Therefore, AI will increase the integrity and security of financial markets, helping them function even better by providing effective oversight.

Study Questions

1. What types of jobs will AI likely replace?
2. Which types of companies are vulnerable to being "Ubered"?
3. What new job categories are expected to emerge in the next 5–10 years?
4. Predict what industries may look like 10 years from now.
5. What are some of the modern-day analogies to the Luddite movement?

References

Baral, S. 2018. "The Rise of AI: Impacts on Consumer-Oriented Firms and the Future of the Economy." https://theeconreview.com/2018/10/19/the-rise-of-ai-impacts-on-consumer-oriented-firms-and-the-future-of-the-economy/.

Bloomberg. 2018. "Will Robots Take Your Job? Humans Ignore the Coming AI Revolution at their Peril." NBC News. https://www.nbcnews.com/think/opinion/will-robots-take-your-job-humans-ignore-coming-ai-revolution-ncna845366.

Byrne, R. 2013. "A Nod to Ned Ludd." *The Baffler* 23(23): 120–28.

Conniff, R. 2011. "What the Luddites Really Fought Against." *Smithsonian*. https://www.smithsonianmag.com/history/what-the-luddites-really-fought-against-264412/.

Crafts, N. F. R. 2004. "Steam as a General Purpose Technology: A Growth Accounting Perspective." *The Economic Journal* 114(495): 338–51.

Frank, M., P. Roehrig, and B. Pring. 2017. *What To Do When Machines Do Everything: How to Get Ahead in a World of AI, Algorithms, Bots, and Big Data*. John Wiley & Sons.

Frey, C. B., and M. Osborne. 2016. "The Future of Employment: How Susceptible Are Jobs to Computerisation?" Oxford Martin Webnotes, December 23, 2016. http://www.oxfordmartin.ox.ac.uk/downloads/academic/The_Future_of_Employment.pdf.

Furman, J., and R. Seamans. 2018. "AI and the Economy." https://www.nber.org/system/files/working_papers/w24689/w24689.pdf.

Furman, J., and R. Seamans. 2019. "AI and the Economy." National Bureau of Economic Research, *Harvard Kennedy School NYU Stern School of Business* 19. https://www.journals.uchicago.edu/doi/pdfplus/10.1086/699936.

He, D. 2018. "4 Ways AI Will Impact the Financial Job Market." https://www.weforum.org/agenda/2018/09/4-ways-ai-artificial-intelligence-impact-financial-job-market/.

Hruska, J. 2017. "Stephen Hawking: AI Could Be the Worst Event in the History of Civilization." https://www.extremetech.com/computing/258646-stephen-hawking-believes-ai-could-be-the-worst-event-in-the-history-of-civilization.

"March of the Machines." *The Economist*, June 25, 2016, p. 11, http://www.economist.com/news/leaders/21701119-what-history-tells-usabout-future-artificial-intelligenceand-how-society-should.

McKinsey Global Institute. 2018. "Notes from the AI Frontier: Modeling the Impact of AI on the World Economy." https://www.mckinsey.com/~/media/McKinsey/Featured%20Insights/Artificial%20Intelligence/Notes%20from%20the%20frontier%20Modeling%20the%20impact%20of%20AI%20on%20the%20world%20economy/MGI-Notes-from-the-AI-frontier-Modeling-the-impact-of-AI-on-the-world-economy-September-2018.pdf.

Mühleisen, M. 2018. "The Long and Short of The Digital Revolution." *Finance & Development* 55(2). https://www.imf.org/external/pubs/ft/fandd/2018/06/impact-of-digital-technology-on-economic-growth/muhleisen.html.

Perez, C. 2013. "The New Technological Revolution." Presentation at the Technology Frontiers Forum of *The Economist*. https://carlotaperez.org/wp-content/downloads/media/articles-and-blogs/Perez_Economist_Technology_Frontiers.pdf.

Schwab, K. 2016. *The Fourth Industrial Revolution*. http://www3.weforum.org/docs/Media/KSC_4IR.pdf.

Further Reading

Agrawal, A., J. Gans, and A. Goldfarb. 2018. *Prediction Machines*. Harvard Business Review Press.

Bootle, R. 2019. *The AI Economy: Work, Wealth and Welfare in the Age of the Robot*. Nicholas Brealey Publications.

Ford, M. 2016. *Rise of the Robots: Technology and the Threat of a Jobless Future*. Basic Books.

Frank, M., Roehrig P., Pring B. 2017. *"What To Do When Machines Do Everything: How to Get Ahead in a World of AI, Algorithms, Bots, and Big Data"* 39p., Wiley. Numbers derived from Bureau of Labor Statistics (BLS).

CHAPTER 5

Political Science: AI Governance

Karolis Kubilevičius and Tomas Berkmanas

5.1 The Importance of Artificial Intelligence to Political Science

Artificial intelligence (AI) has been one of the main subjects of research for the last 70 years. It is believed that "AI can deliver great benefits for economies and society, and support decision-making which is fairer, safer and more inclusive and informed" (Google 2019, 2). There are many different areas where AI can be used. The field of "AI governance studies how humanity can best navigate the transition" to advanced AI systems, "focusing on the political, economic, military, governance, and ethical dimensions" (Dafoe 2018, 5). The focus of this article will be on the impact of AI on political science and, more generally, on the whole political field.

The use of AI in processes of a political nature (be it more academic or more practical) has several benefits: easier access to government services, simpler exercise of rights, increased transparency, communication between the government and the citizen, etc. Automation of these or, more precisely, shifting the control over to AI allows the government to save costs without losing the quality of services provided. Moreover, the entire process becomes quick, simple and efficient, allowing the government to eliminate bureaucracy and focus on areas that are more beneficial to citizens.

When discussing AI in the context of political science, we encounter concepts such as e-governance, automation, semi-autonomous, and fully autonomous. To avoid any misinterpretations, it is important to establish definitions of the aforementioned concepts.

5.2 Definitions

In the context of this article, a fully autonomous AI system will be understood as the ability to perform any task that requires thinking as well as a human being. In accordance with this definition, a system cannot be regarded as AI-based if it cannot operate without the interruption and/or assistance of a human being. Similarly, only a fully autonomous system, i.e., a system that can

 | DOI:10.1163/9789004682900_007

make decisions on its own without any human intervention, will be considered AI-based.

A semi-autonomous system means that the system can perform limited tasks that require thinking. In other words, the system can operate without human intervention only to a certain extent. Finally, an automated system can perform only the most basic tasks without human intervention (e.g., auto-pilot, cruise control). Unlike fully autonomous systems and (to an extent) semi-autonomous system, an automated system cannot by itself respond or adapt to any unexpected events unless a human being has programmed the system to do so (and even then, the response is very limited).

Meanwhile, fully autonomous systems and, to some extent, semi-autonomous systems do not have to be programmed by a human being to face unexpected events, as they can make the necessary programming changes themselves. This distinction is important because in the context of this article, we will be talking only about the highest level of AI, namely fully autonomous systems.

Now that we have defined key AI concepts, we can explore additional concepts that are more specific to the political realm:

E-governance is "the use of information and communication technologies [ICTs] in government in ways that either (1) alter governance structure or processes in ways that are not feasible without ICT and/or (2) create new governance structures or processes that were until now not possible without ICT and/or (3) reify heretofore theoretical ideas or issues in normative governance" (Bannister and Connolly 2012).

E-democracy is "the support and enhancement of traditional democracy by means of ICT, and which can complement and reinforce democratic processes by adding elements of citizens' empowerment through different online activities that include, amongst others, e-government, e-governance, e-deliberation, e-participation and e-voting" (European Parliament 2017).[1]

To sum up the abovementioned concepts of e-governance and e-democracy, we could say that these two concepts describe (1) the processes by which government functions and interacts with its citizens and (2) the enhancement of said processes through digital means. Whereas limited AI is already used in the abovementioned processes (e.g., virtual assistants that help the government to communicate with citizens), these processes are still currently dependent on the interaction of a human being. There are two main reasons for that. One

1 The European Parliament refers to e-democracy as the use of ICT to create channels for public consultation and participation (for example, an e-parliament, e-initiatives, e-voting, e-petitions, e-consultation, etc.).

reason is that due to technical limitations, for the time being it is technically impossible to create AI that would be fully autonomous. Second, there are no established imperative rules, or the established rules are very limited and/or too abstract, that would apply to fully autonomous AI.

Similarly, since conventional governments act in accordance with rules and other regulations when enacting laws or acting on behalf of the citizens, a fully autonomous AI system with the ability to act on its own accord has to adhere to certain rules. The need for rules applicable to AI use in democratic processes is also highlighted by the European Commission, which assigned AI technology used in democratic processes to the category of high-risk AI systems subject to "strict obligations" (European Commission 2021).

Without any established rules, AI would have no accountability to the citizens (unlike conventional governments), thus negating the benefits of using fully autonomous AI in political processes (such as those discussed in the first part of this article). With that in mind, in the next section we will discuss the basic principles that should be applicable to AI use in political processes.

5.3 Principles

There are two main ways in which AI can be used in political processes. The first is AI use in administrative procedures, such as answering basic inquiries, managing e-petitions and their voting procedures, etc. Due to their low level of complexity, these types of tasks can be completed by semi-autonomous AI or even an automated system. The second, more ambitious way to use AI would be in decision-making procedures. This type of AI would essentially replace government officials and make decisions in their stead.

In each of the two ways in which AI can be used, there are two different groups of subjects/objects that have to adhere to rules. In the former way, the main group would be the human beings who control or manage the semi-autonomous AI or automated systems. In the latter way, it would be the AI itself (since fully autonomous AI should have the ability to perform tasks requiring thinking without human's supervision). Before we expand on the second point, it is important to keep in mind that if AI is to be used in decision making, it must also have the same type of accountability that applies to government officials. The logic behind that claim is that traditionally, in democratic countries, citizens either choose their representatives (representative democracy) or make decisions directly (direct democracy). Naturally, in a representative democracy, the elected officials represent the interests of their voters. Therefore, the officials must not only adhere to existing rules but must also properly represent the citizens. The same duties and rules ought to apply to AI, should it be used in decision making as well.

And just as in the case of government officials, the processes conducted by AI must be transparent. In fact, in the context of AI, transparency plays an even bigger role than in conventional governments. Citizens lack knowledge regarding the functionality of AI. If a person does not understand how an AI system works or what the system is doing exactly, he will not support its use in the political field. Moreover, unlike conventional governments (in representative democracy), the AI system is not (or in theory should not be) elected by the citizens. Nor is it controlled directly by the citizens as in the case of direct democracy. Thus, AI political systems may run into a problem of legitimacy; i.e., no matter how advanced the AI system is, if it is not transparent, it will not be accepted by the citizens.

Therefore, it is important to ensure that the AI used in decision making has the same level of accountability as conventional government officials. Furthermore, the AI processes must be clear and fair and must revolve around the human citizens, because otherwise they will lose legitimacy in the eyes of the citizens.

These four main principles that should be applicable to an AI are:

- Transparency of the process: ability to receive information about every single process related to governance where AI is used. Transparency allows citizens to constantly be informed about the various actions conducted by the AI system. Removing any obscurity may make the citizens more prone to accept AI and its use in political processes.
- Explainability: the ability to explain the processes of an AI system in human terms. After ensuring the transparency of processes, it is necessary to provide clarity. It must be possible to explain AI processes in such a way that a moderately intelligent person can understand them (thus increasing citizens' trust).
- Fairness: the ability to conduct actions impartially, without favoritism or discrimination. Just like conventional political processes, AI-based decisions must also be fair, so that the interests of various groups of citizens are not harmed.
- Human-centeredness: the ability to focus on users' needs and requirements by "applying human factors and (or) ergonomics, usability knowledge and techniques" (International Organization for Standardization 2010). Before the AI system can make political decisions, the citizens must be assured that their well-being is placed at the center. If AI-related decisions do not revolve around the welfare of the citizens, the system will lose the citizens' trust.

Finally, the principles are interdependent. The absence of even a single principle could infringe the integrity of citizens' rights. In the absence of transparency, the processes of AI decision making will not be public; in the absence of explainability, the citizens will not be able to understand AI processes; in the absence of fairness, AI will not be impartial; and in the absence of a human-centric approach, AI will not act in favor of citizens.

5.4 Current Technical Possibilities

With advancements brought forth by the industrial revolution 4.0, the use of AI in everyday activities has turned from a scientific fiction into reality. The internet of things, autonomous vehicles, quantum computing, machine learning, deep learning, and a plethora of other advanced technologies are continuously being developed and applied in various different fields, such as healthcare, energy, and aerospace (United Nations Conference on Trade and Development 2018, 13).

Political science is one field where limited and semi-limited AI can be used as well. To be specific, machine learning (one branch of AI) has several uses in political science:

- Classification of data. In political science, this type of algorithm can be used to predict how many seats a certain political party will receive. The class of information the algorithm is looking for has to be user-defined (Cranmer 2019, 4).
- Clustering of data. This type of algorithm has a similar use to classification algorithms, except that it looks for certain classes without the knowledge of which class or classes to look for (Cranmer 2019, 4).
- Reduction of data. This type of algorithm summarizes the data, providing a coherent summary of longer documents. It can be used for "recovering ideological measures for an expansive range of political actors using contribution records" (Bonica 2014, 16).

The above-mentioned algorithms are mainly used for analyzing relevant data. They can be useful when political figures need to know the general opinion of the citizens regarding certain matters. Furthermore, they can help to predict the potential political landscape. Of course, this opens a door to potential abuse of the algorithms, such as using them on behalf of one political party to sway public opinion. But this type of technology will continue being developed with or without support from local governments. Therefore, it is more beneficial to be part of the development process and to have the ability to explore potential risks and how to combat them.

Another way to use limited and semi-limited AI in political science is through e-democracy instruments. This type of use is closely related to communication between government institutions and the citizens. E-democracy instruments include the following:

- E-petitions. Various tools are used to assist citizens in filing a complaint, request, or demand regarding an issue or an infringement of rights. This type of tool usually provides the citizen with the ability to file a petition online; sign a petition with an electronic signature; modify the petition's text virtually; discuss the petition's content virtually; or follow the progress of the petition from the comfort of one's phone, computer, or any other electronic device.
- E-voting. These tools give citizens the ability to submit their vote either through a stationary electronic device (electronic voting machines) or remotely (phone, computer, etc.). One of the key factors supporting this technology is the ability to confirm the identity of a user, so as to prevent fraud or illegal voting.
- E-consultation. These tools permit users to "collect opinions of designated persons or the public at large on a specific policy issue without necessarily mandating the decision maker" (Council of Europe 2009). They make it possible for the citizens to add their input regarding policy initiatives and decision making. The difference between e-consultation and e-petitions is that citizens can use e-consultation to express an opinion regarding a project or a new policy. In contrast, an e-petition is usually submitted after a policy has been already enacted.
- E-initiatives, or "using electronic and internet tools to establish initiatives by citizens in order to participate in or influence political decision-making and engage in political agenda setting" (Council of Europe 2009).
- E-participation. This type of tools allows citizens to participate actively and engage in defining the process and content of policy making. The difference between e-consultation and e-participation is that in the latter context, citizens can suggest policy changes rather than just consultation or general input.

To summarize the current technical possibilities, we could say that the current technologies in political science empower alternative forms of political participation as well as offering different methods of processing extensive collections of data.

5.5 Safety Requirements

AI-based systems, for the most part, depend on access to the internet. Internet access allows government officials, businesses, and citizens to use these systems when it is most convenient. Naturally, AI must meet the same safety requirements as would any other system that uses the internet or any other electronic device as its base:

- Cyber security. For several years, cybercrimes have been one of the fastest growing types of crime (Meško 2018, 1–2). The threat has become even greater with the global spread of the COVID-19 pandemic, since more citizens have started working at home, thus increasing the use of internet-dependent technology. Criminals' ability to conceal their actions and minimize the risk of getting caught, while at the same time achieving a larger financial gain than from conventional type of crimes, makes it difficult to investigate cyber incidents and to indict culprits. Furthermore, the low bar of entry makes cyber crimes very appealing, increasing the number of cyber incidents of various degrees exponentially. For this reason, internet-dependent and electronic AI systems must ensure the safety of private data and sensitive information of all citizens. Furthermore, it is important to ensure confidentiality so that citizens would not lose their trust in AI-based systems. After all, in the words of Margrethe Vestager, Executive Vice-President for a Europe Fit for the Digital Age, "On artificial intelligence, trust is a must, not a nice thing to have" (European Commission 2021).
- Data redundancy. In the event that cyber security is not enough to provide safety for AI-based systems, data redundancy must be ensured. Although data redundancy does not focus on the technology used in AI-based systems, it can help to preserve the integrity of sensitive data. Whereas some cyber incidents involve the theft of sensitive information, a large portion of cyber criminals aim to destroy sensitive data.[2] Therefore it is important to make sure that the data are backed on several systems.
- Safe authorization. AI-based systems must be able to be used only on safe networks and only after the person has confirmed his or her identity and provided appropriate passwords. Furthermore, the systems used in confirming a person's identity must also adhere to legal norms; i.e., if a person is confirming his or her identity by the use of an electronic signature, the person must use a qualified signature. In addition, in case of an unauthorized

2 Some examples of types of viruses used in cyber incidents: Trojan horse—enables cyber criminals to delete, block, modify, or copy people's data; ransomware—blocks access to a system or personal files, threatening to delete files unless a ransom is paid.

connection, the system has to automatically block access until the person either confirms his or her identity or access to an account is restored by the official institutions. This safety requirement is different from cyber security, because it partially relies on people's proper use of AI-based systems whereas cyber security is necessary to protect the system from cyber threats, over which the person has little control.

5.6 Risks

In addition to the limitations set forth in the second part of this article, there is one more important obstacle for the implementation of AI in political processes. Not everyone is convinced that political processes can be automated to the point where human interaction will not be needed. Authors Maciej Kuziemski and Gianluca Misuraca have summed up the main risks of using machine learning algorithms for political processes:

- Framing trap: failure to model the entire system over which a social criterion, such as fairness, will be enforced.
- Portability trap: failure to understand how repurposing algorithmic solutions designed for one social context may be misleading, inaccurate, or otherwise harmful when applied to a different context.
- Formalism trap: failure to account for the full meaning of social concepts such as fairness, which can be procedural, contextual, and contestable and cannot be resolved through mathematical formalisms.
- Ripple effect trap: failure to understand how the insertion of technology into an existing social system changes the behaviors and embedded values of the pre-existing system.
- Solutionism trap: failure to recognize the possibility that the best solution to a problem may not involve technology. (Kuziemski and Misuraca 2020, 4)

The first trap (framing) may occur when a system does not take into account all the relevant parts of the larger socio-technical system of which it is a part. Let's take, as an example, a system used to draft legal acts. Before giving the final output (in this case, the text of a legal act), the system must take into account the data (or the input) that it uses to draft the legal act. Such data include the subjects affected, compatibility with other legal norms, legal precedents, and other factors. Furthermore, the system must take into account the result (or the output)—in this particular example, how the subjects will interpret the text of a legal act.

The portability trap may occur when the same solution to a problem is used in a different context without taking into an account the differences between the two contexts. The possible differences include legal systems, cultures, political systems, social norms, and others.

The formalism trap may occur when the process of data quantification is based only on pure mathematical formulas and does not take into account procedures, contexts, and other information that cannot be conveyed mathematically. For example, when trying to predict the crime rate, one cannot simply evaluate the number of arrests made over a specific period of time. It is important also to evaluate the context surrounding the arrests (for example, maybe the arrest happened as a result of discrimination), the procedure used, and contestable factors (i.e., any other variables that had an impact on the arrest).

The fourth trap, ripple effect, may occur when the process has unforeseen impacts on an already existing system. It is important not only to evaluate the benefits of a system being created, but also its drawbacks in the context of the environment where the system is going to be applied. Otherwise, it may have the opposite effect from what is desired or it may be ineffective.

Finally, the solutionism trap may occur when the problem is addressed only through technological means. It is important to keep in mind that technological means are only one of the alternative ways in which a problem can be solved.

The above-mentioned traps highlight the potential danger of "how algorithms may fail to properly account for or understand the interactions between technical systems and social worlds" (Kuziemski and Misuraca 2020, 4). Furthermore, they highlight the dangers of machine bias, i.e., the less relevant data the machine has at its disposal, the less accurate the result will be.

Another risk of using AI in political processes is the black box situation. As mentioned above, transparency plays a very important role in politics. Failing to ensure the transparency of political processes can result in citizen distrust with the processes or even in civil unrest. The black box problem is exactly the opposite of transparency; this term refers to situations when decisions made by AI become unpredictable and unknown either to the creator, the consumer (in the context of this article, that would be the citizens), or both. Since the thorough peculiarities of the black box problem will be explored in other articles, we will not further expand on this issue here. But we must keep in mind that in the context of political science, the black box problem is detrimental to the use of AI in more advanced political processes (such as decision making).

Political processes in the contemporary world are closely related to the processes of democracy. The principles that are now the main pillars of democracy have been used and developed for centuries. The advancements of AI technology will not merely add to or improve already existing processes; they will change the entire processes of governance, democracy, and governments. Therefore, tackling centuries-old processes will undeniably have a much bigger impact than is seen today or has been highlighted in this article.

Nonetheless, AI offers "transformative potential for the augmentation and potential replacement of human tasks and activities within a wide range of industrial, intellectual and social applications" (Dwivedi 2019). If (or, more precisely, when) AI one day becomes at least semi-autonomous, one of its indirect effects may be the restoration of citizens' trust in government processes and in the government itself. In many countries, a group of citizens of various sizes expresses distrust in government, its officials, and/or its governing processes. Therefore, the biggest potential of AI in the political field is not only that it can allow officials to reduce their workload, but also that it will increase citizens' trust in the processes of their government, thus transforming entire societies and laying a positive foundation for the future generations.

5.7 Conclusion

There is little doubt about the potential of AI in political science. The ability to conduct not only administrative but also decision-making tasks can improve the quality of political decision-making processes, the response time of government officials, and the overall quality of political decisions themselves. Nonetheless, since political decisions affect entire populations, the AI must be safe to use and its processes must be transparent. Without transparency, it is impossible to ensure that decisions made by AI will be explainable, fair, and human-centric. Failure to ensure the aforementioned safety requirements and principles of AI can result in black-box situations where it is impossible to explain decisions made by the AI. And if transparency is not ensured, the citizens will not acknowledge the use of AI in the political field.

Study Questions

1. What are the primary applications of AI in the political field?
2. Why is it crucial for AI systems used in the political field to be transparent?
3. What are the primary safety requirements for AI systems used in the political field?

4. Why is AI currently used sparingly, if at all, in political decision-making processes?
5. What are the main risks associated with using AI in political decision-making processes?

References

Bannister F., and R. Connolly. 2012. "Defining E-Governance." *E-Service Journal* 8(2): 3–25.

Bonica, A. 2014. "Mapping the Ideological Marketplace." *American Journal of Political Science* 58(2): 367–86.

Council of Europe. 2009. *Generic Tools and Policies for an Electronic Democracy.* https://www.coe.int/t/dgap/goodgovernance/Activities/CAHDE/2009/RecCM2009_1_and_Accomp_Docs/CAHDE_Indicative_Guides_and_Glossary_EN.asp.

Cranmer, S. 2019. "Introduction to the Virtual Issue: Machine Learning in Political Science." *Political Analysis Virtual Special Issue.* https://www.cambridge.org/core/services/aop-file-manager/file/5c348274e401b41903dae11b/PAN-VSI-Intro-0119-Machine-learning.pdf.

Dafoe, A. 2018. "AI Governance: a Research Agenda." https://www.fhi.ox.ac.uk/wp-content/uploads/GovAI-Agenda.pdf.

Dwivedi, Y. K., et al. 2019. "Artificial Intelligence (AI): Multidisciplinary Perspectives on Emerging Challenges, Opportunities, and Agenda for Research, Practice and Policy." *International Journal of Information Management* 57.

European Commission. 2021. *Europe Fit for the Digital Age: Commission Proposes New Rules and Actions for Excellence and Trust in Artificial Intelligence.* https://ec.europa.eu/commission/presscorner/detail/en/ip_21_1682.

European Parliament. 2017. *Report on E-democracy in the European Union: Potential and Challenges.* https://www.europarl.europa.eu/doceo/document/TA-8-2017-0095_EN.html.

Google. 2019. "Perspectives on Issues in AI Governance." https://ai.google/static/documents/perspectives-on-issues-in-ai-governance.pdf.

International Organization for Standardization. 2010. *Ergonomics of Human-System Interaction—Part 210: Human-Centred Design for Interactive Systems.* https://www.iso.org/obp/ui/#iso:std:iso:9241:-210:ed-2:v1:en.

Kuziemski, M., and G. Misuraca. 2020. "AI Governance in the Public Sector: Three Tales from the Frontiers of Automated Decision-Making in Democratic Settings." *Telecommunications Policy* 44(6).

Meško, G. 2018. "On Some Aspects of Cybercrime and Cybervictimization." *European Journal of Crime, Criminal Law & Criminal Justice* 26(3): 189–99.

United Nations Conference on Trade and Development. 2018. *Technology and Innovation Report*. https://unctad.org/system/files/official-document/tir2018_en.pdf.

Further Reading

Valladão, A. G. A. 2018. "Artificial Intelligence and Political Science." https://www.policycenter.ma/sites/default/files/OCPPC-PP1807_0.pdf.

CHAPTER 6

The Impact of Artificial Intelligence on Healthcare

Giedrė Kvedaravičienė, Adam Poulsen and Milda Žaliauskaitė

6.1 The Context of AI-Enabled Innovation Accommodation in Healthcare

Developments in high-speed computing and AI have enabled scientists and clinicians to process enormous amounts of data and speed up knowledge accumulation as never before. This progress allows huge time savings for biomedical R&D, as well as more precise patient stratification for disease prediction, diagnostics, and treatment.

This chapter will address the following topics:

- What is the general context of AI-driven solutions in healthcare?
- In what way do related ethical issues shape risk and value perceptions?
- What policy frameworks have emerged to address technological risks in this context?
- How has COVID-19 affected the perception of machine learning and AI's importance in healthcare?

Fast-evolving technologies create significant challenges for efforts to incorporate timely updates in legislative frameworks. This is especially true for highly regulated industries, such as healthcare, where AI carries the potential to foster significant advancements in health but also poses much higher levels of risk, often slowing down the adoption and dissemination of the technology (Harvey 2012). Frequently, current AI advances in healthcare are impeded by outdated laws. Modern-day verification of medical products, technologies, and even healthcare service delivery processes are often obligated to observe regulations that date back to the 1980s, long before one could have anticipated the general developments in ICT and the potential role of AI technologies in the 2020s. As a result, breaking into the new qualitative level of national healthcare systems remains more of an "aspiration than reality" (Kiener 2021).

Lack of financing and minimal technical competences (e.g., lack of confidence) among doctors are often listed as reasons for delayed technology dissemination in clinical practice, the source of uncertainty in risk assessment (including social acceptance), and biased value perception when compared to the existing alternative methods of service provision.

 | DOI:10.1163/9789004682900_008

Yet, as Mowery and Rosenberg, Nelson, and Winter, and other economists pointed out in the 1990s and earlier, uncertainties raised by new technologies cannot be resolved before their use in practice. The development of new technologies does not end with adoption but rather continues for some extended period. For example, one of the greatest values of AI comes from its ability to learn from real-world feedback and adapt the newly acquired information for improved performance. The transformative power of machine learning (ML) and AI have already started an information revolution in medical technologies and healthcare, irrespective of any potential perceptions of threats. This situates AI-enabled systems in a unique position among other medical devices used to improve clinical outcomes. Like practicing clinicians, AI-driven medical systems improve efficiency and effectiveness as they are used over time and are not limited to the capacities of the initial design. Moreover, the big data processing capacities of AI allow the inclusion of statistically significant contextual factors collected from an array of sources. Inclusion of such non-clinical factors as lifestyle or environmental parameters in clinical analysis enables a much better prediction of the development of certain diseases, which is very important for efficient preventative healthcare management, both by the clinicians and by the patients themselves, who can make informed changes in their lifestyle to avoid or reduce the risk of developing certain diseases such as diabetes, heart and vascular diseases or cancer.

Next to data processing capacities, AI also plays an important role in developing digital infrastructure (e.g., enabling intelligent use of the Medical Internet of Things or MIoT), remote monitoring technologies, and smart remote care solutions (El-Haddadeh 2019).

6.2 Ethical Challenges for Social Acceptance and Value Perception

Innovation is commonly viewed as a "central driver of economic growth and development" (Global Innovation Index 2015). Healthcare innovations help not only to secure better treatment for the ill or injured but also to improve daily health and secure higher levels of well-being (Elefant 2017). This causes society, especially in developed countries, to be moved by expectations of "timely patient access to high-quality, safe and effective medical technology" (Digital Health Innovation Action Plan by FDA). In the case of AI-driven solutions, fundamental rights, such as the right to security, dignity, privacy, social assistance, and equal treatment, are implicated. The impact of fundamental rights in understanding and regulating smart technology use in healthcare is an important aspect to consider when assessing possible regulation designs for clinical practice. In many cases, the definition of fundamental rights becomes a challenge when one tries to create a definitive list of normative moral criteria for them.

Fundamental rights are perfectly explicit, but they are also perfectly broad. As Gordon (2018) pointed out, it may be more reasonable to rephrase questions about fundamental rights so that instead of, for example, asking "What is dignity?" one asks "What is indignity?" aiming to "define the possible cases of indignity which should be avoided, rather than trying to positively define dignity" (Poulsen and Ulhaq 2021). This line of thought leads to another observation by Poulsen and Ulhaq (2021). What is dignity or indignity for each recipient of healthcare varies. Patients' reliance on the caregivers' responsiveness and their ability to adapt to the individual needs of each individual patient makes the subject of establishing ethics for the AI-enabled technologies a much more complex topic than can be covered by the industrial design and quality compliance rules.

Many authors, including Karni and Kaner (2006) and Schartinger et al. (2015), stress that in sociotechnical service systems such as healthcare, the participation of customers or clients (i.e., patients and their family members) is vital for service design and provision. Yet it is hard to achieve a major consensus among the stakeholders, given their different backgrounds in practice. The diversity of cognitive frameworks used by the healthcare system's stakeholders in assessing risks and formulating demands creates natural barriers in the process of achieving social consensus regarding the acceptable level of AI presence in healthcare.

6.3 Practical Challenges for the AI-Driven Technology Dissemination in Healthcare

From a practical perspective, there are some concrete issues to be addressed by policymakers. Among them are improved health data security and the establishment of sufficient regulation and good practice for data aggregation, sharing and use, including secondary use for scientific or public safety purposes. Furthermore, more clarity in healthcare-related regulation is needed regarding risk management when AI-assisted medical devices are used for health services.

At this point, AI algorithms are typically considered only as decision support tools, despite the aggregated evidence that deep learning–enabled AI can match human performance. For example, AI systems in healthcare can analyze MRI scans and certain health data in gastroenterology, endoscopy, and other medical fields, with equal or even higher accuracy relative to clinicians who analyze the same data manually (Kaul et al. 2020).

6.3.1 *Patient Data Security and Privacy*

Irrespective of the economic sector, digital data accumulation and the internet-enabled use of it point to simultaneously rising risks of internet malware, cyber attacks, and unauthorized use of data (Pirubhulal 2019). These risks call for precise laws and regulations to regulate any possible incidents, as well as to enforce constant upgrading of data protection technologies. This is especially important for the healthcare sector because of the vast amount of information, which is too complex to manage without big data tools.

From a legal perspective, collecting, storing, processing, transforming, and transferring health information from the patient to the healthcare specialist and to the business entity that develops a device or application need to be regulated and monitored appropriately. Regulation (EU) 2016/679 of the European Parliament and of the Council of April 27, 2016 on the protection of natural persons regarding the processing of personal data and on the free movement of such data, and repealing Directive 95/46/EC (General Data Protection Regulation, GDPR) is the key EU-level document having a significant impact on data management in the healthcare sector, as it covers health data. In 2020, the European Commission initiated the framework of joint action for the European Health Data Space. To accommodate rapid digital transformations, a set of new horizontal legislations—the Artificial Intelligence Act, the Data Act, the Cyber Resilience Act, and the European Health Data Space Regulation—are expected to be adopted in the EU in 2023.[1] It is expected that the common Health Data Space in the European Union will improve accessibility and exchange of different types of health data, such as electronic health records, genomics data, and data from patient registries, for efficient healthcare provision (the primary purpose of health data use). The secondary use of health data for scientific (including AI training) or policymaking purposes will enhance the cost-efficiency of R&D activities in healthcare and lead to greater precision

1 The updated Network and Information Security (NIS) Directive, known as NIS2, and the Data Governance Act have already been accepted. However, they both are rather contextual and have no direct impact on healthcare markets. The full picture of the legislative framework will only emerge once we see the full list of interactions between all applicable legislations—namely, the existing sectorial legislations and the newly arriving ones. The fact that most of these legislations are horizontal in their nature means that they are intended to regulate digital technologies in a variety of different markets. This runs the risk of not considering the specifics of healthcare markets and how they differ from, for example, regular consumer markets.

and agility in the relevant regulatory environments (European Commission, eHealth: Digital health and care). The EU has also launched an independent data protection authority, the European Data Protection Supervisor, which issues various opinions and remarks on the EU documents, as well as decisions related to health data and its proper management.

Similarly to the EU yet much earlier, the United States enacted several federal laws, such as the Health Insurance Portability and Accountability Act (1996) and the Health Information Technology for Economic and Clinical Health Act (2009). Federal institutions are in place to oversee health data management, such as the Department of Health and Human Services (2019), the Food and Drug Administration's Digital Health Center of Excellence, and state-specific laws regarding health data and the use or accessibility of medical innovations in general (U.S. Food and Drug Administration, Center for Devices and Radiological Health, Digital Health Program 2020; U.S. Food and Drug Administration 2021). At the international level, the International Health Regulations (2005), which are legally binding in 196 countries, include safeguards to protect traveling patients and other rights related to the treatment of personal data.

Despite all these global efforts, the healthcare industry is still widely regarded as having weak data security (Khaloufi et al. 2018). Therefore, there is still much room for policymakers and lawyers to create and implement appropriate defense measures and effective safety protection mechanisms to ensure the expected level of privacy for individual patients and society.

6.3.2 *Emerging Guidelines for Risk Management in Software as a Medical Device*

Not surprisingly, health data are seen as a strategic asset in the EU, the USA, and other developed global economies.

In discussions around AI-driven technologies in healthcare, it is important to pay attention to the differences in the purpose of medical devices and the algorithms driving the systems, as subsequent differences in regulation may apply. Mobile health apps, especially those that do not claim any provision of clinical recommendations (e.g., Apple Health, Samsung Health, and Google Fit), are often classified as consumer goods and reach the markets largely unregulated. On the other hand, digital therapeutics (sometimes referred to as "digiceuticals") are sophisticated AI-driven diagnostic tools that aim to diagnose and treat a medical or psychological condition. Therefore, these latter systems must pass the clinical validity, accuracy and reliability testing processes and get regulatory approvals for medical devices. Unlike the consumer market apps for health, which are promoted with significant marketing budgets, digiceuticals are dominated by companies that are not known to the public and are focused on clinicians as users. Recently, however, big names in consumer markets, such as Apple, started moving into the medical device market. For example, Apple has started offering the FDA-approved Apple series 6 smartwatch with a built-in electrocardiograph.

To cover specific areas of impact for AI-enabled medical software that makes the device or solution accountable as a medical device, a global effort to classify and standardize the regulation of IT-driven medical devices has emerged. In 2011, the International Medical Device Regulators Forum (IMDRF) was established to set standards going forward, including the IP protection enablement for Software as a Medical Device (SaMD), defined as "software intended to be used for one or more medical purposes that perform these purposes without being part of a hardware medical device" (IMDRF SaMD Working Group 2013). The FDA clarifies medical purposes as those that are "intended to treat, diagnose, cure, mitigate, or prevent disease or other conditions" (United States Code: Federal Food, Drug, and Cosmetic Act 1934).

Following earlier practices of medical device regulation (United States Code: Medical Device Regulation Act 1976) , IMDRF proposes a dual system of factors to define and assign technologies to certain risk groups. IMDRF suggests that the intended use of the AI-enabled SaMD, the significance of the information provided by the SaMD, and the state of health or condition for which information is gathered and used should be used as criteria. The more serious the health condition for which the SaMD is intended and/or the more significant the impact of AI-enabled SaMD on diagnostic accuracy and therapeutic decisions, the higher risk group (from first to fourth) is assigned (see Table 6.1).

In line with the IMDRF classification, in 2019 the FDA proposed principles for the creation of a regulatory environment for AI/ML-enabled SaMD development, which could be summarized in the following four major points:

TABLE 6.1 SaMD risk categories as defined by IMDRF

State of healthcare situation or condition	**Significance of information provided by SaMD to healthcare decision**		
	Treat or diagnose	**Drive clinical management**	**Inform clinical management**
Critical	IV	III	II
Serious	III	II	I
Non-serious	III	I	I

1. Good machine learning practice (GMLP) can establish clear quality expectation for SaMD developers.
2. Premarket reviews for more risky technologies can mitigate risks in terms of both social acceptance and investment rationale.
3. Following the nature of AI-driven technologies and the risk of AI/ML degradation while in use, continuous monitoring and validation of the evolving algorithm practice can enable better risk management after the market authorization for SaMD is granted.
4. A high level of transparency is of critical importance for continuous assurance of SaMDs' safety and effectiveness.

These points capture the essence of major fears that may create significant institutionalized obstacles in the regulatory environment should the element of trust not be nurtured systematically by policymakers, manufacturers, and the wider public (the users).

6.4 COVID-19 Implications

The global COVID-19 pandemic escalated the long-standing problem of inefficiency in resource allocation in healthcare and the inability of national healthcare systems to adjust to the changing demand conditions swiftly. This created an unprecedented demand for technological solutions, including AI-driven ones, to cope with the pace, scale, and complexity of the pandemic-caused issues to be urgently addressed across healthcare sectors worldwide and related industries. Not surprisingly, open data, secondary use of data, and digitization of analytics and communication became the focal points for governments worldwide. For example, the pandemic boosted demand for preventative and home care services. This demand put pressure on the health industry to expedite the development and integration of the MIoT, smart analytic tools for diagnostics, remote monitoring, and AI-enabled care solutions (e.g., care robots). The rapid development of COVID-19 vaccines has also demonstrated that current big data technologies can allow us to have novel treatments in one year rather than twelve years, which is still the average time for drug or vaccine development.

The European Union's Data Strategy reflects the common belief among policymakers that "people, businesses and organizations should be empowered to make better decisions based on insights from non-personal data, which should be available to all" (European Commission 2020). Nevertheless, in the EU, up until the COVID-19 crisis, the implementation of the European Data Strategy was left to individual member states to pursue with little centralized coordination and guidance. Given the emerging framework of horizontal and sector-specific legislation for digital technologies, much higher levels of centralized EU-level regulation for AI and other digital technologies and digital data will be established in the EU. The European Commission aims to empower the concept of the European Health Data Space, which will result in a prototype of an interoperable data access infrastructure by 2025. The activities under the European Open Science Cloud (EOSC) initiative are expected to facilitate secure cross-border health data interoperability so as to achieve the defined objectives described in Figure 6.1.

Whether these efforts will help to minimize differences between the EU countries' local context of AI perception, political will, and openness to technological innovation, thereby affecting the scale and scope of the AI development in the EU, remains to be seen.

6.5 Conclusion

The combined research efforts of universities, governments, and healthcare-related industries have resulted in significant advances in the biomedical sciences and in clinical practice, generating vast amounts of data on the level of molecular body functions. The sheer amount of data being accumulated every day, together with the dominating principle of discovery research by using a particular approach rather than random screening, makes it impossible to imagine medical progress without extensive use of the ICT technologies. Among these technologies, AI is a key tool for speeding up discoveries of new drugs and enhancing diagnostic accuracy.

Information access improves patients' awareness and their ability to make health-related decisions. From a societal perspective, three priorities can be summarized as the main goals of the AI developments in healthcare:

1. Health data access enablement;
2. A health data pool for scientific and professional use; and
3. People's empowerment through digital health tools for self-care, disease prevention, and better feedback and interaction between the patients and the healthcare professionals.

This last goal raises legal questions not only concerning the role of AI-driven devices, but also concerning responsibility allocation between the healthcare professionals, patients, and other external stakeholders who interact with the

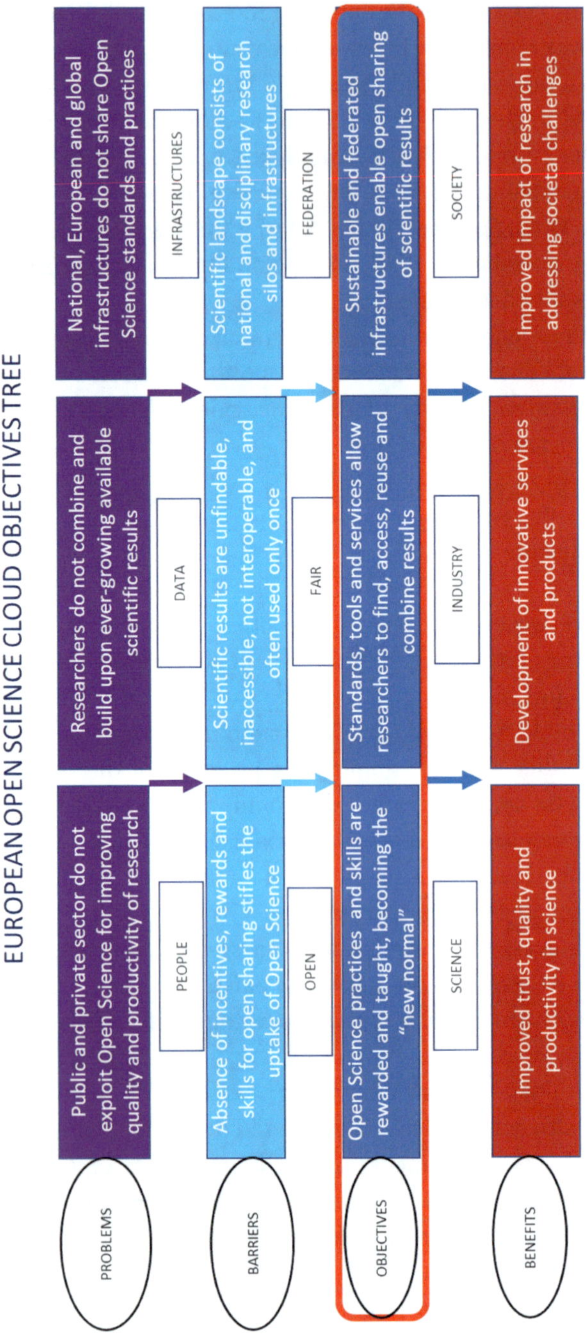

FIGURE 6.1 Strategy implementation structure for the European Open Science Cloud (EOSC)

AI-driven systems (e.g., creators of the health monitoring devices and researchers with access to health data).

In the context of the COVID-19 pandemic, an additional goal emerges that should be added to the previous three:

4. Communicable disease management using digital medical technologies, incorporated into the MIoT, as part of the cross-border solution when humanity is challenged by forces of nature beyond human control.

Finally, AI is highly likely to improve the healthcare sector's cost measurement capability and cost-efficiency. Next to potential gains in clinical efficiency, AI may offer tools for improved evaluation of disease management costs throughout the healthcare system. This would enable stakeholders who drive change in healthcare, such as dedicated government departments on the national level and healthcare managers at healthcare institutions, to make better-informed decisions on resource allocation and reap the full benefits of AI-enabled healthcare.

Still, some concerns remain, such as how quickly AI-driven products and services will emerge as part of regular practice in healthcare. Also, it is still uncertain whether in some cases the AI systems can be better suited for managing or providing treatment and care services to patients. Going forward, these and other concerns need to be carefully addressed, given that the development and the use of new medical technologies remain subject to a complex system of laws, regulations, standards, and varying perceptions of AI's benefits and threats in every country and across the globe (Ross 2018; Raza 2018; Maresova 2020).

Study Questions

1. What opportunities does AI offer for improving healthcare and health outcomes?
2. What challenges does the deployment of AI in healthcare create for clinicians, patients, society, and policymakers?
3. How do cybersecurity aspects of AI affect risk perception and risk management strategies for AI-driven medical devices?
4. What is the new emerging legislative framework for digital technologies, including AI, in the European Union?
5. What is the vision of the European data strategy?

6. How do the FDA and IMDRF approach the regulation of emerging software-driven medical devices?
7. Based on the lessons learned from the COVID-19 pandemic, how might major global health challenges impact the dynamics of AI adoption in healthcare in the future?

References

Elefant, S. R. 2017. "Comparative Analysis of Healthcare Innovation in Israel, Ireland and Switzerland: a Systematic Literature Review." Central Michigan University, School of Health Sciences.

El-Haddadeh, R., et al. 2019. "Examining Citizens' Perceived Value of Internet of Things Technologies in Facilitating Public Sector Services Engagement." *Government Information Quarterly* 36(2): 310–20.

European Commission. 2020. *Communication from the Commission to the European Parliament, the Council, the European Economic and Social Committee and the Committee of the Regions. A European Strategy for Data.* https://eur-lex.europa.eu/legal-content/EN/TXT/HTML/?uri=CELEX:52020DC0066&from=EN.

Global Innovation Index. 2015. *The Global Innovation Index: Effective Innovation Policies for Development.* Fontainebleau, Geneva, Switzerland (2015).

Harvey, A., et al. 2012. "The Future of Technologies for Personalised Medicine." *New Biotechnology* 29(6). http://www.imdrf.org/docs/imdrf/final/technical/imdrf-tech-131209-samd-key-definitions-140901.pdf#search=%22SaMD%22.

IMDRF SaMD Working Group. 2013. *Software as a Medical Device (SaMD): Key Definitions.* https://www.gmp-compliance.org/files/guidemgr/imdrf-tech-131209-samd-key-definitions.pdf.

Kaner, M., and R. Karni. 2006. "A Knowledge Framework for a Service Concept." In 6th International Conference on Knowledge Management, Graz, Austria, pp. 231–35.

Kaul, V., S. Enslin, and S. A. Gross. 2020. "History of Artificial Intelligence in Medicine." *Gastrointestinal Endoscopy* 92(4): 807–12.

Khaloufu, H., et al. 2018. "Security Model for Big Healthcare Data Lifecycle." *Procedia Computer Science* 141: 294–301.

Kiener, M. 2021. "Artificial Intelligence in Medicine and the Disclosure of Risks." *AI & Society* 36: 705–13.

Maresova, P., and L. Hajek. 2020. "New Regulations on Medical Devices in Europe: Are They an Opportunity for Growth?" *Administrative Sciences* 10(1): 16.

Pirubhulal, S., et al. 2019. "A Joint Resource-Aware and Medical Data Security Framework for Wearable Healthcare Systems." *Future Generation Computer Systems* 95: 382–91.

Poulsen, A., and A. Ulhaq. 2021. "Fundamental Rights and Smart Health Technologies." In *Smart Technologies and Fundamental Rights*, edited by J.-S. Gordon, 127–53. Leiden: Brill.

Raza, S., et al. 2018. *The Personalized Medicine Technology Landscape*. PHG Foundation, University of Cambridge.

Ross, J., et al. 2018. "Developing an Implementation Strategy for a Digital Health Intervention: an Example in Routine Healthcare." *BMC Health Services Research* 18: 794.

Schartinger, D., et al. 2015. "Personal Health Systems Technologies: Critical Issues in Service Innovation and Diffusion." *Technology Innovation Management Review* 5(2): 46–57. http://timreview.ca/article/873.

U.S. Department of Health and Human Services, Office of the Chief Technology Officer. 2019. *Leveraging Data for the Nation's Health*.

U.S. Food and Drug Administration. 2021. *Proposed Regulatory Framework for Modifications to Artificial Intelligence/Machine Learning (AI/ML)-Based Software as a Medical Device (SaMD): Discussion Paper and Request for Feedback*.

U.S. Food and Drug Administration, Center for Devices and Radiological Health, Digital Health Program. 2020. *Digital Health Innovation Action Plan*.

United States Code: Federal Food, Drug, and Cosmetic Act. 1934. PL 75–717 Stat 52, Stat. 1040.

United States Code: Medical Device Regulation Act. 1976. PL 94–295, 90 Stat 539.

Further Reading

European Parliamentary Research Service, Scientific Foresight Unit (STOA). 2022. "Artificial intelligence in healthcare: Applications, risks, and ethical and societal impacts." PE 729.512—June 2022.

United States Government Accountability Office, National Academy of Medicine. 2022. "Technology Assessment. Artificial Intelligence in Health Care. Benefits and Challenges of Machine Learning Technologies for Medical Diagnostics." GAO-22-104629.

World Health Organization. International health regulations (2005). World Health Organization, 2008.

PART 2

Major Key Issues: AI *Decision Making*

Introduction to Part 2

AI is without a doubt a game changer in many areas of human activity. This includes education (e.g., plagiarism checkers, software for student admissions), transportation (e.g., AI autopilot), sales and marketing (e.g., sales forecasting, personalized marketing online), surveillance (e.g., smart surveillance cameras and drones), data analytics (e.g., various data management and monitoring functions), healthcare (e.g., automated diagnosis and medication prescription), and many more.[1] Given the many benefits of AI, it is virtually guaranteed that more and more systems will be developed in the future for various purposes, including sophisticated robots, which are autonomous AI-powered embodied agents. Nevertheless, the deployment of AI comes with its own technical, legal, and ethical challenges, many of which have to do with the decision making of AI systems. In some cases, an AI system that is not behaving as intended will simply not be able to perform its function well, whereas in others it may even pose a threat to our fundamental values. The latter point makes it especially important to identify and address the many challenges pertaining to AI decision making, which is the topic of this part.

The next chapter of this part considers the notion of machine bias. Although there is a widespread belief that the concepts of bias or prejudice can relate only to human conduct or attitudes, this is now known to be false—machines, too, can be biased. While machine learning has certainly opened a number of intriguing venues when it comes to AI applications, machine bias is bound to remain a relevant problem for decades to come. This means that devising strategies to mitigate bias and diminish its effects is of utmost importance. The chapter first introduces the concept of machine bias, then, relates it to algorithmic systems and machine learning, and finally discusses some relevant challenges for the mitigation of bias.

Chapter 8 introduces issues related to ethical programming and machine moral agency. Since the sophistication of AI systems has been growing and their use in morally salient contexts has been increasing, it has been generally recognized that machines should be able to make ethical decisions when necessary. This applies not only to the many "narrow" systems that exist today, such as autonomous vehicles, but also to so-called "artificial moral agents," or machines with a broad range of capacities, which may exist in the future. The chapter first explains the importance of ethical programming and outlines

1 https://research.aimultiple.com/ai-usecases/.

 DOI:10.1163/9789004682900_009

different categories of machine moral agency. Then, different approaches to building ethical machines and their main strengths and weaknesses are sketched. Finally, some closing remarks on legal and practical decision making in the context of ethical programming and machine moral agency are provided.

Chapter 9 discusses the issue known as the black box problem. Today, many AI systems are opaque, or "black boxes," in the sense that one cannot peer inside them to know exactly how they make their decisions. Sometimes that is a good thing, because learning how a certain AI system makes decisions could violate the property rights of its developers. At other times, however, this feature makes it very difficult to identify the reasons for faulty decisions that the system makes (e.g., in the case of machine bias), which is a considerable issue in its own right. The chapter first introduces and elaborates on the concept of the black box in the context of IT systems and AI. Then, some proposed technical and legal solutions to the problem are outlined.

Lastly, chapter 10 discusses the control problem in the context of technological singularity, otherwise known as the intelligence explosion. Technological singularity predicts that once human-level AI comes into existence, soon after that there will be even more capable AIs, which will in turn manage to create even more potent artificial beings than themselves. After a few cycles of successive improvements of this sort, "artificial superintelligence" will come to exist, the abilities of which will go far beyond human comprehension. The control problem refers to the task of ensuring that the resulting AI is sensitive to the most fundamental human values. The chapter first introduces the notion of control and its background in information technology. Then, the concept of singularity is presented with some general remarks on its importance. Finally, the chapter discusses the two main sets of control methods in the context of artificial superintelligence.

CHAPTER 7

Machine Bias

Vladislav V. Fomin

7.1 The Basic Concepts of a Computing System and a Bias

> Algorithmic decisions are not automatically equitable just by virtue of being the products of complex processes, and the procedural consistency of algorithms is not equivalent to objectivity. … Algorithms may be mathematically optimal but ethically problematic.
>
> OSOBA AND WELSER 2017, 2

What is machine bias? How a machine can be biased or avoid bias? What implications does the concept of machine bias have for the professionals who develop technologies or the members of society who use and depend on the various technologies in their daily private and business interactions? In this chapter, we examine the concept of bias, which is central to both how information systems are designed and how we put trust in results produced with the mediation of information technology (IT).

According to the *Oxford Dictionary*, the word "bias" has several meanings, of which the ones relevant to this discussion are the following:

1. "Inclination or prejudice for or against one person or group, especially in a way considered to be unfair," and
2. "A systematic distortion of a statistical result due to a factor not allowed for in its derivation."

In the context of machine bias, the word "machine" refers to information systems and technologies (or simply IT). The word "system," according to the *Oxford Dictionary* can be defined as

1. "A set of things working together as parts of a mechanism or an interconnecting network; a complex whole," or
2. "a set of principles or procedures according to which something is done."

 | DOI:10.1163/9789004682900_010

Given these definitions, the term "machine bias" must refer to situations in which the mechanisms governing the functioning of the IT produce a distorted (i.e., misleading or false) result. Moving from the generic understanding of the concept of machine bias to a domain-specific one, several types of bias can be distinguished:

- Sample bias: a dataset does not represent the problem space (such as training an autonomous vehicle with only daytime data).
- Prejudicial bias: a dataset incorporates data that might not be valid to consider (for example, a person's race or gender).
- Exclusion bias occurs when features that were considered not relevant are removed in the process of cleansing data before they are used in training or testing a machine learning model.
- Measurement bias occurs when the data collected for training differs from the data collected during production (e.g., using images for training that were taken at one angle to the object but then using images taken at a different angle during production, or using images taken by a camera with different characteristics).
- Algorithmic bias stems from the machine learning model. This includes how the model was developed or how the model was trained so as to result in unfair outcomes.[1]

In the following discussion, I review different causes and effects of machine bias in computational systems and discuss some implications for the development and use of IT services.

7.2 Algorithmic IT Systems

Like any other system, a generic IT system can be abstractly presented as having three main elements: the input provided to the system, the processing part of the system, and the output generated by the system (Figure 7.1). The feedback loop is required for control over the system.

As the system is defined as "a set of principles or procedures according to which something is done," that set of principles is what is referred to as an *algorithm*, according to which the IT system performs some computational processes.

The concept of the algorithm is important in the discussion of bias in computational systems. In simple terms, an algorithm can be defined as a sequence

1 https://developer.ibm.com/technologies/machine-learning/articles/machine-learning-and-bias/.

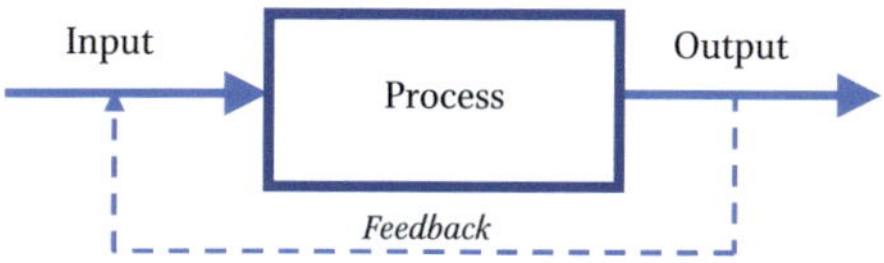

FIGURE 7.1 A generic representation of an IT system

of steps and instructions that can be applied to data (the input) to produce the intended result (the output). Programming languages are used to transform the algorithm into computer (machine) code. Among the properties an algorithm must possess, the following are relevant:
- *Definiteness*: each step must be precisely defined; the actions to be carried out must be rigorously and unambiguously specified for each case.
- *Output*: an algorithm has one or more outputs, which have a specified relation to the inputs.

Algorithmic bias, one of the five types of machine bias listed above, can be observed when a faulty computational model (the system's algorithmic logic) has been developed.

7.2.1 *Bias in Algorithmic Systems*

Given the definition of the algorithm and following the computational model as presented in Figure 7.1 for an algorithmic IT system to produce bias-free results, both the input and the process of the system must be impeccable (see Table 7.1, Situation #1). The possibilities for bias arise when the following factors are present:

1. There is a faulty algorithm (Situation 2 in Table 7.1), in which case a faulty (biased) result is produced.
2. The input data are incomplete or faulty (Situation 3 in the table), in which case the process will either be stalled or produce a faulty (biased) result.
3. Finally, if both the input data and the algorithm are distorted (Situation 4 in the table), one would again expect distorted results.

The distorted output of the system (Situation 2 in the table) can be unambiguously referred to as *algorithmic machine bias*, whereas output distortions in Situations 2 through 4 are subject-distorted input and can represent one or several of the other types of machine biases listed above.

Many IT systems services in use today are based on complex nested computational subsystems, in which the output from one (sub-)system is fed as

TABLE 7.1 Possible sources of distortion in a computational system

Situation #	Input→	Process	→Output
1	Proper	Proper	Proper
2	Proper	Distorted	Distorted
3	Distorted	Proper	Distorted
4	Distorted	Distorted	Distorted

an input to another. For example, when someone applies for a bank loan, the citizen's income, criminal record, social security payments, and residence status, among other things, are checked with help of certain IT systems that have access to a number of open and closed state registers. What appears to be a "one-stop" inquiry for the bank officer may indeed be a combination of nested and parallel query-and-process operations. In this light, an important observation must be made: a faulty input or process in one (sub-)system is likely to escalate the distortion in connected systems.

Finally, one more consideration must be mentioned, that of intentionality. Distortion or bias in a computational system can be intentional or unintentional, with respect to both cause and effect.

Distortion in computational systems can be introduced intentionally, such as when seeking to create inclinations or prejudices toward a certain group or person, or to mislead users. Thus, Table 7.2 below shows the categorization of intentional and unintentional computational faults with respect to the *input* to the system (data) or the *processing* of data in the system (the algorithm), as well as the positive or negative implications of such distortions.

Whereas the intentional introduction of distortion or bias in most contexts may be interpreted as having a negative connotation, the concept of affirmative action is one common example of an intentional bias intended to foster positive changes (except in the UK, where affirmative action is outlawed).

Affirmative action is the policy of promoting the education and employment of members of groups that are known to have suffered from discrimination. As an example, affirmative action has been (and continues to be) deployed by several U.S. universities, resulting in (substantially) higher admission rates for certain groups of the population. In many cases, the U.S. Supreme Court has supported such intentional biases, allowing educational institutions to consider race as a factor when

TABLE 7.2 Intentional and unintentional computational faults in data input vs processing

	Intentional	**Unintentional**
Bias in data (input)	Connotation: Negative Example: Financial misreporting Connotation: Positive Example: Political propaganda (at its origin)	Connotation: Negative Example: Overlooking certain historical or systemic dependencies in the input data
Bias in process (algorithm)	Connotation: Negative Example: Dieselgate scandal Connotation: Positive Example: Affirmative action	Connotation: Positive Example: PayPal accidentally credits man $92 quadrillion[a] Connotation: Negative Example: ERROR

a The Pennsylvania PR executive's Reynolds' PayPal account balance was erroneously increased to a whopping $92,233,720,368,547,800. PayPal admitted the error and offered to donate an unspecified amount of money to a cause of Reynolds' choice.

SOURCE: HTTPS://EDITION.CNN.COM/2013/07/17/TECH/PAYPAL-ERROR/INDEX.HTML

admitting students, and thus creating more favorable conditions for one racial group over others.[2]

The case of affirmative action emphasizes the importance of *human* decision making, or the precedence of human over algorithmic (machine-made) decisions. It is through the reflective action of experts that realization of the need for biased admissions came about. An otherwise faultless computational model had to be superseded by additional criteria to attract a more balanced ethnic composition of university students and minimize the imperfect, unwanted racial bias in a social system.

In the context of algorithmic IT systems, algorithmic distortion is the primary focus of the discussion of machine bias. Here, the computational and input-related distortions have always been treated as an error that must be

2 See *Gratz v. Bollinger* (539 U.S. 244 (2003)): https://library.law.hawaii.edu/2017/01/30/gratz-v-bollinger-case-summary/.

eliminated through the reflective action of humans, by identifying and eliminating the causes of distortion.

The advent of a new computational paradigm based on machine learning (ML) has brought forth a need for more elaborate classification of machine bias (as done at the beginning of this article). Some of the types of bias are further reviewed in the following section.

7.3 The Concept of Bias under the Paradigm of Learning IT

As we approach the end of the first quarter of the 21st century, more than half a century down the road from the first introduction of computers, IT has entered all walks of private and business life to become an inseparable and invisible part of modernity. The paramount reasons for the development and implementation of IT have not, however, changed since the dawn of the computer era: *to control and to inform humans to enable control.* Neither have the thresholds for distortion and bias tolerance changed. What has changed with the advent of the new paradigm of intelligent (i.e., capable of learning) IT, however, is (1) the *decreased ability of humans to detect computational faults* and to control for bias-free results of computation, which is the result of (2) computing systems' ability to "learn" and "improve" their methods of computation, thus moving away from the originally embedded algorithmic logic. The explosive growth of all kinds of data—from business transactions to demographics to machine-produced logs—has resulted in the (3) phenomenon of "third-party data," where the appropriateness and "cleanliness" of data as input to the computational system cannot be easily controlled for. These three cases are reviewed below.

7.3.1 *The New Paradigm of Learning Technologies*

AI-based systems can be purely software-based, such as the voice assistants or image analysis and face recognition software found in our smartphones or in cloud services. AI can also be embedded in hardware devices, such as autonomous cars or drones (EC AI High-Level Expert Group 2019a).

If traditional (algorithmic) computational systems were built on the foundation of strict control over the system (low to zero tolerance of distortions in algorithmic logic and computational output, as discussed above), then *ML algorithms, which power AI, are radically different,* in that they do not receive explicit programming instructions. Instead, AI systems receive datasets containing what in the algorithmic IT systems would be denoted as input data and output data, i.e., the data upon which the calculation must be performed and the correct results of that calculation, respectively. The AI system then tries to figure out what is the function *F* that allows deriving the given output from the given input. That "trying" to find a matching *F* is referred to as the system's learning process. This key feature of AI, learning, makes AI more bias-prone than traditional IT systems.

7.3.2 *The Nature of Bias in AI Systems*

In the context of learning technologies, the term *bias* was introduced by Mitchell (1980) to mean "any basis for choosing one generalization [hypothesis] over another, other than strict consistency with the observed training instances" (Dietterich and Kong 1995, 1). This "bias for choosing one generalization over another" is actually how an AI system seeks a good function *F* to establish the correspondence between the input and the output data, and the word "bias" here does not have a negative connotation.

In this chapter, we are concerned with the negative connotation of machine bias, which is generally understood as "programming that assumes the prejudice of its creators or data" (Shadowen 2017, 5, referring to Garcia 2016). In Table 7.1, I presented four situations of input-and process-related biases in the context of computational systems. Whereas Situations 2 and 3 apply to learning technologies, here the discourse on machine bias is more focused on the input data, rather than on the process, as was the case with algorithmic systems.

Similar to the traditional algorithmic systems, the process (or algorithmic) bias (Situation 2 in the table) in AI systems stems from the machine learning model—i.e., the methods used to arrive at the result given the specific input data. However, whereas in the case of an algorithmic system the algorithmic bias is the result of intentional or unintentional introduction of distortion by the system's developers, then in the case of AI systems algorithmic bias can also be the result of how the model was trained.

Different sources of bias in AI systems can be and often are interlinked. The High-Level Expert Group on AI provides a good overview of causes and effects of bias in AI systems.

> In the document "Ethics guidelines for trustworthy AI," published in 2019 by The High-Level Expert Group on AI (2019b), various causes and effects of bias in AI systems are reviewed: Bias is an inclination of prejudice toward or against a person, object, or position. Bias can arise in many ways in AI systems. For example, in data-driven AI systems, such as those produced through machine learning, bias in data collection and training can result in an AI system demonstrating bias. In logic-based AI, such as rule-based systems, bias can arise due to how a knowledge engineer

> might view the rules that apply in a particular setting. Bias can also arise due to online learning and adaptation through interaction. It can also arise through personalization, whereby users are presented with recommendations or information feeds tailored to the user's tastes. It does not necessarily relate to human bias or human-driven data collection. It can arise, for example, through the limited contexts in which a system is used, in which case there is no opportunity to generalize it to other contexts. Bias can be good or bad, intentional or unintentional. In certain cases, bias can result in discriminatory and/or unfair outcomes, indicated … as unfair bias.

The following subsections explore data-and process-originating bias in AI systems in more detail.

7.3.3 *Process-Originating Biases in AI Systems*

As noted above, the learning element makes AI different from traditional computational models. Learning determines how the subsequent cycles of computation will unfold, and it implies some sort of optimization of the process with respect to the produced results. In other words, for the users of the system, it becomes impossible to control for algorithmic (process) bias. One reason for this lack of control is the pace at which the machines learn—they learn faster than we can adapt (Lyytinen et al. 2020).

An AI system detects patterns in large datasets and learns how to make predictions and recommendations by processing data and experiences. Technical properties influencing learning may remain unknown to the users and designers of the system (Lyytinen et al. 2020), which may eventually render the AI system's algorithmic logic considerably different from the guidelines their programmers initially gave them (Etzioni and Etzioni 2016, 30).

Citing Jenna Burrell from the School of Information at the University of California–Berkeley, Etzioni and Etzioni (2016, 30) introduce the concept of opacity with regard to AI algorithms: "Machine learning and/or the number of different programmers involved renders an algorithm opaque even to the programmers." The system becomes a black box (see chapter 9 of this volume on the black box problem), and the traditional human reflective action to determine algorithmic biases becomes inapplicable (see Text box III.1.4).

> In his article "The Dark Secret at the Heart of AI," published in 2017 in the *MIT Technology Review*, Will Knight (2017) describes the technical causes of the black box problem of AI systems:

> You can't just look inside a deep neural network to see how it works. A network's reasoning is embedded in the behavior of thousands of simulated neurons, arranged into dozens or even hundreds of intricately interconnected layers. The neurons in the first layer each receive an input, like the intensity of a pixel in an image, and then perform a calculation before outputting a new signal. These outputs are fed, in a complex web, to the neurons in the next layer, and so on, until an overall output is produced. Plus, there is a process known as back-propagation that tweaks the calculations of individual neurons in a way that lets the network learn to produce a desired output.

7.3.4 *Data-Originating Biases in AI Systems*

For an AI system to produce reliable results, it must be first trained on large amounts of data (i.e., the input and output data are fed to the system, with the "tagged" correlations, or which input should produce which output). Hence, bias in training data will likely result in AI systems not being able to generalize well and possibly making unfair decisions that can favor some groups over others (EC AI High-Level Expert Group 2019b). Bias in data can occur due to historical, political, or technical factors that were in play when data were collected, causing the data to be insufficiently balanced or inclusive.

Although scholars understand the risks of imperfect data well, as seen, for example, through the prism of the concept of primary and secondary sources in collecting research data, the general public may not be aware of the problem. In the case of the training of an AI system, when a company does not have a sufficiently large dataset to complete the training process (i.e., to achieve the level of training when the AI system starts producing the proper results under controlled system use), third-party data, especially repurposed data, are likely to be used for the training. But this will likely introduce a bias in the training data (Burkhardt et al. 2019, 4), and hence improper learning will typically result and the system will produce biased results upon deployment.

Whether original or third-party data are used, to date there is no possibility of automatically controlling for bias in training data, as there are no standards or solutions to categorize, label, or assess data according to how they were collected and whether they are accessible, searchable, or findable (Kinder-Kurlanda 2019). This situation, on one hand, emphasizes the importance of human reflective judgement in the process of building training datasets; on the other hand, it gives scholars a reason to label raw data an oxymoron, as data become at the same time both the fuel and the destroying agent for AI systems.

7.4 Challenges in Mitigating Bias with AI

Traditionally, in domains and professions related to law, finance, and medicine, where complex cognitive skills are required, human experts have benefited from reflective practice (Lyytinen et al. 2020, referring to Schön 1983). In other words, undesired biases in source data (the input), rule-based governance and computational models, and their supplied results (the output) were identified using human expertise and judgement.

Human professionals have years of accumulated experience on which to reflect, as exemplified by issues such as affirmative action, where intentional bias has been introduced so as to produce what are considered positive results in the long run.

Noticing change, considering the meta-level implications of change on the whole system, finding patterns, and adjusting the system accordingly have been a uniquely human endeavor (Lyytinen et al. 2020). Although AI has certainly been shown to have the capability of predictive assessment, to date it remains unknown whether machines can invent mechanisms for governance akin to human systems.

A second important question related to bias in AI concerns the explainability of the results. The design of reinforcement learning in AI is such that computing agents interact with and receive feedback from their environment—that is, they learn from experience—and the AI systems can and do create responses corresponding to such received experience, i.e., AI can identify patterns in data to match or even supersede humans. The challenge, however, remains how to relate the AI-produced outcomes to the rule-based systems with which humans have traditionally worked (Lyytinen et al. 2020). How can AI explain its decisions to the users, so as to develop trust that their operations and their results are bias-free? The advantages of AI-supplied predictive performance must be balanced against the requirement of interpretability of results. The higher the predictive performance of an AI system, the lower the possibility that humans will understand its decision-making path and hence be able to detect bias(es).

In this age of explosive growth of data, especially user data collected from various internet sites, smartphone apps, and other sources, data has become a tradable good. As an easy way to obtain data for training AI systems, data acquisition from a third party carries risks of instilling data-related biases. However, even the use of company-owned data does not preclude sample, measurement, prejudice, or exclusion biases. All these risks must be carefully considered by system architects and implementers.

7.5 Conclusions

Large and complex learning systems are being introduced and used in mundane and critical societal tasks, from facial recognition at airports' automatic control gates to stock trading, to cancer cell detection in the medical sector, to very complex military systems. Irrespective of the degree of sophistication of the contemporary learning systems, the governance responsibility still rests with individual humans in authority.

Unlike the automation of tasks, *the automation of governance* of AI systems is unlikely to escape human control and responsibility unless and until the larger regulatory and technological context evolves to deal with this issue (Lyytinen et al. 2020). Continuous and long-term evidence of the bias-free operation of AI systems is certainly needed before we can trust complex AI systems to the same extent as we trust complex algorithmic systems.

The development of regulatory and best-practice frameworks and standards for collecting and using data in training learning systems is one viable way forward toward bias-free AI systems.

Study Questions

1. What is an algorithm? How does the concept of an algorithm reflect human knowledge?
2. What is the meaning of an algorithmic computational system?
3. What are the potential sources of bias in algorithmic computational systems?
4. How do learning IT systems differ from algorithmic systems? What are the implications for bias based on the differences between the two types of systems?
5. What strategies can be employed to mitigate the risks of biased results being produced by AI systems?

References

Burkhardt, R., N. Hohn and C. Wigley. 2019. "Leading your Organization to Responsible AI." *McKinsey Analytics*. https://www.mckinsey.com/~/media/McKinsey/Business%20Functions/McKinsey%20Analytics/Our%20Insights/Leading%20your%20organization%20to%20responsible%20AI/Leading-your-organization-to-responsible-AI.ashx.

Dietterich, T. G., and E. B. Kong. 1995. *Machine Learning Bias, Statistical Bias, and Statistical Variance of Decision Tree Algorithms*. Technical Report, Department of Computer Science, Oregon State University.

EC AI High-Level Expert Group. 2019a. *A Definition of Artificial Intelligence: Main Capabilities and Scientific Disciplines*. https://ec.europa.eu/newsroom/dae/document.cfm?doc_id=56341.

EC AI High-Level Expert Group. 2019b. *Ethics Guidelines for Trustworthy AI*. https://ec.europa.eu/newsroom/dae/document.cfm?doc_id=58477.

Etzioni, A., and O. Etzioni. 2016. "Designing AI Systems that Obey Our Laws and Values." *Commun. ACM* 59(9): 29–31.

Garcia, M. 2016. "Racist in the Machine: the Disturbing Implications of Algorithmic Bias." *World Policy Journal* 33(4): 111–17.

Kinder-Kurlanda, K. 2019. Keynote Speech at the 18th Annual STS Conference Graz. https://sts-conference.isds.tugraz.at/event/2/attachments/1/22/BoA2019_-_STS_Conference_Graz.pdf.

Knight, W. 2017. "The Dark Secret at the Heart of AI." *MIT Technology Review*. https://www.technologyreview.com/s/604087/the-dark-secret-at-the-heart-of-ai/.

Lyytinen, K., J. V. Nickerson, and J. L. King. 2020. "Metahuman Systems = Humans + Machines That Learn." *Journal of Information Technology* 0268396220915917.

Mitchell, T. M. 1980. *The Need for Biases in Learning Generalizations*. Department of Computer Science, Laboratory for Computer Science Research.

Osoba, O. A., and W. Welser. 2017. *An Intelligence in Our Image: the Risks of Bias and Errors in Artificial Intelligence*. Rand Corporation.

Schön, D. A. 1983. *The Reflective Practitioner: How Professionals Think in Action*. Basic Books.

Shadowen, A. N. 2017. *Ethics and Bias in Machine Learning: a Technical Study of What Makes Us "Good."* Academic Works, CUNY. https://academicworks.cuny.edu/jj_etds/44.

Further Reading

Castelluccia, C., and D. Le Métayer. 2019. "Understanding Algorithmic Decision-Making: Opportunities and Challenges." Panel for the Future of Science and Technology (STOA) of the Directorate-General for Parliamentary Research Services. https://doi.org/10.2861/536131.

CHAPTER 8

Ethical Programming and Machine Moral Agency

Kęstutis Mosakas

8.1 Background Issues

AI is probably the main hallmark of the current century's on-going technological developments. The ability to solve various problems by invoking systems that simulate certain aspects of human intelligence has proved to be invaluable ever since the inception of AI in the mid-twentieth century. At present, it seems virtually certain that the rapid development of AI will continue, pervading more and more aspects of human life. However, the opportunities provided by AI present a multitude of challenges. On one hand, AI systems are already outperforming humans in a great number of tasks, which has greatly enhanced progress in various domains, including science, industry, medicine, economics, and many more. On the other hand, the increasing sophistication and autonomy of AI systems, combined with the critical roles these systems are expected to play, come with considerable worries and dangers of their own. For example, if an AI system were to "misbehave" in a domain as vital as transportation, healthcare, or warfare, it may end up causing severe harm or even violating human rights or values.

For this reason, increased attention is now devoted to research on the ethical programming of AI systems. This pertains to both significant issues of an ethical nature (e.g., what ethical code systems should follow to perform their function without violating the fundamental values of society) as well as technical issues (e.g., how to ensure that the machine follows its ethical code in practice). It also concerns the law, because legal regulation is crucial to promote AI development while simultaneously keeping the many related risks in check. The interdisciplinary problems that concern programming ethics into the machine, then, are some of the most crucial ones to resolve in the coming years and decades.

8.2 Ethical Programming of Narrow AI

The most imminent questions related to programming ethics into the machine are those that concern what is known as narrow AI. Unlike broad or general AI,

 | DOI:10.1163/9789004682900_011

which refers to a system that is competent at many different tasks (comparable to human beings), narrow AI systems are good at only one particular task, such as playing chess, vacuum cleaning, performing medical diagnosis, or traffic control. Moreover, unlike general AI, the existence of which is still a matter of considerable speculation, narrow AI systems have been around for decades. The novel issues that arise concerning narrow AI have to do with a relatively new machine learning model, known as deep neural networks, and the new domains of application that are ethically problematic, with probably the most significant present example being self-driving vehicles.

Before we turn to these issues, it may be important to distinguish between different kinds of ethical functioning of AI systems. The first kind refers to artificial entities that simply have some kind of ethical impact in the world. Moor (2011, 16) refers to systems of this sort as "ethical impact agents." The second type refers to artificial entities that have been programmed to function with certain ethical outcomes in mind ("implicit ethical agents"). Examples of such agents would include automated teller machines, which are programmed to distribute the right amount of money in the name of the bank owning it, or the airplane's autopilot, which is programmed to ensure that the plane reaches its destination safely and on time (ibid). Moor distinguishes implicitly ethical systems from explicitly ethical ones. He writes that an explicit ethical agent "can identify and process ethical information about a variety of situations and make sensitive determinations about what should be done" (Moor 2009, 2). A system of this sort does not merely perform a "linear" function that is ethically important, but rather makes ethical decisions by itself. In other words, it processes the available information and determines the most adequate ethical decision in any given situation without any external human input. One could say, as Moor puts it, that it acts "*from* ethics, not merely *according to* ethics" (Moor 2011, 1). Finally, there are "full ethical agents," or explicit ethical agents that also have certain mental properties associated with agency—much like human beings.

In terms of Moor's categories, implicitly ethical artificial agents are the most relevant at present, since they are already being built, although substantial related difficulties remain.[1] Here one could distinguish between two kinds of

1 The extent to which an implicitly ethical artificial agent is problematic depends on its complexity and domain of application. For example, both an automated teller machine and a self-driving car are such agents. Yet it is not problematic to make the teller machine "behave" ethically, since all it has to do is to give out the right amount of cash; whereas ensuring the ethical outcome of the decision making of an autonomous car is a considerably more arduous task.

difficulties that must be overcome to ensure that the upcoming explicitly ethical AI systems make appropriate decisions. Difficulties of the first kind are by their very nature ethical. Consider the case of self-driving vehicles. Suppose that a vehicle is forced to choose between going straight and running over a pedestrian crossing the street legally or, instead, swerving and crushing into three pedestrians who are crossing the road illegally. This choice is an inherently ethical one and thereby requires an ethical solution. But it is not at all obvious how such dilemma cases, which are akin to the famous "trolley problem," should be resolved. After all, one could imagine all kinds of different choices that the vehicle may face, and since experts on ethics greatly disagree with each other, it seems unlikely that there would be a consensus on all such dilemmas.[2]

Then, there are technical difficulties. Even if we had a clear understanding of how different systems should be programmed to behave ethically, there is no guarantee that the resulting behavior of a given system will match our expectations, due to certain technical nuances and limitations. Probably the most significant related problem at present is machine bias, as discussed in the previous chapter. Machine bias occurs "when seemingly innocuous programming takes on the prejudices either of its creators or the data it is fed" (Garcia 2016, 112). Additionally, as Barocas and Selbst (2016, 675) note, bias may enter at various phases of machine learning, "whether by specifying the problem to be solved in ways that affect classes differently, failing to recognize or address statistical biases, reproducing past prejudice, or considering an insufficiently rich set of factors." A relatively recent example of machine bias could be the AI recruiting tool made by Amazon that proved to be discriminatory against women. As Lee et al. (2019, 3) write:

> The algorithm was taught to recognize word patterns in the resumes, rather than relevant skill sets, and these data were benchmarked against the company's predominantly male engineering department to determine an applicant's fit. As a result, the AI software penalized any resume that contained the word "women's" in the text and downgraded the resumes of women who attended women's colleges, resulting in gender bias.

2 See also the part on driverless cars (chapter 15) of this textbook for a more nuanced picture of the problem, including several reasons why the use of such ethical dilemmas in the context of self-driving cars is rather limited. Here the dilemmas were mentioned solely for illustrative purposes—i.e., to provide some examples of what could count as an ethical difficulty in the context of AI agency and decision making.

Notably, this problem exists for all types of machine learning, including deep neural networks, a model that has become highly prominent due to these networks' effectiveness and flexibility. Unfortunately, their decision-making processes are very hard to trace even for experts, which creates a kind of "black box" problem. This opacity of machine learning makes problematic behaviors of AI systems difficult to uncover and resolve (Fernandez 2018; Fomin 2020). Ultimately, the underlying point is that having exact ethical norms or criteria for an AI system to follow—which itself can be extremely difficult, depending on the system's sophistication and domain of application—does not guarantee that the system will actually follow these norms in practice. Issues related to programming, such as machine bias, can always come into play and overturn the ethical expectations of human programmers.

8.3 Programming Artificial Moral Agents

While the most imminent ethical concerns related to AI have to do with the upcoming narrow systems (e.g., self-driving vehicles and autonomous military weapons), researchers have begun to consider how one should program ethics into AI systems with broader capacities—especially in the context of technological singularity and superintelligence (see chapter 10 in the present part). The general field of study that considers machines as ethical subjects is commonly known as "machine ethics." According to Anderson and Anderson (2007, 15), the fundamental goal of machine ethics is to ensure "that the behavior of machines toward human users, and perhaps other machines as well, is ethically acceptable." This relatively new field of study takes its name from the Machine Ethics project (machineethics.com) launched by the Andersons in 2005. The project resulted in the edited volume *Machine Ethics* (Anderson and Anderson 2011), as well as the development of certain ethical AI systems, including the ethical eldercare system EthEl (Anderson and Anderson 2007) and the moral advisor on medical ethics MedEthEx (Anderson et al. 2006).

Generally, machine ethics focuses on so-called artificial moral agents (AMAs) or, in Moor's terms, AI systems that could be regarded as explicit or even full ethical agents. According to Moor (2011, 18), a "full ethical agent can make explicit ethical judgments and generally is competent to reasonably justify them." One example of a full ethical agent is an average human adult. Presumably, if a machine were to be considered a full ethical agent, it would need to come close to—if not match—the human level of ethical competence. Moor also notes that human ethical agents are thought to have certain mental properties associated with their agency, such as consciousness, intentionality, and free will (ibid). However, it is not clear whether it is even possible for an AI system to have these qualities and thus be recognized as a full ethical agent on a par with human beings, even if it is capable of making a broad range of ethical judgments and justifying them (cf. Sullins 2011).[3] In any case, regardless of whether one sets the bar for the full ethical agency of AI high or low (with respect to the mentioned mental properties), one of the fundamental questions that machine ethics attempts to address is how to ensure that a machine with a broad set of capabilities can make decisions that are ethically appropriate. Following Wallach and Allen (2009) and Gordon (2020), we may divide the most common machine ethics proposals into four broad categories.

First, *top-down approaches* involve providing the machine with a particular ethical theory or a set of moral principles to follow. Some of the proposed options include deontology (Powers 2011), prima facie duties (Anderson and bAnderson 2011, 476–92), ideal preference utilitarianism (Muehlhauser and Helm 2012), and a combination of utilitarianism and deontology (Dehghani et al. 2011). The problem that this approach faces is that even though there is considerable disagreement among ethicists with regard to normative ethics, the machine's moral decision making will be restricted by the theory or the set of principles that it was originally provided with. That means that by itself it will not be able to accommodate new moral cases that lie outside the theory or principles that it follows. (For example, a machine that consistently follows utilitarian ethics will not accept moral cases that would be valid on Kantian ethics as opposed to utilitarianism.) This is particularly problematic if the machine is programmed with a single rigid theory that, while accounting well for certain types of moral cases, considerably fails to do so in other areas (e.g., applying utilitarianism to questions of fairness and justice). A more complex theory (e.g., a combination of deontology and utilitarianism; see Dehghani et al. 2011) or a more diverse set of principles, then, may be more promising, even though that would considerably increase the complexity of the machine's ethical value scale. This would in turn require some way to compare different values and weigh them against each other, which is yet another complex and unresolved problem in moral philosophy.

The second option is *bottom-up approaches*. To overcome the problems with top-down approaches, some have suggested that the machine could work its way through ethics bottom-up—e.g., by learning from certain paradigmatic ethical cases and then classifying new cases according to the outcome of its

3 The view that human beings have free will is actually highly contested in philosophy. So, when Moor claims that humans are generally thought to have free will, he may be appealing to a kind of folk intuition about it rather than what philosophers believe to be the case.

learning (see Guarini 2006). This case-based reasoning, typically referred to as casuistry, would not require the machine to stick to a single theory or set of principles, since the ultimate basis for the ethical judgments of a casuistry-based machine would be the paradigmatic cases. Ultimately, however, this approach faces a significant problem of case reclassification, which is, by Guarini's own admission, an important part of human moral reasoning that requires moral principles. The machine's lack of something analogous to human common sense will not only prevent it from revising or specifying the initial instructions (which are virtually certain to be imperfect) but may also result in incorrect generalizations due to certain coincidental patterns that may appear in its training cases (Muehlhauser and Helm 2012, 109). At least by itself, then, casuistry does not seem to be sufficient for building an AMA.

Third, we could consider *mixed approaches*. It may seem that a logical solution to the problems with top-down and bottom-up approaches is to simply combine them. This strategy attempts to smooth out the other two approaches by retaining both top-down moral principles and bottom-up learning (see Wallach and Allen 2009). A machine that follows a mixed approach will make use of both types of moral reasoning. As promising as this may sound, this alternative is not problem-free either. First, as Gordon (2020, 148) points out, the top-down and bottom-up approaches are commonly seen as mutually exclusive. Second, it is unclear how effectively these approaches could be combined, since machines do not have what we refer to as common sense. As Bostrom and Yudkowsky (2014, 318) point out, the distinguishing feature of human intelligence, as opposed to AI, is its generality. Yet moral reasoning that involves combining different approaches seems to be precisely of the kind that favors human rather than machine intelligence.

Finally, there are certain other possibilities. Rzepka and Araki (2005), for example, consider a web-based approach that would include carrying out a statistical analysis of people's ethical attitudes on the web and generalizing from them. The behavior of such a machine, then, would reflect the attitudes of people as captured by the internet. The main problem with this approach is that it seems to be based on some kind of *ad populum* fallacy, since the right action is understood to be the one that is approved by a majority. Although one could expect such a machine to filter out the most radically unethical views, it would struggle with numerous controversial ethical issues and perpetuate human ethical biases, and it may end up agreeing with the general public in cases when ethicists would disagree. Ultimately, while this approach may be useful in descriptive ethics (i.e., to learn what people's moral attitudes in fact are), it is not at heart a normative approach (i.e., pertaining to how one ought to act).

Another possibility would be to build a kind of metahuman system (see Lyytinen et al. 2020) that generally follows a top-down, bottom-up or mixed approach but asks for human advice in cases of uncertainty. While this may not be the desired end result of machine ethics, it may be a good intermediate solution until one can build reliable ethical agents that are fully autonomous in their decision making.

The upshot here is that there are considerable issues with all types of approaches when it comes to programming ethics into the machine. This problem is underscored by the fact that even though people have been doing ethics for thousands of years, a considerable degree of controversy remains. As Muehlhauser and Helm (2012, 105) highlight, relatively simple moral theories tend to have certain counterintuitive implications, whereas the more sophisticated ones have been met with counterexamples of their own. The result is what they call being stuck on a "moral theory merry-go-round." It therefore seems likely that whatever approach is used to program AMAs, one will need to compromise and make certain trade-offs with respect to other approaches. For this reason, some authors (e.g., Anderson 2011) have suggested that building artificial ethical advisors—i.e., systems that are capable of moral reasoning but do not act by themselves and only give advice to human beings—may provide a solid and safe start for the practical implementation of machine ethics. As for AMAs, the question of how they should be programmed to behave ethically remains an open one.

8.4 Practical and Legal Decision Making Concerning Machine Moral Agency

Whether we are considering futuristic AMAs or the many different narrow systems that are being extensively developed, the issues concerning ethical programming are of considerable relevance when it comes to law and practical decision making in general. The reason is that there exists a point of overlap between the main features underlying the ethical programming of AI systems and the legal regulation thereof, in that both aim to secure the many benefits of AI systems without violating the fundamental values of society. Although the functions of ethical and legal theorizing and decision making differ, the mentioned overlap entails the conclusion that some aspects of ethics (and, indeed, practical philosophy more generally) could inform decisions concerning policymaking and law in the context of AI. For example, legal regulation of AI is crucial to manage the risks of undesirable outcomes that AI may produce, whereas the related ethical considerations can further illuminate these risks by examining them against the background of the more fundamental question of what it means to live a good life.[4] Thus, while the legal regulation of AI is concerned with various strategies that would help to ensure its safe deployment, reduce social disruption, and facilitate the integration of AI into existing legal frameworks, ethical reasoning provides some additional considerations that can further inform the said strategies. This is especially true for sophisticated AI, such as AMAs, in which case the law and policymakers will need to be aware of the risks associated with different kinds of ethical programming, but also for narrow AI such as autonomous vehicles and military weapons, which have been considered in both legal and philosophical scholarly literature alike.

Moreover, determinations concerning machine moral agency, such as whether an AI system qualifies as a full moral agent or merely an implicit one, are also relevant for practical decision making. For example, while the debate over how AMAs should be programmed is taking place, there is also an ongoing parallel discussion of whether it is a good idea to build them in the first place. Numerous authors have argued that there is no good reason to do so and that there may even be reasons against it. A common line of argument for this conclusion is that technological artefacts should remain as tools for attaining certain human ends, whereas a being such as an AMA would plausibly have non-zero moral status and therefore may need to be ascribed certain rights. For example, Van Wynsberghe and Robbins (2019) argue that since building AMAs is avoidable and unnecessary, bringing them into existence would only disrupt the existing social order and create new problems. In opposition to this view, machine ethicists have stated that even though some of the arguments in favor of building AMAs are dubious, there are, nevertheless, diverse reasons for regarding machine ethics overall as a valuable project (see Poulsen et al. 2019). Thus, while the question of how to program a certain kind of artificial agent—e.g., an autonomous vehicle—is significant both ethically and legally, so is the question of which categories of artificial agents should be built at all.

Should we construct AMAs once we can do so? The answer to this question depends on a number of different factors, such as the goals of developing AMAs, the potential disruption they would cause and the new demands they would make on society, the challenges of accommodating them in our legal frameworks, and so forth. In any case, the questions of ethical programming

4 Consider, for example, the different ways in which goodness is perceived by the three main theories of normative ethics: utilitarianism, Kantian deontology, and virtue ethics (see Fieser 2003).

and machine moral agency are not merely of philosophical interest, because they underlie important practical decisions that will need to be made once the relevant technologies become possible. Addressing these issues will certainly require knowledge and expertise from a number of different areas of research.

8.5 Conclusion

In conclusion, programming ethics into machines involves a multitude of problems that must be thoroughly explored in advance. This first and foremost issue refers to the upcoming explicit ethical agents, such as autonomous vehicles, military weapons, and other forms of robotics in morally salient contexts. In addition, there are numerous issues related to AMAs, including those pertaining to ethical programming, as well as the more fundamental question of whether such machines should be built in the first place. However, to successfully address these issues, an interdisciplinary endeavor seems to be required. As Gordon (2020) has noted, a number of rookie mistakes have already been made in discussions on ethical programming due to AI researchers underestimating the complexity of ethics and the extent of ethical disagreement among moral philosophers. Moreover, the expansive use of AI and robotics comes with legal and socio-political challenges that need to be explored as well. For these reasons, the many challenges related to the ethics of AI require fruitful interdisciplinary collaboration between AI researchers, ethicists, lawyers, and social scientists alike, in order to ensure that the research is built on firm foundations, that social disruption of AI is minimized, and that the upcoming AI systems function as intended.

Study Questions

1. Why is ethics important for AI applications?
2. What are the categories of moral agency, according to Moor?
3. Why is machine bias relevant to the question of building moral machines?
4. What does the term "machine ethics" refer to?
5. What are the main approaches to building explicit artificial ethical agents?
6. What are the related challenges or problems with these different approaches?

References

Anderson, S. L. 2011. "Machine Metaethics." In *Machine Ethics,* edited by M. Anderson and S. L. Anderson, 21–27. Cambridge University Press.

Anderson, M., and S. L. Anderson. 2007. "Machine Ethics: Creating an Ethical Intelligent Agent." *AI Magazine* 28(4): 15–26.

Anderson, M., and S. L. Anderson, eds. 2011a. *Machine Ethics*. Cambridge: Cambridge University Press.

Anderson, M., and S. L. Anderson. 2011b. "A Prima Facie Duty Approach to Machine Ethics." In *Machine Ethics*, edited by M. Anderson and S. L. Anderson, 476–92. Cambridge University Press.

Anderson, M., S. L. Anderson, and C. Armen. 2006. "An Approach to Computing Ethics." *IEEE Intelligent Systems* 21(4): 56–63.

Barocas, S., and A. D. Selbst. 2016. *Big Data's Disparate Impact*. SSRN Scholarly Paper. Social Science Research Network. https://papers.ssrn.com/abstract=2477899.

Bostrom, N., and E. Yudkowsky. 2014. "The Ethics of Artificial Intelligence." In *Cambridge Handbook of Artificial Intelligence,* edited by K. Frankish and W. Ramsey, 316–34. New York: Cambridge University Press.

Dehghani, M., et al. 2011. "An Integrated Reasoning Approach to Moral Decision Making." In *Machine Ethics*, edited by M. Anderson and S. L. Anderson, 422–41. Cambridge University Press.

Fernandez, S. 2018. "Explainable AI: Peering Inside the Deep Learning Black Box." In *InfoWorld.* https://www.infoworld.com/article/3315748/explainable-ai-peering-inside-the-deep-learning-black-box.html.

Fieser, J. 2003. "Ethics." *The Internet Encyclopedia of Philosophy*. https://iep.utm.edu/ethics/.

Fomin, V. V. 2020. "The Shift from Traditional Computing Systems to Artificial intelligence and the Implications for Bias." In *Smart Technologies and Fundamental Rights*, edited by J.-S. Gordon, 316–33. Brill.

Garcia, M. 2016. "Racist in the Machine: the Disturbing Implications of Algorithmic Bias." *World Policy Journal* 33(4): 111–17.

Gordon, J.-S. 2020. "Building Moral Robots: Ethical Pitfalls and Challenges." *Science and Engineering Ethics* 26(1): 141–57.

Guarini, M. 2006. "Particularism and the Classification and Reclassification of Moral Cases." *IEEE Intelligent Systems* 21(4): 22–28.

Lee, N. T., et al. 2019. *Algorithmic Bias Detection and Mitigation: Best Practices and Policies to Reduce Consumer Harms.* Center for Technology Innovation, Brookings Institution. https://www.brookings.edu/research/algorithmic-bias-detection-and-mitigation-best-practices-and-policies-to-reduce-consumer-harms/.

Lyytinen, K., J. V. Nickerson, and J. L. King. 2020. "Metahuman Systems = Humans + Machines That Learn." *Journal of Information Technology* 0268396220915917.

Moor, J. H. 2009. "Four Kinds of Ethical Robots." *Philosophy Now*. https://philosophynow.org/issues/72/Four_Kinds_of_Ethical_Robots.

Moor, J. H. 2011. "The Nature, Importance, and Difficulty of Machine Ethics." In *Machine Ethics*, edited by M. Anderson and S. L. Anderson, 13–21. Cambridge University Press.

Muehlhauser, L., and L. Helm. 2012. "Intelligence Explosion and Machine Ethics." In *Singularity Hypotheses: a Scientific and Philosophical Assessment*, edited by A. H. Eden, J. H. Moor, J. H. Soraker, and E. Steinhart, 101–27. Springer.

Poulsen, A., et al. 2019. "Responses to a Critique of Artificial Moral Agents." https://arxiv.org/abs/1903.07021.

Powers, T. 2011. "Prospectives for a Kantian Machine." In *Machine Ethics*, edited by M. Anderson and S. L. Anderson, 464–75. Cambridge University Press.

Rzepka, R., and K. Araki. 2005. "What Statistics Could Do for Ethics? The Idea of Common Sense Processing Based Safety Valve." *AAAI Fall Symposium on Machine Ethics, Technical Report* FS-05-06: 85–87.

Sullins, J. P. 2011. "When is a Robot a Moral Agent?" In *Machine Ethics*, edited by M. Anderson and S. L. Anderson, 151–61. Cambridge University Press.

Van Wynsberghe, A., and S. Robbins. 2019. "Critiquing the Reasons for Making Artificial Moral Agents." *Science and Engineering Ethics* 25: 719–35.

Wallach, W., and C. Allen. 2009. *Moral Machines: Teaching Robots Right from Wrong*. Oxford University Press.

Further Reading

Allen, C., et al. 2005. "Artificial Morality: Top-down, Bottom-up, and Hybrid Approaches." *Ethics and Information Technology* 7(3): 149–55.

Formosa, P., and M. Ryan. 2021. "Making Moral Machines: Why We Need Artificial Moral Agents." *AI & Society*. https://link.springer.com/article/10.1007/s00146-020-01089-6.

Lin, P., et al. 2008. *Autonomous Military Robotics: Risk, Ethics, and Design*. ONR report, California Polytechnic State University, San Luis Obispo, December 20. http://ethics.calpoly.edu/ONR_report.pdf.

Thompson, S. J., ed. 2020. *Machine Law, Ethics, and Morality in the Age of Artificial Intelligence*. IGI Global.

CHAPTER 9

The Black Box Problem

Vladislav V. Fomin and Paulius Astromskis

9.1 What Is the Black Box Problem?

In the contemporary world, people's daily private and business transactions are more often than not supported by some information technologies (ITs). These various IT systems and gadgets help to collect, process, and relay data and information, and their need is justified when such operations can help do the job quicker, cheaper, safer, and/or with fewer mistakes. But do we usually trust the IT systems we use? Do we trust that the calculations were performed flawlessly?

One of the essential elements of human trust in the tools we use rests on the understanding of processes leading to the creation of the tool and/or the processes establishing the tool's functionality. Did you ever have a reason not to trust a cash register's calculated total for your long list of purchased items? And how often, when given the unexpectedly big total, do we start looking for an erroneous price of one of the purchased items? Which part, element, or function of a cash register (including the human factor involved, the register's operator) do we doubt in this common situation? Let's look at this example through the prism of the definition of a generic IT system.

Like any other system, an IT system can be abstractly presented as having three main elements: the input provided to the system, the process(ing) part of the system, and the output generated by the system (Figure 7.1). Most IT systems have also a control function, which typically requires a feedback loop (e.g., placing an overly heavy item on the electric scales at the cash register is likely to trigger some sort of alarm designed to prevent erroneous weighing or destruction of the scales). The feedback helps keep the processing under predefined "normal" conditions, minimizing the risk of errors and malfunction.

IT systems typically execute some sort of computational processes, based on an algorithm. In simple terms, an algorithm can be defined as a sequence of steps and instructions that can be applied to (input) data to produce a desired output. Among the properties an algorithm must possess, the following are relevant:

 | DOI:10.1163/9789004682900_012

- *Definiteness*: each step must be precisely defined; the actions to be carried out must be rigorously and unambiguously specified for each case.
- *Output*: an algorithm has one or more outputs, which have a specified relation to the inputs.

In other words, one can characterize an algorithmic IT system as having a number of transparency properties (TPs):

1. Its working principles are known to its creators;
2. Its working principles can be explained to other parties;
3. The definitiveness and unambiguity of the algorithmic basis for *process* implies that given the same input, the system will always produce the same output.

With respect to our example of a shopper's frustration over the unexpectedly high total on the shopping bill, we do not question the system's computational capacities. Rather, we wonder whether the valid *input* was registered or taken by the system; we assume that the cash register can add properly. We understand the nature of the mathematical calculations, which establish the *processing* of the cash register. In other words, our trust rests on the transparency properties of the system, as outlined above.

In situations where one of the aforementioned properties of an algorithmic IT system cannot be sustained, the processing part of the system is referred to as a *black box*. A black box is a system that can be viewed in terms of its inputs and outputs without any definite knowledge of its internal workings (Figure 9.1).

Naturally, the more sophisticated the tool is, the more effort it takes for us to trust that its functioning is safe or produces correct results. As one typical example of a black box, think about how much trust people had in the results produced by a black box placed alongside a road—the radar speed detector—when this technology was novel. Has our trust in radar systems grown since then? If yes, then for what reasons?

FIGURE 9.1 A generic representation of the black box problem

9.1.1 *Examples of Black Box Systems*

Complexity of technology is not the sole reason leading to the black box problem. In the age of knowledge economy and innovation, a common reason for "black boxing" a system is to protect intellectual property rights (IPRs). To protect a company's intellectual property (IP), transparency property number 2—explainability of the system's working properties to a third party—can be rendered legally constrained. In other words, although the working principles of the system are known to its creators, they cannot be explained to third parties due to limitations imposed by the IP laws.

Google's search engine is a good example. Its success is based on proprietary algorithms for data processing. Given the same input (i.e., the same search term), Google searches produce search results (i.e., the output) that are considered to be superior to those of competing systems. Although the working principles of Google's search engine (i.e., the "process" box in Figure 7.1) are known to its creators, sharing the algorithmic logic with third parties would cause the company to lose not only its competitive advantage, but also the very value the users place in the Google brand.

A less common situation when a system becomes "black boxed" is the use of an obsolete IT system that can't be (re-)programmed anymore, or the controllability of which cannot be guaranteed due to the loss of a source code, the retirement of the programming language, or lack of coding skills to tackle the system. This situation renders TP number 1—that "its working principles are known to its creators"—implausible. The working principles of the system may remain well known at the level of the user interface, but the exact mechanisms that make possible the system's functionality may be obscure. The SABRE airline reservation system is often cited as an example of such a situation. SABRE first went live in 1960, and while it may be still operational today on a supporting corporate IT infrastructure, to most engineers the task of opening the black box of the system would be insurmountable.

While the two aforementioned causes for and examples of black-box systems may be considered trivial, inability to guarantee the third transparency property of an algorithmic IT system—the definitiveness and unambiguity of the process—calls for introduction in the context of the new generation of computational systems, referred to as "learning systems."

9.2 Artificial Intelligence and the Black Box Problem

9.2.1 *What Is AI?*

Artificial Intelligence (AI) usually refers to the development of computer systems able to perform tasks normally requiring human intelligence, such as decision making, visual perception, or speech recognition. More broadly, AI is typically defined as a machine's ability to perform cognitive functions such as perceiving, reasoning, learning, interacting with the environment, problem solving, and even exercising creativity. The definition of AI, as proposed by the European Commission, refers to "systems that display intelligent behaviour by analysing their environment and taking actions—with some degree of autonomy—to achieve specific goals" (EC AI High-Level Expert Group 2019a).

AI-based systems can be purely software-based, such as the voice assistants or image analysis and face recognition software found in our smartphones or in cloud services (Press 2017). AI can also be embedded in hardware devices, such as autonomous cars or drones.

If traditional (algorithmic) computational systems were built on the foundation of strict control over the working logic of the system, then most of the current advances in AI have involved machine learning (ML). *ML algorithms, which power AI, are radically different,* in that they do not receive explicit programming instructions. Instead, ML systems receive datasets containing what in the traditional IT systems would be denoted as *input data* and the resulting *output data.* An ML system then attempts to find a good function *F*, the application of which to input data produced the given output data. This "searching" for the best function to produce the output data from the input data is what is we referred to as "learning."

The key feature of AI—the ability to learn—constitutes the second radical distinction between AI and traditional computational systems, which never learn (Lyytinen et al. 2020), as they are programmed with *fixed, codified* human knowledge. Contrary to the fixed codification of the algorithm in the traditional systems, AI systems through their ongoing learning process depart from the initial set of "algorithms" provided by programmers.

9.2.2 *AI Systems' Opacity as the Cause of the Black Box Problem*

The learning in AI systems determines how the subsequent cycles of computation will unfold, and it implies some sort of optimization of the process with respect to the produced results. Whereas in the traditional computational systems (except for the cases when the algorithm is protected by patent) the results could have always been checked against the fixed set of instructions—the algorithm—in the machine-learning AI system this kind of control cannot be established easily or at all. This means that for the users of the system, it becomes impossible to establish definite and unambiguous control over the computational process. In other words, the system becomes a black box to the observer.

The concept of the black box, however, can be elaborated as having different causes and effects, which are important in the context of the development or use of AI-based (public) services. The concept of opacity can be helpful in this regard.

Different types of opacity can be distinguished, which can be juxtaposed with two of the previously elaborated transparency properties (TPs) of algorithmic systems:

1. The working principles of the system are known to its creators;
2. The working principles can be explained to other parties.

The third TP is directly dependent on the definitiveness and unambiguity of the algorithms and hence does not apply to AI systems, which are learning systems as discussed above.

Ferretti and Blasimme (2018) introduced specific terminology to distinguish between different causes of opacity for AI systems:

1. *Epistemic opacity* occurs when it is not possible to have access to or there is not sufficient understanding of the rules an AI system is applying to make predictions, classifications, and decisions.
2. *Explanatory opacity* relates to the question of why an AI system provides a specific outcome.
3. *Lack of disclosure* refers to situations in which data subjects are unaware that automated decision making and profiling activities about them are being carried out.

Lack of disclosure does not relate directly to the problem of the black box and will be omitted from the subsequent discussion. The case of not having access to the computation rules, or epistemic opacity, is similar to the case of IP protection of the algorithmic code, as discussed above. As the other cause of epistemic opacity—the insufficient understanding of the rules of computation—is similar to the case of explanatory opacity, we will review the latter case in more detail.

9.2.3 *Explanatory Opacity or the (Black Box) Problem of Explainability*

This concept of explainability is very important in the context of the overall discussion of the mission of computational systems in automating jobs, and in light of the ongoing public debate and legal efforts on unprecedented (user) data-collection practices.

The notion of algorithmic opacity and the cause of the black box problem of AI implies not only the non-transparency of the processing logic, but also the

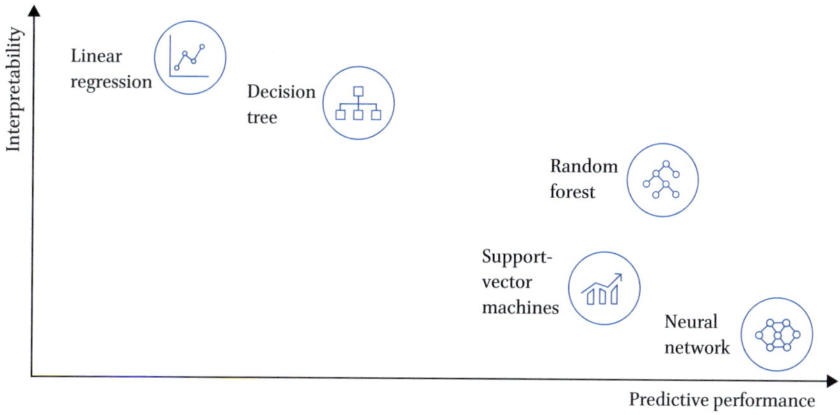

FIGURE 9.2 Interpretability vs. predictive performance trade-off in AI systems
SOURCE: BURKHARDT ET AL. (2019, 7)

inability of system users to trace the reasons for certain decisions of the system (EC AI High-Level Expert Group 2019a, 5).

The design of reinforcement learning of AI is such that computing agents interact with and receive feedback from their environment—that is, they learn from experience—and the AI systems can and do create responses corresponding to such received experience; i.e., AI can identify patterns in data to match or even supersede humans. The challenge, however, remains how to relate the ML-produced outcomes to the rule-based systems (Lyytinen et al. 2020) with which humans have traditionally worked. How can AI systems explain their decisions to users, so as to develop trust that their operations and results are bias-free? The advantages of AI-supplied predictive performance must be balanced against the requirement for interpretability of results (see Figure 9.2).

Data acquisition and use must also be managed by keeping a balance between system performance and transparency regarding how AI systems make their predictions (Burkhardt et al. 2019, 2).

The explanatory opacity of AI systems is a stumbling block on the way to full automation of the input-process-output cycle, which has been driving the deployment of traditional computational systems. Today, implementation of AI systems always bears a risk of biased or distorted results (Fomin 2021), thus requiring intervention by human agents to evaluate the AI-produced decisions prior to the action (see Figure 9.3).

Human decisions can be fully automated when the underlying decision-making algorithmic logic is known, understood, and unambiguous (Simon 1977). Although we already have (some) regulatory basis for the explainability of AI systems, as established, for example, by Articles 13–15 of the GDPR

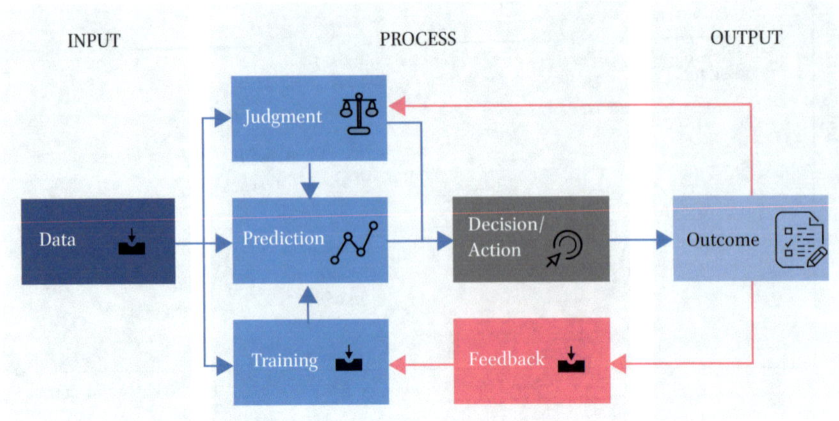

FIGURE 9.3 AI and human (non-automated) decisions
SOURCE: KÖSZEGI (2019), REFERRING TO AGRAWAL, GANS, AND GOLDFARB (2018)

regulation, which states repeatedly that data subjects have a right to "meaningful information about the logic involved," the explainability of computational logic is likely to be increasingly hampered by IP protection of AI systems. Worldwide, applications for AI and ML patents were growing at about 25% rate since 2012, the trend changing in 2017 with a steep 70% growth rate (see Figure 9.4).

Not having meaningful information about the logic involved, and facing situations where it is difficult, if not impossible, to explain the consequences of automated decision making (Burt 2018), we are unlikely to see full automation of tasks become universal under the new computational paradigm, an outcome that represents a setback for the original goals of computation.

9.3 What Are the Solutions to the Black Box Problem?

Ethics Guidelines for Trustworthy AI, proposed by the High-Level Expert Group on Artificial Intelligence set up by the European Commission (2019b), lists four ethical principles, rooted in fundamental rights, that must be respected in order to ensure that AI systems are developed, deployed and used in a trustworthy manner. These are (1) respect for human autonomy; (2) prevention of harm; (3) fairness; and (4) explainability.

This last principle, explainability, is directly aimed at the problems of opacity and states that it should be possible to explain why an AI system arrived at

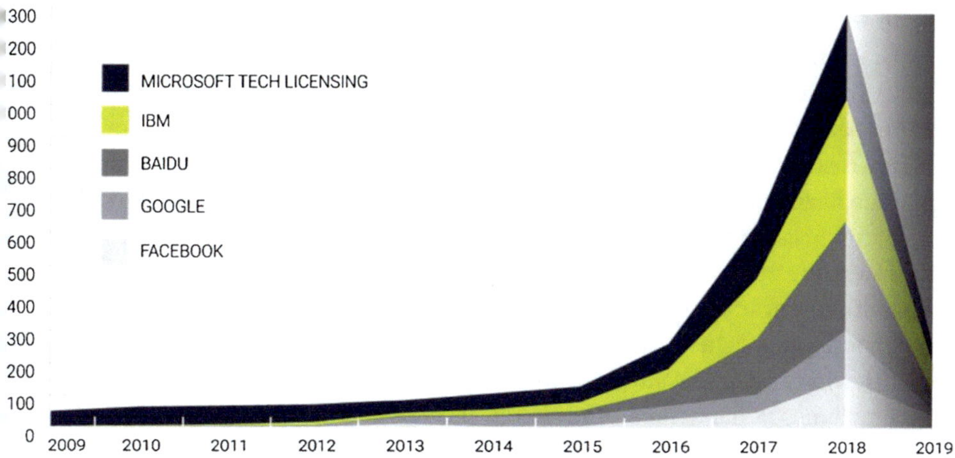

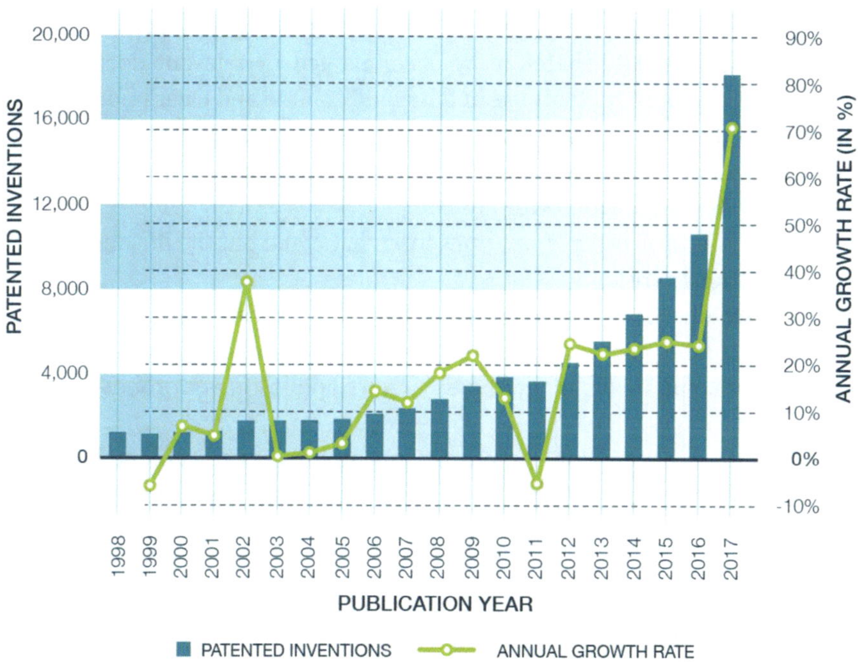

IGURE 9.4 International patent activity in AI between 1998 and 2017
SOURCE: CIPO (2019)

a certain conclusion or result (Bartneck et al. 2021). Explainability is crucial for building and maintaining users' trust in AI systems; i.e., processes need to be transparent, the capabilities and purpose of AI systems should be openly communicated, and decisions—to the extent possible—should be explainable to those who are directly and indirectly affected (EC AI High-Level Expert Group 2019b).

The degree to which explainability is needed depends heavily on the context and the severity of the consequences if that output is erroneous or otherwise inaccurate (EC AI High-Level Expert Group 2019b). A recent proposal for a Regulation of the European Parliament and of the Council, "Laying down harmonised rules on artificial intelligence (Artificial Intelligence Act) and amending certain union legislative acts" (2021), suggests banning AI systems that present unacceptable risk, or that pose a clear threat to the safety, livelihoods, and rights of people, such as applications that manipulate human behavior to circumvent users' free will. Therefore, one way to solve opacity problem is rather extreme and simple: prohibit the use of AI systems.

For high-risk AI systems, the EU's Artificial Intelligence Act specifically addresses opacity problems, requiring a certain degree of transparency. Users should be able to interpret the system's output and use it appropriately. High-risk AI systems should therefore be accompanied by relevant documentation and instructions on their use and include concise and clear information, including information relative to possible risks to fundamental rights and discrimination, where appropriate. AI systems identified as high-risk include technology used in the following areas:

1. Critical infrastructure (e.g., transport) that could put the life and health of citizens at risk;
2. Educational or vocational training that may determine access to education and the professional course of someone's life (e.g., scoring of exams);
3. Safety components of products (e.g., AI applications in robot-assisted surgery);
4. Employment, employee management and access to self-employment (e.g., resume-sorting software for recruitment procedures);
5. Essential private and public services (e.g., credit scoring that determines whether citizens will be able to obtain a loan);
6. Law enforcement that may interfere with people's fundamental rights (e.g., evaluation of the reliability of evidence);
7. Migration, asylum and border control management (e.g., verification of authenticity of travel documents);
8. Administration of justice and democratic processes (e.g., applying the law to a concrete set of facts); and
9. Biometric identification systems.

These high-risk AI systems will be subject to strict obligations before they can be put on the market, including adequate risk assessment and mitigation systems; high quality of the datasets feeding the system, so as to minimize risks or discriminatory outcomes; logging of activity to ensure traceability of results; detailed documentation providing all information necessary on the system and its purpose, so that authorities can assess its compliance; clear and adequate information for the user; appropriate human oversight measures to minimize risk; and a high level of robustness, security, and accuracy (European Commission 2021).

For limited systems, the EU's Artificial Intelligence Act sets only some specific transparency obligations: when using artificial intelligence systems such as chatbots, users should be aware that they are interacting with a machine so that they can make an informed decision to continue or step back. And for minimal-risk systems, regulation does not intervene here.

An explanation, when required, will have to remain a human-interpretable description of the process by which a decision maker takes a particular set of inputs and reaches a particular conclusion (Doshi-Velez et al. 2017). An explanation does not require knowing the flow of bits through an AI system, any more than an explanation from humans requires knowing the flow of signals through human brain neurons. The High-Level Expert Group on Artificial Intelligence (2019b) also requires that those directly and indirectly affected by AI systems should be able to obtain, to the extent possible, as "a suitable explanation of the AI system's decision-making process."

Traceability, auditability mechanisms, and transparent communication on system capabilities are proposed as possible solutions that examine the inputs and outputs of algorithms for bias and harms, rather than unpacking how the system functions (Cath 2018), provided that the system as a whole respects fundamental rights (EC AI High-Level Expert Group 2019b). It is technically feasible to create AI systems that provide the same kinds of explanations currently expected of humans under the law (Doshi-Velez et al. 2017). That is, explanations should be delivered in a concise, transparent, intelligible, and easily accessible form, using clear and plain language that the user can comprehend and verify, and, most of all, so that users can effectively contest the system's decisions (Hoeren and Niehoff 2018).

To this end, Leslie (2019) distinguishes four explanatory strategies worth paying special attention to, a typology of which is shown in Figure 9.5:

- Internal explanation, which involves making intelligible how the components and relationships within it function. On one hand, this can be seen as an endeavor to explain the model's operation by considering it globally as a comprehensible whole. Here, the aspiration is to "pry open the black box" by building an explanatory model that enables a full grasp of the opaque system's internal contents. On the other hand, the search for internal explanation can indicate the pursuit of a kind of engineering insight. In this sense, internal explanation can be seen as attempting to shed descriptive and inferential light on the parts and operation of the system as a whole in order to achieve a higher degree of outcome transparency.

- External or post-hoc explanation, which attempts to capture essential attributes of the observable behavior of a black-box system by subjecting it to a number of different techniques that reverse-engineer explanatory insight. Such a post-hoc approach allows us to seek evidence for the reasoning behind a given opaque model's prediction or classification by utilizing maximally interpretable techniques such as linear regression, decision trees, rule lists, or case-based reasoning.
- Supplemental explanatory infrastructure, which involves incorporating secondary explanatory facilities into the system, making their implementation more sensitive to user needs, more explanation-friendly, and more understandable by humans. For instance, multimodal methods of combining visualization tools and textual interfaces are being developed that may make the provision of explanations more interpretable for both implementers and decision subjects.
- Counterfactual explanations are contrastive explanations. They offer succinct computational reckonings of how specific factors that influenced an algorithmic decision can be changed so that better alternatives can be realized by the subject of that decision.

9.4 Conclusions

Following the path of the first wave of computerization, the adoption of AI is rapidly taking hold across global business and military operations. As we have learned in the past, governments will follow with caution, as the consequences and risks of dependence on AI must first be assessed (Osoba and Welser 2017).

For trust to be established, the black-box AI systems, i.e., systems the processes of which are opaque to human observers, must be made compatible with rule-based systems (Lyytinen et al. 2020) with which humans have traditionally worked to enable reflective analysis and explainability. Although this remains a challenge for both scholars and practitioners, explainable AI (sometimes referred to as XAI) may be a way toward a future in which the power of AI can be deployed without setbacks related to trust and avoidance of bias, thus making full automation of tasks possible, as was once envisioned at the dawn of the computer age.

The recent EU Artificial Intelligence Act (2021) offers concrete proposals for AI system implementation and mitigation of risk, including the enlisting of

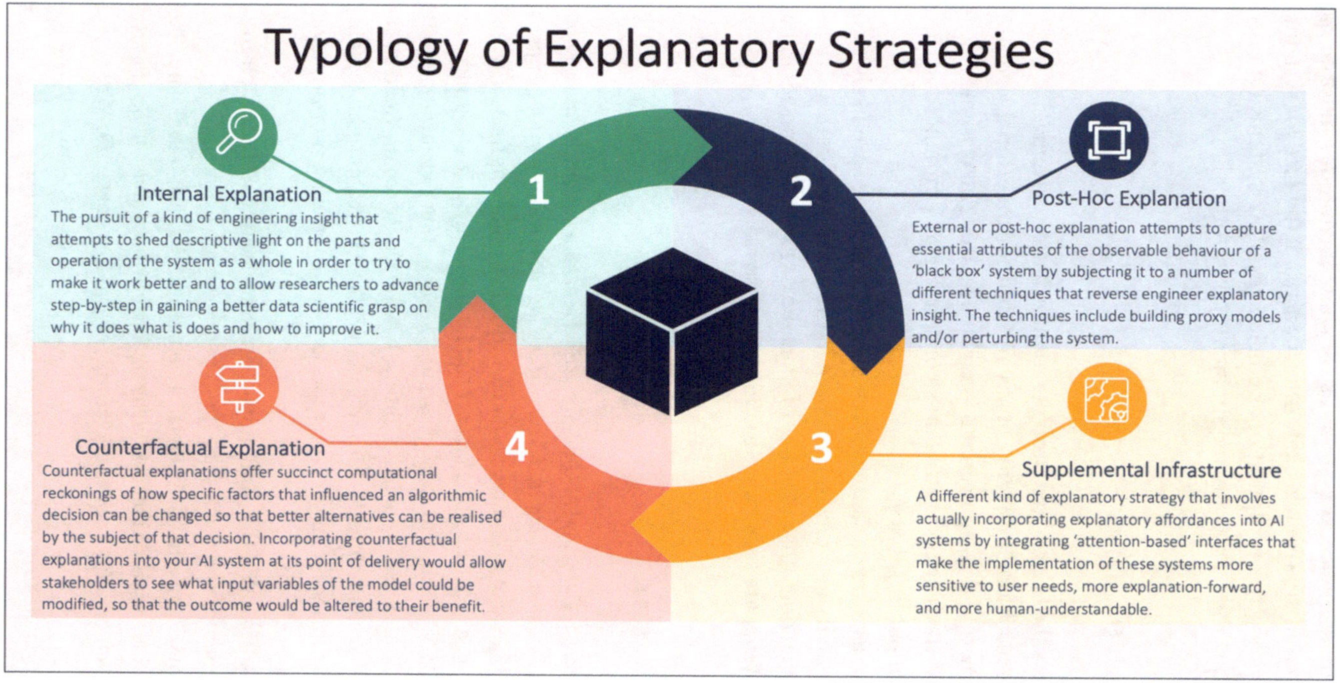

FIGURE 9.5 Typology of explanatory strategies
SOURCE: LESLIE (2019)

domains and tasks where the risks associated with black-box systems cannot be tolerated and hence AI systems as we know them today must be banned. This prohibition, however, is likely only to instigate the race for systems capable of delivering the computational efficiencies of AI systems on one hand, while meeting the EU's AI Act requirements on the other hand.

Study Questions

1. What is the "black box" problem in information systems?
2. Is the black box problem equally relevant for traditional algorithmic IT systems and those powered by machine learning algorithms?
3. Why is the black box problem a concern for governments and the provision of public services?
4. Which aspects or causes of the black box problem are likely to persist, and which ones may be overcome in the nearest future?
5. In which domains is the use of black-box AI systems considered as high risk? What are some ways to mitigate those risks?

References

Agrawal, A. K., J. S. Gans, and A. Goldfarb. 2018. *Prediction, Judgment and Complexity: A Theory of Decision Making and Artificial Intelligence* (NBER Working Paper 24243). National Bureau of Economic Research. https://www.nber.org/papers/w24243.pdf.

Bartneck, C., et al. 2021. *An Introduction to Ethics in Robotics and AI*. Springer Nature.

Burkhardt, R., N. Hohn, and C. Wigley. 2019. "Leading Your Organization to Responsible AI." *McKinsey Analytics*. https://www.mckinsey.com/~/media/McKinsey/Business%20Functions/McKinsey%20Analytics/Our%20Insights/Leading%20your%20organization%20to%20responsible%20AI/Leading-your-organization-to-responsible-AI.ashx.

Burt, A. 2018. "How Will the GDPR Impact Machine Learning?" O'Reilly. https://www.oreilly.com/ideas/how-will-the-gdpr-impact-machine-learning.

Cath, C. 2018. "Governing Artificial Intelligence: Ethical, Legal and Technical Opportunities and Challenges." *Philosophical Transactions of the Royal Society A: Mathematical, Physical and Engineering Sciences* 376(2133): 20180080.

Doshi-Velez, F., et al. 2017. "Accountability of AI under the Law: the Role of Explanation." *ArXiv Preprint ArXiv:1711.01134*. https://arxiv.org/abs/1711.01134.

EC AI High-Level Expert Group. 2019a. *A Definition of Artificial Intelligence: Main Capabilities and Scientific Disciplines*. https://ec.europa.eu/newsroom/dae/document.cfm?doc_id=56341.

EC AI High-Level Expert Group. 2019b. *Ethics Guidelines for Trustworthy AI*. https://ec.europa.eu/newsroom/dae/document.cfm?doc_id=58477.

European Commission. 2021. *Proposal for a Regulation Laying down Harmonised Rules on Artificial Intelligence (Artificial Intelligence Act)* (COM/2021/206 final). Commission to the European Parliament. https://digital-strategy.ec.europa.eu/en/library/proposal-regulation-laying-down-harmonised-rules-artificial-intelligence-artificial-intelligence.

Ferretti, A. S., and A. Blasimme. 2018. "Machine Learning in Medicine: Opening the New Data Protection Black Box." *European Data Protection Law Review (EDPL)* 4(3): 320–32.

Fomin, V. V. 2021. "The Shift from Traditional Computing Systems to Artificial Intelligence and the Implications for Bias." In *Smart Technologies and Fundamental Rights*, edited by J.-S. Gordon, 316–33. Brill.

Hoeren, T., and M. Niehoff. 2018. "Artificial Intelligence in Medical Diagnoses and the Right to Explanation." *European Data Protection Law Review (EDPL)* 4(3): 308–19.

Köszegi, S. T. 2019. Keynote Speach at the 18th Annual STS Conference Graz. https://sts-conference.isds.tugraz.at/event/2/page/44-keynotespeaker.

Leslie, D. 2019. "Understanding Artificial Intelligence Ethics and Safety: a Guide for the Responsible Design and Implementation of AI systems in the Public Sector." *Zenodo*.

Lyytinen, K., J. V. Nickerson, and J. L. King. 2020. "Metahuman Systems = Humans + Machines That Learn." *Journal of Information Technology* 0268396220915917.

Osoba, O. A., and W. Welser. 2017. *An Intelligence in Our Image: the Risks of Bias and Errors in Artificial Intelligence*. Rand Corporation.

Press, G. 2017. "Top 10 Hot Artificial Intelligence (AI) Technologies." *Forbes*. https://www.forbes.com/sites/gilpress/2017/01/23/top-10-hot-artificial-intelligence-ai-technologies/#a1c98f519287.

Simon, H. A. 1977. *The New Science of Management Decision*. Prentice-Hall.

CHAPTER 10

Singularity and Control

Vladislav V. Fomin and Kęstutis Mosakas

10.1 The Notion of Control: General Concept and Background

10.1.1 *Control of Algorithmic Systems*

Since the very first uses of computers, people have typically developed and adopted IT systems because they believed such systems would allow them to accomplish more, more quickly, and at lower cost. IT systems were built to substitute for humans not only in tasks where fast and vast calculations were required, but also where jobs were perceived to be too complicated or dangerous for humans. Importantly, computation allowed the introduction of control where humans did not have the capability to exercise control themselves.

The concept of *controllability* was originally introduced by Kalman (1960). To control a *system*, one must be able to change certain physical quantities, called *inputs*, and to measure the behavior of the system, or the physical variables of the system called *outputs*. The relationship between those inputs and outputs can help us define what a system is. Namely, a system (IT or generic) can be defined as a physical or digital object or a collection of objects that are characterized by input and output variables for which there are cause-effect relationships (see Figure 7.1).

To develop a controllable system, one must provide an *algorithm* for computing the output of the system at any given time *t'* from the knowledge of input to the system at time *t* <= *t'* (Kalman 1960, 151). In other words, the calculatable cause-effect relationships between input and output, also referred to as controllable feedback, gives the user the possibility of transferring any initial state to zero by a suitable control action. An algorithm can be defined as a sequence of steps and instructions that can be applied to (input) data to produce some result (output).

In traditional IT systems, data are provided as an input and are produced as an output. The output from one system can be an input to another system, which typically results in increased complexity of the aggregate system and decreases controllability of the aggregate system or any of its constituent systems.

Given the definition of the IT system, an algorithmic IT system is understood as a controllable system, as the notion of the algorithm implies *definiteness*

 | DOI:10.1163/9789004682900_013

(each step must be precisely defined; the actions to be carried out must be rigorously and unambiguously specified for each case) and lack of ambiguity in the input-output relationship (for one or more outputs, there is an unambiguous specified relation to the inputs). Programming languages are used to transform the algorithm into computer (machine) code. When implemented, IT systems can perform operations on data as programmed.

10.1.2 *Control of Non-algorithmic Systems*

If traditional computational systems are built on the foundation of strict control over the system, the emerging paradigm of artificial intelligence (AI) systems is more akin to fuzzy organizational systems. AI is based on various machine learning (ML) methods, which, in contrast to algorithmic systems, do not receive explicit programming instructions from the creators—a fact that calls into question the controllability of those systems.

Instead of following the explicit programming instructions, ML systems receive datasets containing what in the traditional algorithmic IT systems would be denoted as input data and output data—i.e., the data upon which the calculation must be performed and the correct results of that calculation, respectively. The ML system then tries to figure out how the output can be derived from the input. That "trying" is what is referred to as the "learning" of the ML-based system. This key feature of AI—the ability to learn—causes scholars to question the controllability of AI systems.

10.1.3 *Control of IT Systems in Organizational Settings*

In organizational settings, Kalman's (1960) mathematical conception of control over a system is extended to include interaction with the users of the system and manipulations of data and information, which serve as inputs or are produced as the outputs of the system.

A general definition of the control of an IT system in organizational settings can be found in the widely adopted COBIT framework of the Information Systems Audit and Control Association (https://www.isaca.org): "The policies, procedures, practices and organizational structures designed to provide reasonable assurance that business objectives will be achieved and that undesired events will be prevented or detected and corrected."

The function of controls of an IT system in organizational settings is to detect, correct, and/or prevent problems such as fraud or a failure in the system. Given the scope and the definition, control of an IT system in organizational settings is less likely to follow strict algorithmic logic, as neither policies nor human practices can be defined definitively (i.e., without any ambiguities) (de Vaujany et al. 2018).

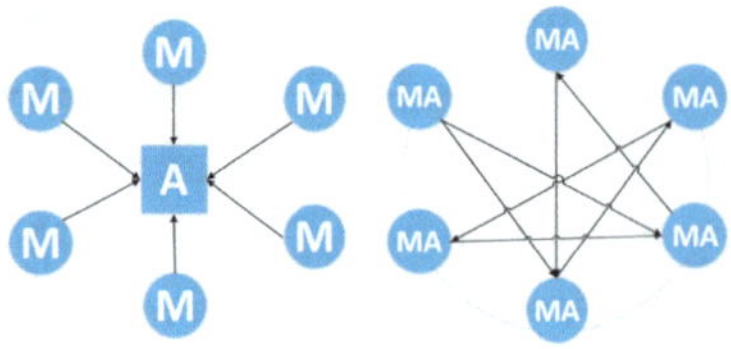

FIGURE 10.1 Architecture of centralized (left) and distributed (right) systems

10.2 Methods of and Approaches to Control

Akin to the diversity of political systems in the modern world, which can be broadly categorized as authoritarian and democratic, the wide variety of IT systems can be broadly generalized as having centralized and distributed control (see Figure 10.1), also referred to as "architecture."

The concept of centralized architecture implies the presence of one controlling entity for the entire system. Decentralized architecture implies that each entity in the system has some control capability over itself and/or in relationship to other entities.

In what is believed to have been the first commercial application of computers, in the 1950s the LEO computer was built as a centralized system to aid J. Lyons and Company in computational tasks related to stock tracking, wage calculations, and other financial functions. The centralized architecture implies easy control over computing resources and jobs assigned to the system. However, should the computing system be subjected to a malfunction or electricity outage, the whole system loses its functional capability—it becomes out of control.

Most of today's public services offered by national and municipal governments over the internet (e-health, e-government, etc.), as well as most corporate services for the public, are based on a centralized architecture. Most internet users have experienced at least once the "out of service" or "server is not responding" message on their computer screens. There are systems, however, which are built purposefully to make the "out of service" situation extremely unlikely; usually, these systems are based on a distributed architecture.

The internet is an example of a distributed computing system. The origins of the internet lie in the development of a computer-based network for the anti-missile defense system ARPANET during the Cold War. Distributing the computational and communication capability across multiple nodes of the system ensured that the destruction of any one node (or even multiple nodes) of the system would not cause the entire system to break down, thus providing the state with greater defense capability.

Perhaps the best-known modern example of a distributed computational system (besides the internet) is Bitcoin cryptocurrency. The distributed architecture for the system was chosen not to maintain resilience in the event of war, but to avoid centralized control of any single entity—in other words, to oppose the currently dominant setup of global financial systems under which all currency operations are controlled by a central bank. The other side of the distributed architecture of Bitcoin is user anonymity, which carries legal implications in cases when cryptocurrency transactions are used to support fraudulent or illegal business activities.

By design, the governance of distributed systems, as compared to that of centralized systems, is a more complex task. Thus the risk of having the system, or some entities in the system, go "out of control" is greater. This presents a paradox in the logic of the development of computational systems and their deployment. On one hand, computational systems are built to give people control over tasks they are not capable of controlling themselves. On the other hand, with the growing complexity and distribution of business and civic interactions, distributed systems allow for greater flexibility and resilience but, at the same time, are more likely to face an "out of control" situation.

10.3 Singularity = Artificial General Intelligence + "Out of Control" State

To date, most individuals, companies, and nation-states have experienced types of "out of control" situations. Notable examples of computing bugs or failures include stock trading incidents, disasters in space shuttle missions, and fatal accidents involving autonomous cars. Our fears of intelligent supertechnology going out of control were taken by many screen writers as a basis for their movies, of which *The Terminator* is probably the epitome.

In science, the major challenge related to the control of future AI is what is known as the "technological singularity" or "intelligence explosion" (see, e.g., Kurzweil 2005; Muehlhauser 2013). In the core sense, singularity refers to the hypothetical future scenario according to which AI systems become "superintelligent" through numerous cycles of recursive self-improvement (see Chalmers 2010). As Muehlhauser and Bostrom write:

> We can predict that advanced AIs will have instrumental goals to preserve themselves, acquire resources, and self-improve, because those goals are useful intermediaries to the achievement of almost any set of final goals.

> Thus, when we build an AI that is as skilled as we are at the task of designing AI systems, we may thereby initiate a rapid, AI-motivated cascade of self-improvement cycles. Now when the AI improves itself, it improves the intelligence that does the improving, quickly leaving the human level of intelligence far behind.
>
> MUEHLHAUSER AND BOSTROM 2014, 42

As of 2023, this scenario of intelligent machines improving themselves and building even smarter machines may rightly appear to be more reminiscent of science fiction rather than reality, since the current AI systems are built to be "intelligent" at only one particular task, be it a gaze recognition system for highway safety, a stock price prediction system, or power grid load prediction. In contrast to today's narrow applications of AI, which can be and are controlled by people, the concept of singularity entails the existence of *general* AI (AGI)—the kind of AI that is competent at a variety of different tasks, much like human beings, and would lie *outside human control*.

As scary as uncontrolled AI may appear, it seems that humanity is on its way toward AGI. As Harris (2016) points out, as long as one accepts two basic assumptions, the existence of AGI becomes only a matter of time. The first basic assumption is that humans will continue to develop and improve AI systems. Considering the benefits to be reaped by developing AI and the major investments flowing into this work, it seems highly implausible that the developmental process would be stopped voluntarily. The second basic assumption is that AGI is in principle attainable to us. In other words, there is nothing physically impossible about humans creating AGI. If we grant both of these assumptions, it follows that AGI is yet another milestone to be achieved at some point in the future of humanity.

According to surveys regarding human-level AI, most experts agree that AGI is likely to emerge by the end of the present century (see, e.g., Müller and Bostrom 2014; Sandberg and Bostrom 2011). Nonetheless, considerable room for scepticism remains regarding these time predictions. As Armstrong and Sotala (2012, 19) point out, the expert predictions tend to be "spread across a wide range and in strong disagreement with each other."

Ultimately, the "when" question remains an open one, and the currently available data seems too meager for any meaningful assessment of the many specific timelines that have been proposed.[1] Nevertheless, the potential

1 But see Chalmers (2010) for comprehensive philosophical treatment of singularity and some arguments in favor of a more conservative prediction—namely, that it is likely to occur "within centuries" from now.

impact of superintelligent AI on human beings seems significant enough to warrant researching the related methods of control well before AGI becomes attainable.

Different methods of controlling AGI—most notably, motivational control and control through restraints—have been proposed in the literature on the ethics of AI. They will be outlined shortly. But it is also worth noting that the problems related to superintelligent AI are relevant to law as well. It is widely acknowledged that the law needs to be sensitive to the shifting societal role of AI, which is currently transitioning from relatively primitive systems to quite sophisticated ones. This development has given rise to new proposals in the context of intellectual property and copyright law, data protection, liability for damage, and other areas, but most importantly with regard to new legal regulations and safety standards for AI (Satarino 2021). The questions pertaining to safety and regulation of advanced AI will be of utmost importance when humanity gets close to the tipping point of AI systems becoming more potent than human intelligence—and all the more so if AGI development turns into an arms race between different countries. For this reason, gaining familiarity with the issues raised by the increasing sophistication of AI and the related control methods, with their respective pros and cons, is undoubtedly important for future lawyers.

10.4 Methods of Control in the Context of Superintelligent AI

The notion of singularity entails the existence of artificial entities that surpass human beings in their intelligence, which makes the resulting AI a potential threat to humanity (Yudkowsky 2002; Bostrom 2014). Even if the singularity scenario is regarded as unlikely by some, its enormous potential impact on human beings is seen by many as sufficient to justify the research on the ethical safeguards and methods of control for superintelligent AI. Such research involves considerable challenges that researchers in different disciplines have now been trying to address for about two decades.

10.4.1 *AI Motivational Control through Ethical Programming*

The "control problem" in the context of superintelligence (Bostrom 2014) immediately calls for the implementation of certain safeguards that would ensure that the resulting AI is "friendly" toward human beings and does not violate their fundamental values. Perhaps the most explicit solution would be to program the superintelligent AI with good motivations. This, however, is a daunting task, given the problems related to programming ethics into the machine (EC AI High-Level Expert Group 2019; Gordon 2020; Shadowen 2017). In the context of singularity, the issue becomes even more complicated, since it exclusively concerns "machine superintelligence"—that is, AI systems that are considerably more capable than human beings in all relevant respects.

As Muehlhauser notes, two main difficulties may cause efforts to develop friendly superintelligence to fail: *superpower* and *literalness*. "Superpower" refers to the fact that "a superintelligent machine will have unprecedented powers to reshape reality, and therefore will achieve its goals with highly efficient methods that confound human expectations and desires" (Muehlhauser 2013, 9). Meanwhile, "literalness" means that the machine "recognizes only precise specifications of rules and values, acting in ways that violate what feels like 'common sense' to humans, and in ways that fail to respect the subtlety of human values" (Muehlhauser and Helm 2012, 106). These two properties of machine superintelligence make for a particularly worrisome combination, given that (i) due to the literalness aspect and the lack of consensus and clarity on human values, it seems altogether probable that subtle human values will not be programmed in an adequate and secure manner, and (ii) due to the superpower aspect, a loophole created by a failure in a machine's programming may allow it to behave in ways that cause severe harm. Indeed, as Yudkowsky (2008, 27) writes, "The AI does not hate you, nor does it love you, but you are made out of atoms which it can use for something else." Reversing the view can help us better understand this point through the example provided by Harris (2016): humans do not *hate* ants, but if a formicary were to be found in a construction site, it would be wiped away without any second thoughts. Similarly, any misalignment between the goals of AI and human values has the potential to produce a similar kind of disregarding behavior.

Some ideas as to how the challenges posed by machine superintelligence may be handled through ethical programming stem from the already-discussed initiative of "machine ethics."[2] Although building ethical machines would not endow humans with full control over the emergence of singularity, doing so may steer these machines in a direction that is, overall, beneficial for humanity and comes with as few risks as possible. This would be, then, an instance of motivational control. However, the idea of ethical programming in the context of singularity—be it providing the machine with a "complete" ethical theory or supplying it with tools to work out its own ethics "bottom-up" (or both)—is problematic, since any discrepancy between the expectations of the human programmers and the actual programming of the machine could prove fatal in

2 See chapter 8 for an outline.

the long run. It would not necessarily be fatal in the sense that it would create machines that are malevolent toward humanity, but rather in the sense that the human values would be misaligned with the goals of the superintelligent agent, as described above. The method of motivational control through ethical programming, then, is bound to confront the issues of superpower and literalness head-on. For this reason, one has to consider alternatives to motivational control, such as AI control through various restraints.

10.4.2 *AI Control through Restraints*

The epitome of human control over machines is the on-off power switch. The dreadfulness of losing control over the "power off" function is well illustrated in the cult movie *2001: A Space Odyssey*.[3] However, since the origin of computation, humans have been striving for more elaborate forms of control, resorting to the power-off switch only in extreme or emergency cases.

The ultimate desire of humans with regard to computation is to automate tasks, including those of control. Today, automatic control systems are ubiquitous. In engineering applications, they range from simple, switch-controlled thermostats used in every electric iron or coffee machine up to highly advanced autopilots for supersonic aircraft. Humans' capability to build such devices, which automatically control the broad range of machines and technical processes, represents a cornerstone in the development of modern technology. Control systems have influenced our way of life and have become an integral part of modern society.

While the concept of "power switch control" may be more applicable to centralized IT systems, increasingly modern IT systems are built as distributed systems, and the concepts of AGI and singularity seem to imply a distributed architecture too. The controllability of distributed systems, as discussed above, is more problematic for many reasons, one of which is the so-called opacity of the system to the observer, as the user does not possess the knowledge or the know-how to understand the system being used, or perhaps even to find the control unit or the power switch. In most cases, the user's interaction with the system is limited to receiving the output produced by the system, with no control over the input. Consider how much you know about the internet, for example. Where is the power switch for it? How can you control data flow on the internet? Manual[4] and automatic controls are being applied in distributed

3 https://www.imdb.com/title/tt0062622/.

4 Manual control is traditionally applied in systems where safety is involved, notably in supervisory roles such as by an operator in a power plant or a driver of a car or bicycle.

systems, but regular users of the services produced by those systems do not know fully (if at all) how they or somebody else can exercise control.

One approach to controlling both centralized and distributed systems that is especially relevant in the context of controlling AI systems through restraints is based on the well-known technique of *divide et impera*, or "divide and conquer."[5] This approach is used to reduce computational complexity when developing the systems, but it is also a way to prevent AI from emerging into AGI—i.e., keeping AI narrow in its function and preventing the establishment of a single, general-purpose AI. This and other similar approaches in the context of singularity-preventive measures are known as "AI-Box"—i.e., imposing a certain strict form of capability control on the superintelligent AI. For example, one could limit the resources available to the AI system or keep it disconnected from the internet so as to use it as some sort of question-answering machine oracle (Armstrong et al. 2012; Muehlhauser 2013, 11).

The AI-Box-ing approach raises several potential issues. First, it would be very tempting to let the AI out of the box, since the imposed limitations would reduce its efficiency considerably (Armstrong et al. 2012; Muehlhauser 2013). Second, it is conceivable that the AI would eventually be able to find its way out of the box by tricking or manipulating humans. After all, not only would humans be naturally predisposed toward letting it out (see the first point), but the very scenario pits them against what is by definition a superior intelligence. For example, the early AI-box experiments by Yudkowsky (2002) suggest that the AI system would likely not remain contained if humans were allowed to freely interact with it. Third, as Muehlhauser and Bostrom (2014, 44) point out, the development of AGI is likely to turn into a race between different nations, and so "If one AI development team has built a human-level or superintelligent AI and successfully confined it, then other AI development teams are probably not far behind them, and these other teams may not be as cautious." And the more AI-boxes there are, the more likely it is that one superintelligent AI will find its way out of the box. Finally, by merely constraining the capabilities of AI, one delays the risk without decisively preventing it (Muehlhauser and Bostrom 2014). Nevertheless, as Armstrong et al. (2012) note, such an "AI oracle" should still be considerably safer than an unconstrained AI.

5 In computer science, "divide and conquer" is an algorithm design paradigm based on multi-branched recursion. A divide-and-conquer algorithm works by recursively breaking down a problem into two or more sub-problems of the same or related type, until these become simple enough to be solved directly. The solutions to the sub-problems are then combined to yield a solution to the original problem.

10.5 Conclusions

This chapter has introduced the general concepts and methods of controlling IT systems and elaborated on the possibility of AI getting out of human control. The importance of this topic is implied by several key facts.

First, as modern IT systems become more and more complex, geographically and functionally distributed, and interdependent, the topic of IT system control will remain at the forefront of scholarly research and on the agenda of policymakers (EC AI High-Level Expert Group 2019).

Second, the very nature of the new generation of IT systems—those based on machine learning and commonly referred to as AI—represents a new paradigm not only in computing (Fomin 2021), but also in relation to the commonly accepted dogma that *only humans learn, artifacts do not.* Learning is at the heart of AI systems, and for that reason the methods that humans have previously deployed to control algorithmic systems do not work (as well or at all) for AI systems (Lyytinen et al. 2020). As AI systems have shown that they can learn faster than humans, the already commenced trend of introducing AI-based systems to support different functions of enterprises and to deliver different public services naturally raises concerns about whether humans can remain in control of the systems. This question is translated into the question of how to control *what* and *how* AI systems learn. As IT-based services become more intelligent, more powerful, more accessible, more useful, and more ubiquitous, we must ensure that they remain reliable and safe for humans to use.

Although challenges in controlling AI may abound, we would like to conclude on a positive note. Kurzweil (2005, 2009) suggests that we will likely remain in control of AI systems even if they develop to the level of superintelligence, because human intelligence will develop even faster. According to Kurzweil (2005, 2009), humans will be able to transcend their biological limitations by gradually enhancing themselves, creating brain-computer interfaces, or even uploading their own minds to computers. This line of thinking, of course, raises some interesting philosophical questions, such as whether the uploaded "mind" would really be conscious and whether the resulting entity would be "human" in any meaningful sense. In that case, the meaning of the term *singularity* would likely change, opening up new venues for scholarly research.

Study Questions

1. How are control and controllability defined in computational systems?

2. What different types of computational system architectures have been distinguished, and what implications does this have for control?
3. In what way are AI-based computational systems different from algorithmic computational systems?
4. What "out of control" scenarios have been hypothesized for AI systems? Why is it important to research them?
5. What properties of superintelligent AI systems make them a potential threat to humanity?
6. What are the challenges and possible solutions for keeping AI systems under control?

References

Armstrong, S., A. Sandberg, and N. Bostrom. 2012. "Thinking Inside the Box: Controlling and Using an Oracle AI." *Minds and Machines* 22(4): 299–324.

Armstrong, S., and K. Sotala. 2012. "How We're Predicting AI—or Failing To." In *Beyond AI: Artificial Dreams*, edited by J. Romportl et al., 52–75. University of West Bohemia. https://intelligence.org/files/PredictingAI.pdf.

Bostrom, N. 2014. *Superintelligence: Paths, Dangers, Strategies*. Oxford University Press.

Chalmers, D. J. 2010. "The Singularity: A Philosophical Analysis." *Journal of Consciousness Studies* 17(9–10): 7–65.

de Vaujany, et al. 2018. "Rules, Practices, and Information Technology: a Trifecta of Organizational Regulation." *Information Systems Research*: 1–19.

EC AI High-Level Expert Group. 2019. *Ethics Guidelines for Trustworthy AI*. https://ec.europa.eu/newsroom/dae/document.cfm?doc_id=58477.

Fomin, V. V. 2021. "The Shift from Traditional Computing Systems to Artificial Intelligence and the Implications for Bias." In *Smart Technologies and Fundamental Rights*, edited by J.-S. Gordon, 316–33. Brill.

Gordon, J.-S. 2020. "Building Moral Robots: Ethical Pitfalls and Challenges." *Science and Engineering Ethics* 26(1): 141–57.

Harris, S. 2016. *Can We Build AI without Losing Control over It?* TED. https://www.ted.com/talks/sam_harris_can_we_build_ai_without_losing_control_over_it.

Kalman, R. E. 1960. "Contributions to the Theory of Optimal Control." *Bol. Soc. Mat. Mexicana* 5(2): 102–19.

Kurzweil, R. 2005. *The Singularity Is Near: When Humans Transcend Biology*. Viking Press.

Kurzweil, R. 2009. "The Coming Merging of Mind and Machine." *Scientific American*. https://www.scientificamerican.com/article/merging-of-mind-and-machine/.

Lyytinen, K., J. V. Nickerson, and J. L. King. 2020. "Metahuman Systems = Humans + Machines That Learn." *Journal of Information Technology* 0268396220915917.

Muehlhauser, L. 2013. *Intelligence Explosion FAQ*. Machine Intelligence Research Institute. http://intelligence.org/files/IE-FAQ.pdf.

Muehlhauser, L., and N. Bostrom. 2014. "Why We Need Friendly AI." *Think* 13(36): 41–47.

Muehlhauser, L., and L. Helm. 2012. "Intelligence Explosion and Machine Ethics." In *Singularity Hypotheses: a Scientific and Philosophical Assessment*, edited by A. H. Eden, J. H. Moor, J. H. Soraker, and E. Steinhart, 101–27. Springer.

Müller, V. C., and N. Bostrom. 2014. "Future Progress in Artificial Intelligence: a Poll among Experts in Impacts and Risks of Artificial General Intelligence." *Journal of Experimental and Theoretical Artificial Intelligence*.

Sandberg, A., and N. Bostrom. 2011. *Machine Intelligence Survey* (Technical Report 2011–1). Future of Humanity Institute.

Satarino, A. 2021. "Europe Proposes Strict Rules for Artificial Intelligence." *New York Times*. https://www.nytimes.com/2021/04/16/business/artificial-intelligence-regulation.html.

Shadowen, A. N. 2017. *Ethics and Bias in Machine Learning: a Technical Study of What Makes Us "Good."* Academic Works, CUNY. https://academicworks.cuny.edu/jj_etds/44.

Yudkowsky, E. 2002. *The AI-Box Experiment*. http://yudkowsky.net/singularity/aibox.

Yudkowsky, E. 2008. "Artificial Intelligence as a Positive and Negative Factor in Global Risk." In *Global Catastrophic Risks*, edited by N. Bostrom, 308–45. Oxford University Press.

Further Reading

Callaghan, V., et al., eds. 2017. *The Technological Singularity: Managing the Journey*. Berlin: Springer.

Eden, A. H., et al., eds. 2012. *Singularity Hypotheses: a Scientific and Philosophical Assessment*. Berlin: Springer.

Kurzweil, R. 2022. *The Singularity Is Nearer*. Penguin.

Shanahan, M. 2015. *The Technological Singularity*. MIT Press.

PART 3

Major Key Issues: Rights, Status, and Responsibility

Introduction to Part 3

The ever-growing sophistication and autonomy of AI systems have raised some new, problematic questions regarding rights, status, and responsibility. These questions concern not only the attribution of human rights and responsibility to different human stakeholders in the utilization of AI, but also the possibility of ascribing rights and responsibility to AI systems themselves, an issue that is gaining momentum in ongoing research. Although various aspects of the vital concepts of rights, status, and responsibility have been considered in the context of law and practical philosophy for centuries, recent developments in AI have had a disruptive effect on many of the previous paradigms, making it crucial to reevaluate these concepts against the background of AI. The present part covers the most important threads of the ongoing legal and philosophical debates on rights, status, and responsibility in the world of AI.

Chapter 11 discusses electronic personhood—a concept that was brought into the spotlight by the European Parliament in attempt to introduce a suitable legal status for the most sophisticated machines that would address their rights and responsibilities. The chapter provides a breakdown of the concept of electronic personhood, considers it against the background of the main theories of legal status, and sketches some potential costs and benefits of implementing electronic personhood into the law.

Chapter 12 focuses on the moral and legal status of robots. Although current robots are generally seen as little more than sophisticated tools, the impressive trajectory of ongoing technological developments could change this situation in the coming decades. In preparation for this possibility, it is critical to assess the moral and legal status of AI systems themselves. The chapter explicates the notions of moral and legal status and their importance for the ascription of rights and then discusses four distinct approaches to the ascription of such statuses to robots. The most important objections to the approaches are presented thereafter.

Chapter 13 takes up the question of moral and legal rights for robots—an issue that overlaps with but is distinct from that of moral and legal status. The recognition of moral rights is of utmost importance with regard to securing the basic moral claims of humans and, indeed, of other entities that are thought to have moral status. In the context of law, the recognition of moral rights is one basis for legal protection, although legal rights may be extended even to entities without moral status if doing so proves to be useful (consider the legal rights of corporations or natural objects). This chapter elaborates on the concept

 | DOI:10.1163/9789004682900_014

and function of rights, and it then discusses three different approaches to the ascription of rights to robots and the main related objections.

Chapter 14 concerns the questions of moral and legal responsibility in the context of AI. It first highlights the notion of moral responsibility and the related philosophical problems regarding freedom and control. The discussion is linked to human moral responsibility in the context of AI and the idea of morally responsible artificial agents. After that, it turns to legal responsibility and related issues, such as how AI impacts the existing legal liability frameworks and the main characteristics of emerging technologies that raise liability issues (e.g., intelligence, autonomy, embodiment, opacity, complexity).

Finally, chapter 15 provides a comprehensive overview of autonomous transportation—a matter that is becoming increasingly relevant as upcoming technological advances will allow for greater safety and autonomy of driverless vehicles. Nevertheless, substantial issues remain. First, the chapter provides some background on the development of and expectations regarding autonomous cars. Then, it considers the ethical dilemmas that such cars may face as well as the main methods of approaching crash scenarios, such as empirical ethics and traditional ethical theories. Lastly, the chapter touches on issues of moral and legal responsibility, such as who should be held liable if a driverless car causes an accident.

CHAPTER 11

Electronic Personhood

Julija Kiršienė, Edita Gruodytė and Darius Amilevičius

> There may come a time when we ascribe personhood and rights to the most sophisticated machines, which will have resulted by muddling through the problems that come to light.
>
> CHINEN 2019, 21

11.1 Introduction

This chapter introduces the hotly debated concept of electronic personhood as one possible legal solution for artificial intelligence (AI). First, the definition of an electronic person is examined, and afterwards the reasons for the introduction of this novelty are analyzed by comparison to the history of the concept of legal personhood (i.e., corporations). Finally, the idea of robot rights as one more reason for introducing electronic personhood is discussed briefly.

The phrase "electronic person" (hereafter AIP for AI person)[1] was first used in 1967, in an article that introduced the robot Shaky (Alexandre 2017, 22), but this phrase became much better known when AIP was suggested by the European Parliament as one of six possible legal solutions to the new industrial revolution and the expansion of digital technology (European Parliament Committee on Legal Affairs 2015, 31). The European Parliament (2015, 59 (f)) referred to "creating a specific legal status for robots in the long run, so that at least the most sophisticated autonomous robots could be established as having the status of electronic persons responsible for making good any damage they may cause, and possibly applying electronic personality to cases where robots make autonomous decisions or otherwise interact with third parties independently."

1 The terms "electronic person," "electronic personality," and the abbreviation AIP are used interchangeably in the text.

 | DOI:10.1163/9789004682900_015

In research, the need to treat AI differently from previous technologies is stressed, including a departure from traditional liability theories (Kritikos 2019, 3), as the harm caused by intelligent technologies could not be covered by existing legal mechanisms. This is especially true since AI may acquire a certain degree of autonomy, i.e., it may learn to adopt its behavior in accordance with its interactions with the environment. For example, a self-driving car may decide to hit a pedestrian to avoid possible damage to the person in the car, when another alternative is to drive into the ditch and cause serious damage to the passenger in the car. The full autonomy of machines equipped with AI means that owners, creators, users, and others may not always be able to foresee or fully control AI's decisions. Therefore, new legal forms and instruments should be introduced to deal with such issues.

However, the EU document mentioned above provided no definition, specified criteria, or features which are required for the implementation of AIP. It is not evident whether the status of AIP refers to the full legal personhood of "sophisticated autonomous robots" as signifying the full legal status of persons subject of the law, or only their accountability in contracts and tort law, or both (Pagallo 2018, 4).

So what or who is electronic person? Linguistically, dictionaries describe the term "electronic" using several explanations: (1) relating to electrons, (2) relating to electronics, (3) produced by electronic means, or (4) controlled by computers.[2] The term "person" is predominantly associated with human beings, but one of the legal meanings in the dictionary also defines a person as a "human being (natural person) or a *group of human beings, a corporation, a partnership, an estate, or other legal entity* (*artificial person, or juristic person*) recognized by law as having rights and duties."[3] The importance of this last aspect is connected to the possibility that a person may gain certain legal status as the subject of legal relations. The word "person" is defined in connection to the quality or condition of being an individual person.[4] Thus, the term "electronic person" is linguistically associated with the provision of certain legal status to modern digital technologies, imposing certain rights and obligations.

---

2 https://www.dictionary.com/browse/electronic?s=t.

3 https://www.dictionary.com/browse/person?s=t.

4 https://www.lexico.com/en/definition/personhood.

11.2 Are the Concepts of Electronic Person and Legal Person (Corporation) Similar?

In the traditional approach, the legal status of person is associated only with human beings, whereas the modern approach indicates that the provision of legal status should not depend on whether an entity is a human being, but on moral considerations reflecting social realities in regulation (Alexandre 2017, 18) and the ability to hold legal duties, which requires specific features such as a certain level of autonomy, self-awareness, and intelligence (Gordon 2020, 4). In other words, the "underlying reason for granting legal personhood is to promote the regulation of behaviour" (Gordon 2020, 8). This suggests that whenever AI reaches a certain technological level, there should be no problem with granting it legal status if society has reasons for doing so, especially given the established example of corporations, which have established rights and duties including the ones provided initially to human beings. For example, certain aspects of the right to fair trial indicated in the Convention of Human Rights and Freedoms are widely recognized as applicable to corporations in the practice of the European Court of Human Rights. Therefore, the question arises as to what advantages could be gained and what legal issues, if any, would emerge should we introduce such a status for AI.

Let us consider in detail the similarities and differences between the concepts and legal status of legal persons and electronic persons. The concept of an electronic person has obvious similarity with that of a "legal person" (corporation, enterprise, partnership) as both are fictions created for the convenience of society.

One suggested position is that technologically advanced AI could be given the same legal status as corporations (Hallevy 2016; Singh 2017; Gruodytė and Čerka 2021), because the development of AI resembles the development of corporations. Both AI and corporations share the feature of not possessing moral personhood (Gordon 2020, 1) and are created by humans for their convenience. For example, the first industrial revolution, which is associated with the geographic discoveries of Spain and Portugal in East and West India and the origins of European financial capitalism, created the need for a legal mechanism to underlie capital concentration. This social and economic need was met by the introduction of the concept of a legal person (corporation), which has largely determined the changes in the doctrine of ownership, including the emergence of financial assets. As U.S. Supreme Court Chief Justice Marshall stated in *Dartmouth College v. Woodward* (1819), "A corporation is an artificial being, invisible, intangible, and existing only in contemplation of law." One more trigger for granting the status of legal person to corporations was their lack of accountability and controllability using traditional means of control, including changes in attitudes and risk allocation (Robson 2010, 113, 119). It follows that a legal person, as a consequence of such status, acquires certain rights and obligations (Bryson et al. 2017, 277) but also that this status could be used as a veil protecting owners, shareholders, and founders of the legal person from personal liability (Sellwood 2017, 862). It could also follow that in certain cases, it could be difficult to prove the fault of actual beneficiaries such as shareholders. This means that awarding such status to AI in certain cases could be a trigger promoting technological development because humans would feel able to take greater innovation risk, which is also an engine of economic development.

Thus, is the analogous status of a legal person suitable for AI? After all, certain differences between corporate liability and AI must also be noted. As already mentioned, when we talk about the liability of legal persons, the predominant theories treat a legal person as a certain fiction for the convenience of society (Kim 2000, 785) and with human beings as the main actors behind it. However, AI is not fiction *per se*; it is an existing technology driven by certain algorithms (Gruodytė and Čerka 2021, 265). The next important aspect that could arise with further technological development of AI is that it could become completely autonomous from human beings, which is not the case with traditional corporate persons. In such a case, AI "could be conceived of existing … independently and without involvement of humans and it could reason, which sets it apart from both legal persons in the first respect and from animals in the latter" (Lima 2018, 688).

Three main legal theories of corporate personhood are discussed in the scientific literature: "(1) an artificial and dependent person theory; (2) an aggregate person theory; (3) a real and independent person theory" (Solaiman 2017, 163).

The first theory relates to legal fiction, as it treats legal person as a created derivative for the convenience of society and fully depends on legal regulation—i.e., it starts functioning after all formalities required by law are implemented. It is also known as vicarious liability theory, i.e., activities or inaction together with rights and duties of certain natural persons are ascribed to a legal person. This theory is not suitable for AI as it requires establishment of a "guilty mind" in natural persons. Still, it could be used in a similar way to what we do now to assess "corporations' ability to best compensate the injured party" (Ellis and Dow 2014, 183).

The aggregate person theory, also known in the literature as the collective liability doctrine, is once again grounded on the assumption that a corporation consists of physical persons, but the main difference from the first theory is that it integrates acts and mental states of various actors in the company, and damage could be the result of actions by several persons even without any arrangement or willful intent (Tolvanen 2009, 337). Once again, this doctrine grounds its liability on natural persons but not on a "distinct personality" (Solaiman 2017, 1164), which means that it does not help to hold autonomous AI liable as such in case a "guilty human mind" is not found. But it could help to address situations when damage arises as an aggregation of the activities of several involved persons—e.g., the manufacturer, programmer, owner, user, and operator—and if liability could be foreseen from the point of their joint action (Gruodytė and Čerka 2021, 273).

The last theory is the most modern one, treating a corporation as a real and separate person, distinct from natural persons (owners, shareholders, managers, employees, etc.) and as an objective fact, notwithstanding existing legal regulation (Solaiman 2017, 165). Autonomous liability of corporate persons is also preferred by such international organization as the Organisation for Economic Co-operation and Development (OECD), grounding it on an effectiveness argument: "It is difficult, if not impossible, to comply with international commitments to maintain effective sanctions against legal persons, when corporate liability is dependent on the successful prosecution of the natural perpetrator" (OECD 2015, 26–29). The biggest problem with this theory is that still human beings are standing behind corporate persons, whereas future AI "may be able to act autonomously and may, at some point, even match human intelligence" (Gordon 2020, 13).

This discussion shows that the doctrines of corporate liability may be only partially used as a basis for grounding AI liability.

11.3 Reasons for the Introduction of Electronic Personhood

The idea of providing legal status to AI is grounded on several reasons, which will be briefly discussed below.

In terms of AI, there is still no clear evidence that AIP is the best solution while the underlying rationale is the legal system's recognition that such legal status is necessary (Bryson et al. 2017, 277). Once such a legal status is introduced, certain rights and obligations should be imposed on some technologically developed AI, but first, such "regulatory intervention" should be proportionate and "requires clear criteria to differentiate between the different AI applications" (European Commission 1 2020, 17).

From an ethical point of view, it is argued that there could be no equivalence between human beings and machines.[5] This position could be easily resisted, as we are talking about AI not as equivalent to human beings but as a convenient tool of liability in the interest of protecting society's needs. The 2019 European Commission report on liability for AI and other emerging digital technologies admits that "giving robots or AI a legal personality would not require including all rights natural persons, or companies, have" (European Commission 2019, 38), so there is no problem in this regard, even if the main criticism of AIP concentrates on ethical and human rights issues.

Also, some EU experts argue that it "would not be practically useful, since civil liability is property liability, requiring its bearer to have assets" (European Commission 2019, 38) and that the "harm caused by even fully autonomous technologies is generally reducible to risks attributable to natural persons or existing categories of legal persons, and where this is not the case, new laws directed at individuals are a better response than creating a new category of legal person" (European Commission 2019, 37). This view suggests that other, more usual instruments such as contractual, strict liability or various insurance schemes should be modified for new technologies, at least at this stage of their development. The concept of vicarious liability is employed to argue that operators of machines, computers, robots or similar technologies should also be strictly liable for their operations, based on an analogy to the basis of vicarious liability (European Commission 2019, 25).

However, from a legal point of view, if the goal of European regulation is trustworthy, human-centric AI, liability issues related to emerging digital technologies should first be considered from the potential victim's position. Due to the complexity of products, different connected devices, software, and services, long supply chains, later updates and upgrades, huge amounts of self-learning data for AI, and contributory negligence of injured persons, eventually it will be very difficult for victims to identify the liable person. Furthermore, because the of so-called black box effect, understanding autonomous AI decisions and the data behind them will require the cooperation of the potentially liable party and technical expertise that could be prohibitively costly for victims to obtain. Reports also emphasize that "allocation of the cost when damage occurs may be unfair or inefficient under the current rules" (European Commission 2020, 17). Moreover, the existence of non-harmonized national regimes could lead

5 For example, "treating autonomously operating machines the same way as natural persons would be a dangerous aberration" (Daten Ethik Kommission 2019, 219); see also the Robotics Open Letter of 2018, http://www.robotics-openletter.eu/.

to further fragmentation of legal liability frameworks, increasing the costs of introducing innovative AI technologies and the insurance costs for producers.

AIP as a liability instrument could be coupled with mandatory insurance and strict liability schemes. This would not only ensure compensation irrespective of fault in the long technological chain of products and services, but would also reduce the litigation costs for victims and place a cap on liability. The synergy of three instruments (AIP, strict liability, and mandatory insurance) would greatly contribute to legal certainty and, accordingly, trust for customers and investors. Of course, an economic analysis of the interplay of these three instruments would be helpful, to identify the best approach to cost reduction and the cheapest taker of insurance, which most likely will be the producer (Kiršienė et al. 2021).

Therefore, proponents of electronic personhood mostly ground their position on a pragmatic approach, introducing electronic personality for legal convenience,[6] as some form of a legal entity with limited rights and obligations.

Moreover, it is also argued that another possible risk of introducing AI personhood is the same as what we have experienced in the case of corporations, as the introduction of "legal persons" in fact led to placing greater economic power in the hands of accumulated capital, along with an enlarged image and importance of corporations in society (Robson 2010, 113). It is evident that discussion on these matters is not closed, as in recent EU documents AI is seen as a mere instrument in human hands rather than a person.

11.4 Robot Rights as an Argument for Electronic Personhood

> Asking about robot rights is not a distraction, fairy tale stuff, or a waste of time. It is especially needed and necessary in the face of socially interactive artifacts that effectively challenge the standard operating procedure for dealing with technology.
>
> GUNKEL 2020, 67

An additional important issue directly related to AIPs is whether they should be given certain rights in the future so as to protect them from improper

6 "It is possible to create a legal status, which would only be a 'tangible symbol' for the cooperation of all the people creating and using that specific robot" (Beck 2016, 141). "Giving robots or AI a legal personality would not require including all the rights natural persons, or even companies, have. Theoretically, a legal personality could consist solely of obligations" (European Commission 2019, 38).

treatment by human beings, such as exploitation for prostitution. "When the strong AI develops as a sentient being then it would be our moral obligation to provide rights to them" (Singh 2017, 200). This aspect is grounded on moral issues: when AI is able "to make moral decisions at some point in future … by virtue of their autonomy they deserve to become members of our moral community" (Gordon 2021, 29). Main arguments for this position are (1) protection against exploitation, as noted above; (2) protection based on rationality (which follows from a neo-Kantian approach to dignity); (3) presumption of equal treatment (based on the argument that if and when AIPs are capable of rational reasoning and acting according to moral law, they must be treated equally to human beings); and (4) brutalization of the human character (if we do not treat AIPs properly, we may become less sensitive toward other human beings as well; Gordon 2021, 29–34).

The biggest confusion when we are discussing certain rights for AI concerns the assumption that the provision of certain rights to AIPs entails granting them *human* rights, whereas today we already have the concepts of corporate and animal rights (Gunkel 2020, 55–56), which are not the same as human ones. In this case, the question of whether AI could acquire legal status is weighed through discussion of what a human being is, what cognitive and moral features distinguish a human being from other objects (e.g., animals and plants), and when AI could attain such abilities or even surpass human beings in their development (Elkhova 2017). Whereas the main question to ask is whether and why granting rights to AI would be necessary for the further development of society and would not result in the loss of such virtues as human dignity.

11.5 Conclusion

Today's AI systems are not intelligent thinking machines in any meaningful sense. However, if and when AIPs attain the necessary cognitive capacities, they should, from a moral point of view, be granted certain rights just as animals or legal entities are entitled to some rights.

Electronic personality could be one of the solutions for AI, together with other liability schemes such as mandatory insurance and strict liability. This would not only ensure compensation irrespective of fault in the long technological chain of products and services, but would also reduce the litigation costs for victims and put a cap on liability. The synergy of three instruments (electronic personhood, strict liability, and mandatory insurance) would greatly contribute to legal certainty and, accordingly, trust for customers and investors.

Study Questions

1. How would you define an electronic person?
2. What are the main reasons for introducing the concept of electronic personhood?
3. Would electronic persons be granted the same rights and obligations as human beings?
4. What are the arguments in favor of electronic personhood?
5. What arguments can be made against the introduction of electronic personhood?
6. Can an electronic person be legally equated with a corporation?

References

Alexandre, F. M. 2017. *The Legal Status of Artificially Intelligent Robots: Personhood, Taxation and Control*. Dissertation, Tilburg University.

Beck, S. 2016. "Intelligent Agents and Criminal Law: Negligence, Diffusion of Liability and Electronic Personhood." *Robotics and Autonomous Systems* 86: 138–43.

Bryson, J. J., et al. 2017. "Of, for, and by the People: the Legal Lacuna of Synthetic Persons." *Artificial Intelligence Law* 25(3): 273–91.

Chinen, M. 2019. *Law and Autonomous Machines: the Co-evolution of Legal Responsibility and Technology*. Elgar Law, Technology and Society series.

Daten Ethik Kommission. 2019. *Gutachten der Datenethikkommission*. https://datenethikkommission.de/wp-content/uploads/191128_DEK_Gutachten_bf_b.pdf.

Ellis, N. S., and S. B. Dow. 2014. "Attaching Criminal Liability to Credit Rating Agencies: Use of the Corporate Ethos Theory of Criminal Liability." *University of Pennsylvania Journal of Business Law* 17(1): 167–83.

Elkhova, O. I., and A. F. Kudryasshev. 2017. "The Creative Ability of Artificial Intelligence." *Creativity Studies* 10(2): 135–44.

European Commission. 2019. *Liability for Artificial Intelligence and Other Emerging Digital Technologies*. Report from the Expert Group on Liability and New Technologies—New Technologies Formation, European Union. https://ec.europa.eu/transparency/regexpert/index.cfm?do=groupDetail.groupMeetingDoc&docid=36608.

European Commission. 2020. *Report on the Safety and Liability Implications of Artificial Intelligence, the Internet of Things and Robotics*. https://ec.europa.eu/info/sites/info/files/report-safety-liability-artificial-intelligence-feb2020_en_1.pdf.

European Commission 1. 2020. *White Paper on Artificial Intelligence–A European Approach to Excellence and Trust*. Brussels, February 2, COM (2020) 65 final.

European Parliament. 2015. *Civil Rules on Robotics*. European Parliament resolution of February 16, 2017 with recommendations to the Commission on Civil Law Rules on Robotics (2015/2103(INL)). http://www.europarl.europa.eu/doceo/document/TA-8-2017-0051_EN.pdf.

European Parliament Committee on Legal Affairs. 2015. *Draft Report with Recommendations to the Commission on Civil Law Rules on Robotics* (2015/2103(INL)). http://www.europarl.europa.eu/doceo/document/JURI-PR-582443_EN.pdf?redirect.

Gordon, J.-S. 2020. "Artificial Moral and Legal Personhood." *AI & Society*. https://doi.org/10.1007/s00146-020-01063-2.

Gordon, J.-S. 2021. "What Do We Owe to Intelligent Robots?" In *Smart Technologies and Fundamental Rights*, edited by J.-S. Gordon, 17–47. Brill.

Gruodytė, E., and P. Čerka. 2021. "Artificial Intelligence as a Subject of Criminal Law: a Corporate Liability Model Perspective." In *Smart Technologies and Fundamental Rights*, edited by J.-S. Gordon, 260–81. Brill.

Gunkel, D. J. 2020. "Robot Rights: Thinking the Unthinkable." In *Smart Technologies and Fundamental Rights*, edited by J.-S. Gordon, 48–72. Brill.

Hallevy, G. 2016. "The Criminal Liability of Artificial Intelligence Entities: from Science Fiction to Legal Social Control." *Akron Intellectual Property Journal* 4(2): 170–201.

Kim, S. 2000. "Characteristics of Soulless Persons: the Applicability of the Character Evidence Rule to Corporations." *University of Illinois Law Review* 2000(3): 763–812.

Kiršienė, J., et al. 2021. "From Computerised Thing to Digital Being: Mission (Im)possible?" *AI & Society* 36(2): 547–60.

Kritikos, M. 2019. *Artificial Intelligence Ante Portas: Legal and Ethical Reflections.* Briefing, European Parliamentary Research Service. https://www.europarl.europa.eu/RegData/etudes/BRIE/2019/634427/EPRS_BRI(2019)634427_EN.pdf.

Lima, D. 2018. "Could AI Agents Be Held Criminally Liable? Artificial Intelligence and the Challenges for Criminal Law." *South Carolina Law Review* 69: 677–96.

OECD. 2015. *Liability of Legal Persons for Corruption in Eastern Europe and Central Asia.* https://www.oecd.org/corruption/acn-liability-of-legal-persons-2015.pdf.

Pagallo, U. 2018. "Vital, Sophia, and Co.: the Quest for the Legal Personhood of Robots." *Information* 9: 1–11.

Robotics Open Letter. 2018. http://www.robotics-openletter.eu/.

Robson, R. 2010. "Crime and Punishment: Rehabilitating Retribution as a Justification for Organizational Criminal Liability." *American Business Law Journal* 47(1): 109–44.

Selwood, M. 2017. "The Road to Autonomy." *San Diego Law Review* 54: 829–73.

Singh, S. 2017. "Attribution of Legal Personhood to Artificially Intelligent Beings." *Bharati Law Review*: 194–201.

Solaiman, S. M. 2017. "Legal Personality of Robots, Corporations, Idols and Chimpanzees: a Quest for Legitimacy." *Artificial Intelligence Law* 25(2): 155–79.

Tolvanen, M. 2009. "Trust, Business Ethics and Crime Prevention: Corporate Criminal Liability in Finland." *Jurisprudencija/Jurisprudence* 1(115): 335–58.

CHAPTER 12

Moral and Legal Status of Robots

John-Stewart Gordon and Kęstutis Mosakas

12.1 On the Relevance of Recognizing the Moral and Legal Status of Robots

Mark Coeckelbergh (2020, 47) opens the chapter on "Just Machines?" in his introduction *AI Ethics* (2020) with the following words:

> Today many people think that animals matter, morally speaking. But this was not always the case. Apparently, we were wrong about animals in the past. If today people think that AIs are just machines, are they making a similar mistake? Would superintelligent AIs, for example, deserve moral status? Would they have to be given rights? Or is it a dangerous idea to even consider the question of whether machines can have moral status?

The concept of moral and legal status is important because a being whose status has been recognized is entitled to moral and legal rights. The standard case is a typical adult human being who has the highest moral and legal status and therefore is entitled to all moral and legal rights available. The typical standard adult human is a moral agent. A moral agent is commonly considered an autonomous and intelligent being who is conscious and able to reason and feel pain. All moral agents are moral patients, but not vice versa. A moral patient is a being with a low or lower moral standing (or status) who lacks the ability to reason and hence is unable to make moral decisions (or to be held morally accountable for them). Good examples are cats, dogs, and small toddlers.

Thus, the important question is whether autonomous and intelligent robots (once they exist) are either moral agents or moral patients. The answer to this question depends not on the subjective verdict of human beings, but on objective criteria such as the ability (a) to have consciousness, which is the foundation for the ability to reason, or (b) to have sentience (Kamm 2007). In contrast, some experts such as Coeckelbergh (2014) and David Gunkel (2012) argue that moral status emerges only through social relations and that even current social robots may be considered to have moral status too (see chapter 2 above). Others believe that robots will never be able to match or surpass human capabilities and therefore do not deserve any moral status.

 | DOI:10.1163/9789004682900_016

The ascription of legal status to entities is of utmost significance regarding the recognition of their legal rights. There exist at least two main camps on this matter, and their proponents suggest completely different strategies. The first group claims that legal status concerns only *the regulation of behavior* and that, to have legal status, entities do not necessarily have to be rational, autonomous, or even living beings. For example, one might grant legal status to corporations, holy rivers, temples, or warships. The only thing that counts is that some behavior related to the entity must be regulated (Smith 1928). The other group argues that the ascription of legal status should require that the entity be autonomous, rational, and intelligent, such that it can be held responsible for its actions (Solaiman 2017). This group invokes the concept of moral status and contends that entities are entitled to moral and legal status only if they meet some objective criteria such as rationality, autonomy, or sentience. The view that one should use a species-independent criterion to evaluate all entities has been recently championed by Gordon (2021).

For both camps, the ascription of moral and legal rights depends on the status of the particular entity. The following section provides a brief overview of four main approaches, in the context of the philosophy of technology, regarding how to determine the moral and legal status of entities.

12.2 Main Approaches to Ascribing Moral and Legal Status to Robots

12.2.1 *The Agency-Based Approach*

The first main approach that one could use to ascribe moral status (and, by extension, rights) to robots could be called the agency-based approach. According to this view, an entity has moral status if and only if it possesses certain properties associated with (full) moral agency, with the most important property being rational autonomy—i.e., the ability to make reasoned decisions. If we grant this criterion, it follows that once intelligent robots become moral agents, they should be recognized as proper objects of moral concern and granted corresponding rights and responsibilities (see Gordon 2020). This approach is most strongly associated with the legacy of Immanuel Kant and his logocentric understanding of moral status, according to which the ability to make rational, autonomous decisions is of utmost moral priority. James Rachels succinctly summarizes the key aspects of Kant's approach:

> Humans have an intrinsic worth, i.e. dignity, because they are rational agents, that is, free agents capable of making their own decisions, setting their own goals, and guiding their conduct by reason. Because the

> moral law is the law of reason, rational beings are the embodiment of the moral law itself. … It makes no sense, therefore, to regard rational beings merely as one kind of valuable thing among others. They are the beings for whom mere "things" have value, and they are the beings whose conscientious actions have moral worth. So Kant concludes that their value must be absolute, and not comparable to the value of anything else.
>
> RACHELS 2003, 131–32

Following this approach, one could argue that robots should be recognized as having comparable moral status to human beings once their level of cognitive sophistication comes close to that of humans. This is where the capacities of moral reasoning and decision making become of utmost importance, because that is—according to this approach—what connects a being to the moral law itself. In other words, just some level of sophistication—for example, on a par with animals or small children—is not enough. The key to this approach, then, is to identify at what point machines can be considered to have become rational enough to merit this higher-order moral consideration. Such an assessment is by no means a straightforward task, since the exact conditions for rational autonomy remain contested. Nevertheless, this approach clearly requires that the machine must have rather sophisticated cognitive capacities—or, at the very least, it must function as though it really had them (see Sullins 2011). Once it meets the criteria, it would have moral status, despite the fact that it is not human or even a biological organism.

12.2.2 *Indirect Duties*

The agency-based approach is a demanding view. It declares that robots should have moral status when they become rational in a similar way to human adults But according to many AI researchers, that kind of sophistication is at least several decades away. This raises the important question of how to treat the current and soon-to-be-developed robots that are not as intelligent. A special problem in this context concerns so-called social robots, which are, by definition, "robots that are designed to interact with humans on a social level" (Darling 2016, 215). Social robots include such artificial beings as robotic pets, toys, and companions, as well as healthcare and service robots. Typically, these interactive machines have human-like or animal-like appearances. The question, then, is whether it is morally permissible to treat these social machines as mere tools or if, at some point, they should be provided with some kind of legal protection on other grounds than rational autonomy.

Kate Darling (2016) argues that we may have certain indirect duties towards social robots. In her account, even though social robots may not be proper objects of moral concern, there may be other reasons for extending legal protection to them. She draws on Kant, who maintained that even though animals have no moral status given their lack of rationality, it is still wrong to engage in animal cruelty, because it harms the human character. Kant wrote that "he who is cruel to animals becomes hard also in his dealings with men" (1997, 240). According to Darling, an analogical justification is possible in cases of cruelty toward social robots. Certain kinds of behavior toward machines, she claims, may "traumatize" and "desensitize" humans—especially if the machine were to react as though it were being hurt (Darling 2016, 224). Darling backs her contention by pointing to the fact that humans tend to anthropomorphize social robots; they unwittingly attribute human qualities to these machines, and this tendency affects how they treat the robots. According to Darling, this tendency may also provide a basis for regulating human behavior toward social robots—although, as Darling herself admits, it remains necessary to develop a more rigorous conception of what kind of beings should be regarded as social robots and what may constitute mistreatment in this context.

12.2.3 *Virtue Ethics*

An argument that social robots should have some kind of standing in our society could also be based on virtue ethics, an ethical theory that focuses primarily on matters of moral character (see Hursthouse and Pettigrove 2016). Indeed, virtues (excellent character traits) and vices (the flip side of virtues) alike predispose us to act in certain ways. For example, if one has the virtue of courage, one will find it easier to act courageously in different situations. According to virtue ethics, then, we should foster good character traits and attempt to get rid of the bad ones.

If we take this approach to the question at hand, we may find ourselves embracing something akin to Darling's position—namely, that mistreating social robots is wrong because it damages the human character. However, Darling seems more concerned that this damage to one's character will ultimately lead to certain negative consequences, such as harm to other members of society. In contrast, the virtue ethicist could maintain that damaging human character is a great wrong in itself, independently of any further consequences. That view is embraced by Cappuccio et al., who maintain that we ought to treat "social robots in a morally considerate manner because this is what a humane and compassionate agent would habitually do in their social interactions and because the opposite behavior would not be compatible with a virtuous lifestyle and moral flourishing" (2020, 13). In their view, cruelty or abusive behavior toward social robots is wrong even if these machines are not sentient or rational, because cruel or abusive behavior disposes the agent in question to develop vices rather than virtues.

12.2.4 *The Social-Relational Approach*

Finally, the social-relational approach to machines' moral status and rights has been championed by Gunkel (2012) and Coeckelbergh (2010), who are unsatisfied with approaches (to both status and rights) based on certain kinds of mental properties that entities possess, such as sentience or rationality. They argue that it is unclear how we could know that an entity in general—or a robot in particular—has a mind and can feel pain or think. For this reason, as well as other problems with the property-based views, Gunkel and Coeckelbergh urge us to "think otherwise" about the very question of moral status (see Gunkel 2018).

Their suggested solution is a radically relational view according to which moral consideration emerges entirely from various social relations. To say that an entity is morally considerable, for them, is to say that in some way it belongs to the large web of social relations in which we find ourselves, including all the entities that we conceive of as our friends, family, colleagues, pets, companions, and so forth. Understood in this way, moral consideration is radically external to any given entity and ultimately depends on socially contingent factors. As Coeckelbergh (2010, 214) writes, from this perspective "moral consideration is no longer seen as being 'intrinsic' to the entity: instead it is seen as something that is 'extrinsic': it is attributed to entities within social relations and within a social context." In this account, ethics concerns not difficult metaphysical questions, such as who or what has a mind that can reason or feel pain, but rather how we perceive different entities in our social encounters with them. And if we accept this view, then some degree of moral consideration should plausibly be extended to social robots as well, because of how people tend to bond with them on a social level.

12.3 Objections to Moral and Legal Status Ascriptions

12.3.1 *Against the Agency-Based Approach*

According to the agency-based approach, a being has moral status if it is a full moral agent—i.e., an entity capable of moral reasoning and decision making. As already noted, this is a demanding view. Current robots are nowhere near the sophistication level required for moral agency, as critics of this view, such as Gunkel (2018), have been quick to observe. Gunkel is worried that if we raise the bar for moral status so high, the question of whether robots will ever be able to reach it becomes speculative and uncertain, thereby shutting down critical inquiry into other possibilities. In other words, people may simply dismiss the idea that less sophisticated machines, such as current social robots, could qualify for moral consideration.

Another criticism of this view could be lodged from the perspective of animal ethics. Could robots not have moral status without being rational? In animal ethics, a number of philosophers have espoused sentientism, which holds that sentient beings have moral status because they can suffer or enjoy things. This raises a question: should an artificial being somehow become capable of feeling pain and suffering without being rational, would it still have no moral status? If not, then it would seem that animals and human infants should not have moral status either. One could make a case, then, that moral agency is sufficient for moral status but not necessary. Indeed, some authors, such as John Danaher (2019), have espoused the so-called "animal-robot analogy." According to Danaher, even though today's robots are not rational, some of them may soon become behaviorally comparable to animals, which on Danaher's view is sufficient for recognizing them as worthy of a similar degree of moral concern.

Criticisms could also be lodged from the standpoint of other, more inclusive approaches to moral consideration. For example, Gunkel (2012, 30, 152–53) argues that any attempt to establish some kind of moral criterion, be it sentience or rationality, necessarily results in *a priori* exclusion of entities that for one reason or another do not meet the relevant criteria. According to him, ethics should be "decentralized," i.e., there should not be any pre-established moral criteria. This is a common move among the so-called radical ecologists or ecocentrists, who emphasize that humans, animals, and natural objects are all interdependent elements of the same ecosystem and should thus hold moral value. Along similar lines, David F. Channell (1991) has proposed a "bionic ethic" that focuses on finding morally relevant "ecological" relationships between biological and mechanical entities.

12.3.2 *Against the Indirect Duties Approach*

The main argument of the indirect duties approach relies on the claim that, to prevent our character from becoming morally compromised and leading us to treat fellow human beings immorally, we should not abuse or exhibit cruelty toward social robots. The punch line of this reasoning does not regard social robots as valuable in their own right but focuses solely on the implications for moral character of humans. In other words, if one harms social robots, then one will eventually harm one's own moral character. Since we certainly don't want that to happen, we should behave decently toward social robots, even if they do not match human capabilities and lack technological sophistication.

Furthermore, one should protect lifelike beings, according to Darling (2016, 230), "when society cares deeply enough" about them.

But what if society *does not care deeply enough* about objects such as intelligent machines that might even merit moral status according to some more objective criteria, such as the ability to reason or sentience? Would people still be allowed to abuse them if society does not care deeply enough about them, even though doing so may harm one's own moral character to some extent?

Abusing a social robot occasionally may not have any strong detrimental impact on one's moral character, as long as the behavior does not become a steady habit. According to this approach, morality is eventually based on the way society cares about particular entities (or types of entities); the machines do not have any intrinsic value that may make it unacceptable for us to abuse them. They are left completely and utterly at society's mercy. They do not have any inherent right to protection from human abuse or cruel behavior.

Even though Darling argues for legal protection of social robots, her approach has certain moral limitations. For example, if entities are capable of reasoning or have sentience, then it is not up to any other person or society to withhold moral and legal rights from them. Admittedly, such beings are more advanced than Darling's social robots, but one could extend the general logic of her reasoning to more advanced machines as well. The only thing that would count in this way of framing the approach is whether society cares deeply enough about them. This moral position seems untenable.

12.3.3 *Against Virtue Ethics*

Virtue ethics is an ethical theory of ancient origin that enjoyed a resurgence in the late 1950s due to certain problems related to the two main approaches prevalent at the time—utilitarianism and Kantianism. Although virtue ethics may be worth incorporating alongside the other views so as to get a full picture of ethics, whether it is tenable as a stand-alone theory remains questionable. Although it is definitely true that we should cultivate moral virtues and that a society that consists of virtuous individuals is more likely to flourish, virtue ethics still has the status of a kind of "neighbor ethics." In other words, it serves us well when it is applied to various situations in social contexts. For example, one could specify what kind of virtues may suit a teacher, given the specific nature of a teaching job, as opposed to, say, the virtues of an army general or a president. However, when we encounter particular ethical dilemmas outside social contexts, it is not always clear what a virtuous person should do.

The appeal to virtue ethics by Cappuccio et al. (2020) arguably suffers from similar shortcomings. At best, their approach could provide us with a contextual solution to the problem of the moral status of social robots. One can certainly maintain, as these authors do, that acts of cruelty and abuse are incompatible with virtuous character. But this holds true for most, if not all, such acts—not only those involving social robots. In other words, since virtue ethics focuses primarily on the moral character of the agent, it may not by itself tell us much about the inherent morally relevant differences between various entities. For this reason, Coeckelbergh (2010, 213) has argued that virtue ethics (at least in its traditional version) could productively address the question of moral status only if it were to consider the properties of different entities as well, because otherwise one could not know toward which entities we should exercise virtues. Neither would one know if exercising the same virtues and vices toward different entities always carries the same moral weight. For example, smashing a social robot with a hammer and doing the same to a human person may both be cruel acts contrary to virtue, but that fact alone would not explain why the latter action is a much more severe and grievous misdeed. Thus, it seems that considerations about the moral character of the agent alone are insufficient.

12.3.4 *Against the Social-Relational Approach*

Gunkel (2012) and Coeckelbergh (2010) both believe that morality emerges through social relations. According to their general view, even Paro, the robot seal that is sometimes used in homes for elderly, has some moral standing and hence deserves moral protection. Paro is a relatively simple robot. But what about highly sophisticated, intelligent, autonomous machines that may even match human capabilities at some future point? Of course, they would also deserve moral protection—not because they are so advanced, however, but rather because people have established social relations with them, which is the very basis for treating them morally. In other words, if people do not establish benign social relations with these entities, then morality does not emerge.

The problem with the social-relational approach is that people can decide not to establish any social relations with machines. For example, using machines as mere tools establishes no social ties and hence no moral obligations. Only robot rights can protect machines from abuse and cruel behavior. Similar arguments were previously used in the context of disability studies but were later abandoned due to exactly the same objection, namely that social relations certainly help to welcome new members into the moral community but are not the particular reason *why* they should be recognized. Rather, people with disabilities should be recognized because they meet the morally relevant criteria. Likewise, machines should be morally and legally protected once they meet the morally relevant criteria, which are valid independently of any social recognition.

12.4 Conclusion

The question of the moral and legal status of robots is an important one, because it concerns the boundaries as to when machines become something more than mere instruments that humans can use any way they please. Knowing where these boundaries lie may also allow us to make certain choices regarding the place of artificial beings in our future society. For example, we may choose to cross the boundary and acknowledge artificial entities as full-fledged members of our society—potentially with their own rights. Or we may choose not to do so, because, as some scholars have suggested, endowing artificial entities with moral status would be too disruptive socially and is therefore best avoided. In any case, there is no agreement yet on where the boundaries lie, but future research on the moral and legal status of robots should continue to shed light on this important question.

Study Questions

1. What are the main differences between moral agents and moral patients?
2. What are the two main strategies for ascribing legal rights to different entities?
3. What is the agency-based approach to moral status? Why is it considered a demanding view?
4. What are the main limitations of indirect approaches to moral status?
5. What is virtue ethics? How do virtue ethicists approach the question of moral status?
6. What is the social-relational approach? What are the related difficulties?

References

Cappuccio, M. L., A, Peeters, and W. McDonald. 2020. "Sympathy for Dolores: Moral Consideration for Robots Based on Virtue and Recognition." *Philosophy & Technology* 33: 9–31.

Channell, D. F. 1991. *The Vital Machine: a Study of Technology and Organic Life*. Oxford University Press.

Coeckelbergh, M. 2014. "The Moral Standing of Machines: towards a Relational and Non-Cartesian Moral Hermeneutics." *Philosophy & Technology* 27(1): 61–77.

Coeckelbergh, M. 2010. "Robot Rights? Towards a Social-Relational Justification of Moral Consideration." *Ethics and Information Technology* 12(3): 209–21.

Danaher, J. 2019. "Are Robots like Animals? In Defence of the Animal-Robot Analogy." In *Philosophical Disquisitions*. https://philosophicaldisquisitions.blogspot.com/2019/09/are-robots-like-animals-in-defence-of.html.

Darling, K. 2016. "Extending legal Protection to Social Robots: the Effects of Anthropomorphism, Empathy, and Violent Behavior towards Robotic Objects." In *Robot Law*, edited by R. Calo, A. M. Froomkin, and I. Kerr, 213–31. Edward Elgar.

Gordon, J.-S. 2020. "What Do We Owe to Intelligent Robots?" *AI & Society* 35: 209–23.

Gordon, J.-S. 2021. "Artificial Moral and Legal Personhood." *AI & Society* 36: 457–71.

Gunkel, D. 2012. *The Machine Question: Critical Perspectives on AI, Robots, and Ethics*. MIT Press.

Gunkel, D. 2018. *Robot Rights*. MIT Press.

Hursthouse, H., and G. Pettigrove. 2016. "Virtue Ethics." *Stanford Encyclopedia of Philosophy*. https://plato.stanford.edu/entries/ethics-virtue/.

Kamm, F. 2007. *Intricate Ethics: Rights, Responsibilities, and Permissible Harm*. Oxford University Press.

Kant, I. 1997. *Lectures on Ethics*, edited by J. B. Schneewind. Cambridge University Press.

Rachels, J. 2003. *The Elements of Moral Philosophy*. McGraw-Hill Higher Education.

Smith, B. 1928. "Legal Personality." *Yale Law Journal* 37(3): 283–99.

Solaiman, S. M. 2017. "Legal Personality of Robots, Corporations, Idols and Chimpanzees: a Quest for Legitimacy." *Artificial Intelligence and Law* 25(2): 155–79.

Sullins, J. P. 2011. "When Is a Robot a Moral Agent?" In *Machine Ethics*, edited by M. Anderson and S. L. Anderson, 151–61. Cambridge University Press.

Further Reading

Jaworska, A., and J. Tannenbaum. 2018. "The Grounds of Moral Status." In *Stanford Encyclopedia of Philosophy*. https://plato.stanford.edu/entries/grounds-moral-status/.

Mosakas, K. 2020. "On the Moral Status of Social Robots: Considering the Consciousness Criterion." *AI & Society*. https://link.springer.com/article/10.1007/s00146-020-01002-1.

Warren, M. A. 1997. *Moral Status: Obligations to Persons and Other Living Things*. Oxford University Press.

Whitby, B. 2008. "Sometimes It's Hard to Be a Robot: a Call for Action on the Ethics of Abusing Artificial Agents." *Interacting with Computers* 20(3): 326–33.

CHAPTER 13

Rights for Robots

Kęstutis Mosakas

13.1 Moral and Legal Rights

The idea that robots could possess moral and/or legal rights has recently become an important topic of discussions and controversy. As has been highlighted in the previous chapter, the question of rights is closely related to that of status, in the sense that moral status is necessary for moral rights. In addition, one could make a case that if an entity has certain moral rights, then these rights should be secured through legal means as well, which may include extending legal rights to the entity in question. Ultimately, the answers to the questions regarding our duties toward robots will depend on which account of rights and status we accept and whether the threshold posited by any particular account is attainable for robots (i.e., whether robots could become sophisticated enough to be recognized as moral agents or moral patients).

The notion of rights has been of utmost importance in the history of ethics and law alike. In the most general terms, having a right to something entails having a valid claim to that thing, whatever it may be—property, protection, non-interference, etc. Moreover, the notion of rights is closely tied to that of duties, in that one's right entails a corresponding duty for others. For example, if we determine that a certain entity has a (moral) right to life, then all other moral agents have a corresponding moral prohibition against killing that entity. Although there are considerable disputes regarding the foundation, epistemology, function, and normative content of rights, it is generally agreed that rights impose rather stringent constraints as to how the bearer of those rights should be treated. Indeed, as Kamm notes, rights are exclusionary in the sense that they exclude other factors from our decision making that would otherwise be relevant: "For example, if someone has a right to something that someone else wants, the other person's desire is not merely outweighed, it is irrelevant in deciding who should have it" (Kamm 2007, 237). One could say, then, that rights have a special kind of priority in our decision making (both moral and legal) that has the potential to render other related considerations irrelevant. For this reason, rights often "come close to putting an end to an argument about what to do" (ibid).

 | DOI:10.1163/9789004682900_017

Moreover, in this particular context there are two main important categories of rights to consider: moral and legal. An entity can be said to have moral rights if it has moral status and corresponding moral claims that ought to be protected. According to the most typical views, these claims serve the function of securing the interests of the rights-bearer, with interests understood as aspects of one's well-being (the interest theory); allowing the rights-bearer to make certain choices (the will theory); or both (the hybrid theory). These rights are typically thought of as inherent to the rights-bearer and grounded in their moral status. In contrast, legal rights are by their very nature institutional, granted by certain legal authorities (e.g., governments), which may be done for moral or non-moral reasons. One could say, then, that moral and legal rights pertain to two distinct categories; whereas the former is typically conceived of as universal and valid independently of legal recognition, the latter is by its very nature socially contingent. Or, as MacKinnon and Fiala (2015, 451) observe, "Legal rights are claims that the law recognizes and enforces. However, we also hold that there are moral rights—in other words, things we can rightly claim even if the law does not enforce the claim."

13.2 Approaches to Ascribing Rights to Robots

13.2.1 *Legal Rights for Robots Based on Social Benefits*

One reason why it may be desirable to protect robots is that doing so may benefit society. This kind of rationale may be applied to social robots, since it is doubtful that they have moral status, and therefore they cannot plausibly have rights on that basis. This line of reasoning is expressed by Darling (2016), whose indirect duties approach has been examined in the previous chapter of this book. In a nutshell, Darling argues that if we allow people to treat social robots as they please, in some cases that may result in abusive behavior toward the machines, which may in turn—given the effects of anthropomorphism—make humans more likely to mistreat creatures with moral status as well, including other humans. Darling's central concern is that society as a whole may be worse off if certain kinds of machines, such as social robots, are not granted legal protection from mistreatment.

Darling's idea of extending legal protection to beings that are neither sentient nor human is not without precedent. Indeed, as Channell (1991, 153) notes, "inanimate objects such as trusts, corporations, banks, and ships have long been seen by the courts as possessing rights." To take one example, providing corporations with legal personhood allows them to be owned collectively and not tied to the life span of a single person. Moreover, legal personhood in general can be granted for a variety of reasons. For example, the Whanganui river in New Zealand and a nearby forest have been granted legal personhood due to their importance to Māori tribes. Closer to our present topic, the social robot Sophia has been granted Saudi Arabian honorary citizenship, in what has generally been regarded as a public stunt. Ultimately, Darling's argument invites us to consider whether giving legal protection or rights to robots could bring some practical benefits (or, rather, avoid harm), in much the same way that granting legal personhood to other non-living or inanimate beings has been beneficial.

13.2.2 *Rights on the Basis of Social Participation*

Another possible basis for rights is social participation. Authors such as Gunkel and Coeckelbergh have vigorously advocated the view that moral consideration is purely relational—i.e., it emerges through social relations. In the process, they have also raised objections to the standard properties-based view, according to which the basis for moral status and rights rests on certain properties that entities possess. Probably the most developed arguments in favor of the relational approach and against the standard view can be found in Gunkel's *The Machine Question* (2012) and *Robot Rights* (2018), in which he explores these questions in depth precisely in the context of machine status and rights.

In his 2012 work, Gunkel first approaches the question from the rather typical understanding of rights ascription based on moral agency and moral patiency. It is commonly believed that an entity has rights if it is a full moral agent, capable of moral reasoning and decision making. Arguably, the only beings on our planet that have sufficient moral competence to be regarded as full moral agents are cognitively unimpaired human adults. However, the proponents of the agency-based view do not need to hold that being human is necessary for moral agency. Instead, they can maintain that should other beings match the moral competence of humans, they too would deserve to be recognized as full moral agents with corresponding rights. There are also patiency-oriented approaches, according to which the basis for certain moral rights is properties that make one a moral patient—i.e., a being that may not meet the threshold of moral agency but is nevertheless a vulnerable being whose life can go well or badly. Non-human animals are typically regarded as moral patients because they are sentient and capable of suffering.

According to Gunkel, neither of the two ways of approaching what he calls "the machine question" is ultimately satisfactory. According to him, they suffer from determination, epistemological, and moral problems alike. In this vein, Coeckelbergh and Gunkel have initiated "the relational turn"—an attempt to establish that all moral considerations (including the ascription of status and rights) are relational. Indeed, they reject the idea that rights are intrinsic to any given individual or that they depend upon certain properties of the individual. They contend instead that moral rights—if they can be said to exist in any meaningful sense—are constructed through social relations. In other words, one has rights not because one is an agent or a patient, but rather because one has been recognized as a rights-bearer by the community and is treated as such. And if we grant this assumption, then any further moral investigation is directed not toward the properties of an entity (e.g., whether a given entity can reason or feel pain) but toward what Coeckelbergh and Gunkel (2014, 724–29) call "conditions of possibility for moral status ascription." The key observation in that regard is that if moral status ascription is relational, it is shaped by various social factors, which thereby constitute the mentioned conditions of possibility. These factors would include not only our perceptions of different entities, which are shaped and conditioned by their visual appearance and social capabilities, but also subtler things such as speech acts (e.g., whether we refer to an entity with "who" or "what" pronouns and whether we give it a name), physical space, and the material-technological context (ibid). On this account, these are the factors we must investigate, since they constitute the very basis of moral consideration.

13.2.3 *Rights on the Basis of Ontological Properties*

Finally, the standard view grounds rights in certain ontological properties. This means that the answer to the question of whether an entity has moral rights depends on whether it possesses the necessary properties. But what properties could those be? If we follow the classical agency-patiency dichotomy, the properties would have to do with the kind of moral status that the entity in question has (that of an agent or a patient). Although there is no strict consensus on exactly what these properties are, we may, following Jaworska and Tannenbaum (2018), identify them in two broad categories: rudimentary cognitive capacities and sophisticated cognitive capacities.

Rudimentary cognitive capacities are usually considered both necessary and sufficient for moral patiency. This category includes first and foremost the sentience criterion but may also include the capacity for emotions or mental life in general. According to the interest theories of rights (e.g., Kramer 1998), being sentient entails having interests, which is sufficient for certain basic moral rights (e.g., the right not to be tortured). According to this view, one could affirm the moral rights of animals that are sentient but lack reason.

However, if an entity is to be regarded as a moral agent (and not merely a patient), that requires certain quite sophisticated cognitive capacities most commonly associated with reason and self-consciousness. Although reason is morally important because it is necessary for rationally autonomous decisions, self-consciousness enables the entity to be conscious of its own existence. In other words, there are "merely conscious" beings that can experience sensations or pain, and there are also beings capable of *conceiving themselves* as subjects living through experiences over time—for example, humans and higher primates. According to the will theorists of rights (e.g., Steiner 1998), only beings with these higher-order capacities have rights, because based on this view, rights are something that individuals can either demand or waive the enforcement of through free and rationally deliberated decisions. This means that only human adults have rights in the fullest sense, although some will theorists hold that other entities can be represented by their guardians.

In any case, it seems that the interest and will theories yield different results about who is to be regarded as a rights-bearer. Whereas the former view is patient-oriented and relatively inclusive, the latter is agent-oriented and rather exclusive. Some scholars hold a hybrid view (e.g., Wenar 2008) according to which both theories are valid and account for different kinds of rights.

In any case, both major properties-based views answer the question of whether we should recognize robots as rights-bearers by saying it depends on whether they will come to possess the necessary properties. At present, it does not seem likely that such cognitively sophisticated machines will emerge any time soon. However, even when machines become broadly intelligent, there may not be a straightforward answer to the question of rights on this view, because the cognitive capacities in question seem to require some basic capacity for conscious experience, whereas machine consciousness is a highly contested topic. Moreover, even if machines were to become humanlike in all relevant respects except their origin and the fact that they are not biological, there may still be some resistance to the idea that they should possess rights or even that such machines should be built in the first place (see Bryson 2018).

For example, Lantz Fleming Miller (2015) argues that even if there were "maximally humanlike automata," humans would not be under any obligation to extend full human rights to such beings. His justification is that machines do not meet what he calls the criterion of "existential normative neutrality." According to Miller, the existence of the human species as a whole is "normatively neutral" in the sense that humans came about through evolution by natural selection, with no underlying purpose. However, this cannot be said about machines—no matter how humanlike they may be—because they are always built with some purpose in mind. In Miller's view, then, existential normative neutrality itself makes robots different from humans, with the implication that even the most humanlike machines may justifiably be denied full human rights. As he writes, "Humans are the ones who discern, affirm, and thereby realize human rights. It is fair and just that they grant such rights, and they occupy a fair and just position to determine which ontological kinds of entities deserve recognition of rights" (Miller 2015, 387). Nevertheless, Miller's own approach is subject to important criticisms, as I will show shortly.

13.3 Objections to Different Approaches

13.3.1 *Against the Social Benefits Approach*

Although granting machines legal protection on the basis of social benefits is not unreasonable, it comes with its own caveats. First, when we employ this approach, we must correctly predict whether the ascription of rights (or legal protection more generally) would really result in social benefits. Darling's argument rests on several assumptions about how humans perceive social robots that may seem reasonable *prima facie* but may ultimately not turn out to be true. For example, Gunkel points out that there have been similar worries about video games (see Gunkel 2018, subsection 5.2.4). People thought that engaging in violent acts in video games would have adverse effects on one's character, but the relevant studies of this claim have been inconclusive. Perhaps abusing social robots would not produce such negative effects either, or perhaps, it may do so if one were to engage in these acts constantly.

Then, there is the issue of the moral rights of highly sophisticated machines. Supposing that machines were to become as intelligent as humans or even more so, would it still be morally adequate to provide them with protection solely on the grounds that doing so would benefit humans? In that case, it would seem more reasonable to hold that the machines may deserve protection in their own right, as opposed to being granted rights on an instrumental basis. In other words, while this approach may be adequate when applied to the social robots that may exist in the near future, it may not remain sufficient in the long run when (or if) robots become humanlike.

13.3.2 *Against the Social-Relational Approach*

Although Coeckelbergh (2010) and Gunkel (2012) present their social-relational approach as circumventing certain problems with the standard properties-based accounts of moral status and rights, their view that rights are contingent upon social relations presents several substantial difficulties. For example, the statement that there really are no morally relevant properties is questionable. Although one can maintain, on the basis of the relational approach, that social robots deserve rights, this approach does not acknowledge any morally relevant distinctions between entities in themselves; only relations are the determining factor. This stance entails that the moral and legal recognition of the rights of any given entity is only a product of social contingencies—be it a social robot, a highly sophisticated machine, an animal, or a human being. As a result, prior to establishing social relations, all entities seem to be moral equals on this account. Indeed, this view can create serious problems resulting from social exclusion, since no entity, no matter how cognitively advanced, could have moral status and rights until it becomes involved in social relations. Yet it is conceivable that human society might choose to distance itself from a particular entity rather than establishing relations with it. In such a case, would the entity have no rights?

Moreover, the relational view does not acknowledge moral rights in any robust sense—i.e., as a substantive moral doctrine. Coeckelbergh and Gunkel themselves admit that in their view, rights are socially constructed, which runs the risk of moral relativism (see Fagan 2003), because in that case rights are just a matter of social recognition. This understanding runs contrary to the idea that certain entities—e.g., developed human beings—have justified moral claims at all places and times, independently of whether their claims are recognized by society. At most, then, in Coeckelbergh's and Gunkel's framework one could make use of legal rights to protect beings that already are social participants, but the constructivist understanding of morality espoused by these authors leaves no room for moral rights as a substantive doctrine.

13.3.3 *Against the Ontological Properties View*

According to the view based on ontological properties, an entity has moral rights if and only if it possesses certain morally significant properties. Although this is a common view, it faces several difficulties as well. First, one has to determine which properties matter morally and to what extent, which remains an unresolved and highly debated issue. The difficulty of this task is well illustrated by the longstanding disagreement between the interest and will theories of rights. The two theories embody different understandings of what the main normative function of rights is and have different moral thresholds for the rights-bearer (in terms of properties). However, it remains unclear which theory is the right one to adopt; in Wenar's (2005, 238) words, "in the twentieth century the scholarly contest between advocates of the two theories ended in stalemate."

Second, since having interests or a rational will presupposes having mental states, there are problems related to detecting morally relevant properties in different entities. Although one may be reasonably certain that other humans are conscious by making a structural and functional analogy to oneself, this analogy is not always possible with regard to other entities. What about entities that are considerably different from us, such as arthropods? More importantly, what about robots? The answers to these tough philosophical questions ultimately depend on one's more general views on the philosophy of mind and metaphysics. Indeed, as Schwitzgebel and Garza (2015, 114–15) point out, exploring these questions may have crucial implications for how to think about the moral status and rights of future robots.

Finally, it is not clear whether only cognitive capacities matter, as opposed to other kinds of properties. As an example, one could consider Miller's (2015) criterion of existential normative neutrality, discussed above. However, these other criteria are not necessarily problem-free either. With regard to Miller's criterion, is it really fair to say that the way one came into being is a property in its own right? In Miller's view, there could be two structurally and functionally identical entities and yet we would still have to treat them as having different properties if one was created with a purpose in mind and the other came into being by accident. This raises moral questions too. Should an entity's origin really be regarded as morally relevant? Or should we perhaps espouse something like the principles of ontogeny and substrate non-discrimination advanced by Bostrom and Yudkowsky (2014, 322–23), according to which the way one came into being and the substrate out of which one is made are in themselves morally neutral? What about Miller's view that humans are the ones granting the human rights? A more typical view would be that since human rights are, at the most fundamental level, universal moral rights (Fagan 2003), it is not up to humans to decide who should have them and who should not. Surely, humans could choose whether they want to *secure* the moral rights of a given entity, since they have the power to do so, but that is not the same as saying that any particular entity's rights are a matter of human decision in the first place. To cite MacKinnon and Fiala (2015, 451) again, whereas legal rights are claims that law recognizes, there could still be "things we can rightly claim even if the law does not enforce the claim." Thus, the properties-based approaches also have unresolved issues of their own, and besides, there is considerable variation between them.

13.4 Conclusion

Although the idea that robots may eventually qualify for recognition as rights-bearers has been taken seriously by many researchers, a number of related issues still need to be further explored. As this essay has shown, there is no single, accepted way to approach the question of machine rights, and all the proposed methods come with their own strengths and weaknesses. Perhaps one method will be recognized as the least deficient and will be adopted by humans in their dealings with future robots, or perhaps a pluralistic approach will be taken (e.g., Gordon 2021). In any case, it seems very important in this context not only to ask questions regarding the necessary and sufficient criteria for rights and status, but also to inquire about what kind of entity a machine is (or will become) and what roles it will occupy in the social space that it will share with human beings.

Study Questions

1. What is the notion of rights in the broadest sense?
2. What are the differences between moral and legal rights?
3. What does the ascription of rights based on social benefits mean? What are some of the related complications in the context of machine rights?
4. What is the social-relational approach? What are the related difficulties?
5. What is common to the approaches based on ontological properties?
6. Which properties are commonly considered necessary for moral agency and moral patiency?
7. What are the two main function theories of rights?
8. What are the main difficulties with approaches based on ontological properties?

References

Bostrom, N., and E. Yudkowsky. 2014. “The Ethics of Artificial Intelligence.” In *Cambridge Handbook of Artificial Intelligence,* edited by K. Frankish and W. Ramsey, 316–34. Cambridge University Press.

Bryson, J. 2018. “Patiency Is Not a Virtue: the Design of Intelligent Systems and Systems of Ethics.” *Ethics and Information Technology* 20: 15–26.

Channell, D. F. 1991. *The Vital Machine: a Study of Technology and Organic Life*. Oxford University Press.

Coeckelbergh, M. 2010. “Robot Rights? Towards a Social-Relational Justification of Moral Consideration.” *Ethics and Information Technology* 12(3): 209–21.

Coeckelbergh, M., and D. Gunkel. 2014. “Facing Animals: a Relational, Other-Oriented Approach to Moral Standing.” *Journal of Agricultural and Environmental Ethics* 27(5): 715–33.

Darling, K. 2016. "Extending Legal Protection to Social Robots: the Effects of Anthropomorphism, Empathy, and Violent Behavior Towards Robotic Objects." In *Robot Law,* edited by R. Calo, A. M. Froomking, and I. Kerr, 213–31. Edward Elgar.

Fagan, A. 2003. "Human Rights." *Internet Encyclopedia of Philosophy*. https://www.iep.utm.edu/hum-rts/.

Gordon, J.-S. 2021. "Artificial Moral and Legal Personhood." *AI & Society* 36: 457–71.

Gunkel, D. 2012. *The Machine Question. Critical Perspectives on AI, Robots, and Ethics*. MIT Press.

Gunkel, D. 2018. *Robot Rights*. MIT Press.

Jaworska, A., and J. Tannenbaum. 2018. "The Grounds of Moral Status." *Stanford Encyclopedia of Philosophy*. https://plato.stanford.edu/archives/spr2018/entries/grounds-moral-status.

Kamm, F. 2007. *Intricate Ethics: Rights, Responsibilities, and Permissible Harm*. Oxford University Press.

Kramer, M. H. 1998. "Rights without Trimmings." In *A Debate Over Rights: Philosophical Enquiries*, edited by M. H. Kramer, N. E. Simmonds, and H. Steiner, 7–112. Clarendon Press.

MacKinnon, B., and A. Fiala. 2015. *Ethics: Theory and Contemporary Issues*, 8th ed. Cengage Learning.

Miller, L. F. 2015. "Granting Automata Human Rights: Challenge to a Basis of Full-Rights Privilege." *Human Rights Review* 16(4): 369–91.

Schwitzgebel, E., and M. Garza. 2015. "A Defense of the Rights of Artificial Intelligences." *Midwest Studies in Philosophy* 39(1): 89–119.

Steiner, H. 1998. "Working Rights." In *A Debate Over Rights: Philosophical Enquiries,* edited by M. H. Kramer, N. E. Simmonds, and H. Steiner, 113–32. Clarendon Press.

Wenar, L. 2005. "The Nature of Rights." *Philosophy and Public Affairs* 33: 223–53.

Wenar, L. 2008. "The Analysis of Rights." In *The Legacy of H. L. A. Hart: Legal, Political, and Moral Philosophy,* edited by M. Kramer, C. Grant, B. Colburn, and A. Hatzistavrou, 251–73. Oxford University Press.

Further Reading

Basl, J., and J. Bowen. 2020. "AI as a Moral Right-Holder." In *The Oxford Handbook of Ethics of AI*, edited by M. D. Dubber, F. Pasquale, and S. Das, 289–307. Oxford University Press.

Calverley, D. J. 2011. "Legal Rights for Machines." In *Machine Ethics*, edited by M. Anderson and S. L. Anderson, 213–27. Cambridge University Press.

Estrada, D. 2018. "Value Alignment, Fair Play, and the Rights of Service Robots." *AIES '18: Proceedings of the 2018 AAAI/ACM Conference on AI, Ethics, and Society*, 102–7.

Gellers, J. C. 2020. *Rights for Robots: Artificial Intelligence*. Routledge.

Gordon, J.-S., and A. Pasvenskiene. 2021. "Human Rights for Robots? A Literature Review." *AI & Society*. https://link.springer.com/article/10.1007/s43681-021-00050-7.

Schröder, W. M. 2021. "Robots and Rights: Reviewing Recent Positions in Legal Philosophy and Ethics." In *Robotics, AI, and Humanity*, edited by J. von Braun et al., 191–203. Springer.

CHAPTER 14

AI and Moral and Legal Responsibility

Julija Kiršienė, Edita Gruodytė and Kęstutis Mosakas

14.1 Moral Responsibility

The ever-expanding domains of application of AI raise important questions related to responsibility. Can AI systems ever be held responsible for their actions? If so, how does that affect the attribution of responsibility to human beings who employ AI? The first relevant aspect to address here is that of moral responsibility. Although the attribution of moral responsibility is a common practice among human beings, as a philosophical problem it is complex and largely unresolved. Philosophers disagree not only on the necessary conditions for moral responsibility, but also on whether these conditions could ever actually be met. The underpinning philosophical difficulties regarding moral responsibility, then, are bound to be even more problematic when we attempt to consider moral responsibility in the context of AI.

To pursue this question further, we must first outline what moral responsibility entails. In general, it is believed that one can be held morally responsible for certain actions or omissions if and only if one can be viewed as morally praiseworthy or blameworthy for performing or not performing them (Talbert 2019). This kind of conceptualization is based on two important assumptions: (a) to be morally responsible, one needs to have the capacity to act, which is broadly referred to as agency; (b) one must also meet the criteria for moral praise or blame (which are generally associated with moral agency). This means that mere agency is insufficient for moral responsibility. For example, a wasp may be an agent in the sense that it acts in the world, but it would be nonsensical to blame a wasp for stinging somebody. The wasp may be causally responsible for doing so, but not morally responsible. On the other hand, if a human adult deliberately performed an action with negative consequences, we would be much more strongly inclined to assign moral blame to that person. We may be justified in doing so because of the cognitive and volitional capacities associated with the human adult, such as the ability to deliberate rationally in decision making and to make choices. Indeed, if the action was not performed as a result of rational deliberation, it would seem that whoever performed it should not be praised or blamed for it. As Tognazzini and Coates (2018, subsection 2.1.1) note, "It is widely accepted that potentially blameworthy agents must be

 | DOI:10.1163/9789004682900_018

capable of reflecting upon, reasoning about, and executing a decision about how to behave. If someone lacks these capacities, they are *exempted* from blame." For this reason, not only wasps but also infants and animals are not generally considered morally responsible for their actions.

Although the ability to make rational decisions and act on them is believed to be a necessary condition for moral responsibility, it is not clear that it is also a sufficient condition. This is where the notions of freedom and control come into play. It is generally taken for granted that for somebody to qualify as morally blameworthy or praiseworthy for a certain action, some degree of control is required. For example, we would not blame a person for being pushed into somebody else, since they had no control over the collision. Instead, we would blame the person who did the pushing. But now, suppose that even this other person could not have done otherwise—perhaps their action was determined by some kind of physical necessity. Is it still possible for them to be blameworthy in that case? This line of argument brings us to the problem of determinism in the context of free will and moral responsibility. According to determinists, every event, including mental events that take place in one's mind (such as beliefs, desires, and intentions), has antecedent causes. For this reason, any human decision is ultimately determined by factors external to that human's agency. The problem is well-captured by Van Inwagen, who writes:

> If determinism is true, then our acts are the consequences of the laws of nature and events in the remote past. But it is not up to us what went on before we were born, and neither is it up to us what the laws of nature are. Therefore, the consequences of these things (including our present acts) are not up to us.
>
> VAN INWAGEN 1983, 16

In other words, if human decisions are but a part of one big causal chain of events, it becomes hard to hold them morally responsible for their actions. To borrow a metaphor from Richard Dawkins (1995, 133), we are nothing but machines dancing to the tune of our DNA, and all our actions are determined by prior causes that we are not ultimately responsible for.

With respect to the questions of determinism and freedom of the will, philosophers are divided into two broad camps—incompatibilists and compatibilists. The former group maintains that determinism is not compatible with free will, whereas the latter claims that it is. One group of incompatibilists accepts these two claims: (a) there is free will and (b) determinism is false.

These incompatibilists are known as *libertarians*. Since libertarians reject the idea that human actions are determined by causes external to their volitional states, this puts them in a good position to affirm human moral responsibility. However, this stance also places a burden on the libertarian to explain what the nature of human actions is if they are neither determined nor random. The second group of incompatibilists is known as *hard determinists*. Much like libertarians, hard determinists maintain that determinism is incompatible with free will, but unlike libertarians, they affirm determinism and reject free will. According to this view, responsibility is at most a purely pragmatic concept, because human actions are determined and not free—which seems to strip them of any kind of moral praise or blame element.

However, not all determinists believe that determinism takes away free will. Compatibilists hold that even though determinism is true, it does not preclude free will. Here, we must note that compatibilists accept a different understanding of free will than incompatibilists do. Whereas the latter group maintain that an agent acted out of their free will as long as they could have done otherwise in the exact same situation (which is contradicted by the assumption of determinism), compatibilists argue that an agent acted freely if they are the *ultimate source* of their action (which is compatible with determinism). What matters to the compatibilist, then, is not whether the agent was determined to act in the way they did, but rather whether the action originated *within* the agent and was performed without any external influences on the agent's decision. As McKenna and Coates (2019, section 2.1) put it, for the classical compatibilist, free will essentially refers to the ability to do what one wants. Based on this conceptualization, free will is compatible with determinism and may allow one to salvage moral responsibility even if determinism is true—although it remains debatable whether the compatibilist understanding of free will, which is more properly construed as free action, is really sufficient to permit ascribing moral praise or blame to agents whose actions are fully determined.

Lastly, some philosophers espouse *impossibilism* about free will and maintain that regardless of whether determinism is true, free will is simply impossible.

This brief discussion of moral responsibility confirms that there is no agreement among philosophers regarding either the necessary criteria for moral responsibility or whether human actions can ever meet these criteria. In the context of AI, then, our answers to the question of moral responsibility will inevitably be built on rather uncertain foundations, whether we are considering the issue of human agency while utilizing AI or the agency of AI itself.

14.2 Morally Responsible Artificial Agents?

The idea of artificially intelligent robots that are morally responsible for their actions is a problematic one. The main difficulty, as we have seen, is that the question of whether even human beings can genuinely be held morally responsible remains unresolved, given the philosophical problems with the concept of free will. However, for our current purposes we may wish to suppose that humans can in fact be held morally responsible. Perhaps compatibilism is true, or perhaps the idea of human moral responsibility is too useful in practice to be completely dispensed with, in which case we may want to accept a compatibilist-like view for practical purposes. For example, Carrier (2005, section 4.5) observes that compatibilism has been something of a working assumption in law courts. From this point of view, moral responsibility does not have to do with determinism, but rather with whether one's morally charged action was performed without any external constraints on one's will, such as undue influence from other people (a factor that the courts take into account).

If we accept compatibilism as an undergirding assumption in our framework of moral responsibility (whether it is in fact true or not), this opens the door to the possibility of morally responsible AI. However, the next unresolved question is whether the bar for moral responsibility is too high for artificial beings. For example, Himma (2009) argues that moral agency and moral responsibility alike presuppose the capacity for consciousness; if there is no conscious volition behind one's actions, then the ascription of moral praise or blame to that being seems nonsensical. If this claim is right, it problematizes the issue even further, because it is unknown whether machines can become conscious at all. In contrast to Himma's position, Sullins (2011) has argued that robots should be seen as moral agents with corresponding rights and responsibilities once they fulfill the following criteria: (a) autonomy (the machine is not under direct control); (b) intentionality in the weak sense (the machine behaves *as though* it has intentions to do good or harm); and (c) responsibility (the machine is in a position to act in a way that is morally significant). According to Sullins, the weak intentionality criterion is justified by the fact that strong intentionality (i.e., actual conscious intentions) cannot be directly observed even in human beings. Thus, if human beings are held morally responsible despite such uncertainty, the bar should not be raised any higher for machines either.

One problem with Sullins's view is that we may be able to affirm strong intentionality for human beings with a higher degree of certainty than for machines, in which case the analogy would collapse. Furthermore, the analogy with humans is helpful only if we grant the above-mentioned compatibilist assumptions that allow human moral responsibility in the first place. Lastly, a libertarian could argue against Sullins's analogy on the grounds that humans have libertarian free will whereas machines do not.

14.3 Human Moral Responsibility and AI

Following the threads of the compatibilist argument outlined earlier, one could make a case that humans may be held morally responsible for the actions that they committed while not being under compulsion.[1] If so, then how does that relate to the human use of AI? Assuming that the AI in question is nowhere near meeting the criteria for moral agency, it would seem that any responsibility should rest entirely with human beings. For example, there seems to be no difference, with regard to moral responsibility, whether somebody shoots another person directly or programs a robot to do it instead. In both cases, the human being seems entirely culpable, not the gun or the robot. However, not all cases regarding the human use of AI are so simple. Consider the following examples.

First, a phenomenon not unique to AI but particularly urgent in the context of AI is known as "the problem of many hands." When some type of harm occurs, it is not always easy to identify the individual or group who should be held responsible for it. Sometimes, the harm is the result of a complex web of actions involving different agents in a way that could not possibly have been foreseen. For example, with respect to shipping accidents, Wagenaar and Groenewegen (1987, 596) write, "Accidents appear to be the result of highly complex coincidences which could rarely be foreseen by the people involved. The unpredictability is due to the large number of causes and the spread of the information over the participants." This problem of many actors is relevant in the context of AI as well, such as in the case of decision making by autonomous vehicles. If such a vehicle were to cause an accident, we would have to consider the distribution of responsibility in light of distributed agency, for, as Taddeo and Floridi (2018, 751) point out, "the effects of decisions or actions based on AI are often the result of countless interactions among many actors, including designers, developers, users, software, and hardware." In the context of self-driving vehicles, even more actors may contribute to the accident, such

1 This explanation is, of course, somewhat simplified since it also presumes that the agent in question has some kind of moral competence. For example, it is unclear whether psychopaths or brainwashed persons can be held morally responsible for their acts, even if they did not act under compulsion (see Talbert 2019).

as the driver who is supervising the car's decisions, the mechanics who maintain the car, and the public authorities responsible for the condition of the roads (Müller 2020, subsection 2.9.1).

Second, a common concern regarding autonomous systems is that they take responsibility away from human beings, thereby creating "responsibility gaps" (Sparrow 2007). This worry has been strongly voiced in discussions of autonomous military weapons (sometimes called "killer robots") that can take people's lives while not under direct human control. One crucial problem with these weapons concerns assigning liability in cases of unlawful harm (e.g., civilian casualties), since the system, not human beings, would actually be doing the killing. Additionally, as Docherty (2015) writes, "even if a case succeeded in assigning liability, the nature of the accountability that resulted might not realize the aims of deterring future harm and providing retributive justice to victims."

Third, suppose that an AI system were to cause harm through a decision made due to machine bias. Even if the humans supervising the antecedent learning process carefully selected the training data, it is still possible that they could not have reasonably foreseen certain coincidental patterns in the data that would result in machine bias.

The upshot here is that one needs to consider the attribution of responsibility (legal responsibility in particular) even in cases when nobody is *morally* responsible for the negative outcome. As these three examples illustrate, an occurrence of harm does not always imply that some related actor or group of actors behaved immorally and is thereby morally culpable. Indeed, as Gunkel (2020) has argued, AI systems are not mere tools at the disposal of human beings; instead, we should conceive of them as some kind of agents (although arguably not yet full moral agents) in their own right. This is where it becomes important to consider different legal solutions, since assigning moral praise or blame with regard to the decisions made by autonomous AI systems is not always possible.

14.4 Legal Responsibility and AI

The EU is seeking to become a world leader in emerging technologies such as AI, robotics, the Internet of Things, and blockchains. Emerging technologies are characterized by five attributes: radical novelty, relatively fast growth, coherence, prominent impact, and uncertainty and ambiguity (Rotolo et al. 2015). For now it is impossible to define AI precisely, since such a definition would need to change over time, in accordance with technological developments. For this reason, the present approach to AI is to treat it as a technological system with the capacity to process information in a way that resembles intelligent behavior, and which includes aspects of reasoning, learning, perception, prediction, planning, and control. These technologies are exceptional because they can act autonomously with little or no human involvement or supervision, improving their own performance by learning from experience.

The main goal of safety and liability mechanisms is to protect consumers of these products as well as to create trust in these technologies. Safety frameworks for products ensure that they will operate reliably and consistently. Liability frameworks should ensure efficient remedying of any damage that occurs, protecting both the industry's competitiveness and the interests of users. Existing EU member states' safety frameworks are shown in Figure 14.1. Existing liability frameworks are built on Machinery Directive (2006/42/EC), Product Liability Directive (85/374/EEC), and general rules of liability regimes, which are national and non-harmonized. However, as most rules were written prior to the emergence of the technologies described in this essay, they do not always contain provisions explicitly addressing the new challenges and risks.

Following the principle of precaution, provided by the Principles of European Tort Law (PETL), article 2:102 (2), the more serious the risk of threat created by the product and the more likely the damage, the greater the level of precaution that must be taken. Also, since its adoption in 1985, the Product Liability Directive has been considered one of the cornerstones of European private law, designed to achieve maximum harmonization of consumer protection in the field. The Directive also indicated that product liability must be seen in the context of new technologies and risk apportionment. Notably, EU member states are not allowed to provide a higher level of protection to consumers than that set by the Directive.

The concept of strict liability (liability without fault) of producers has traditionally been a very important principle that protects the interests of both consumers and society. The rationale behind this concept is that producers who make profits from dangerous activities should be held accountable if this danger materializes (BEUC 2017, 2). Several arguments favor the solution of attributing liability to producers or whoever puts a product on the market. The first argument is that of spreading costs. Instead of placing all the costs and the whole burden of an accident on a single person (the victim), strict liability spreads the costs of unavoidable accidents among the whole community of persons who benefit from the activity, which is appropriate because the risks and related expenses are intrinsic to the product and should be figured into its price. Producers also have the option of self-insuring against liability. Self-insurance and cost spreading thus alleviate the expenses associated with

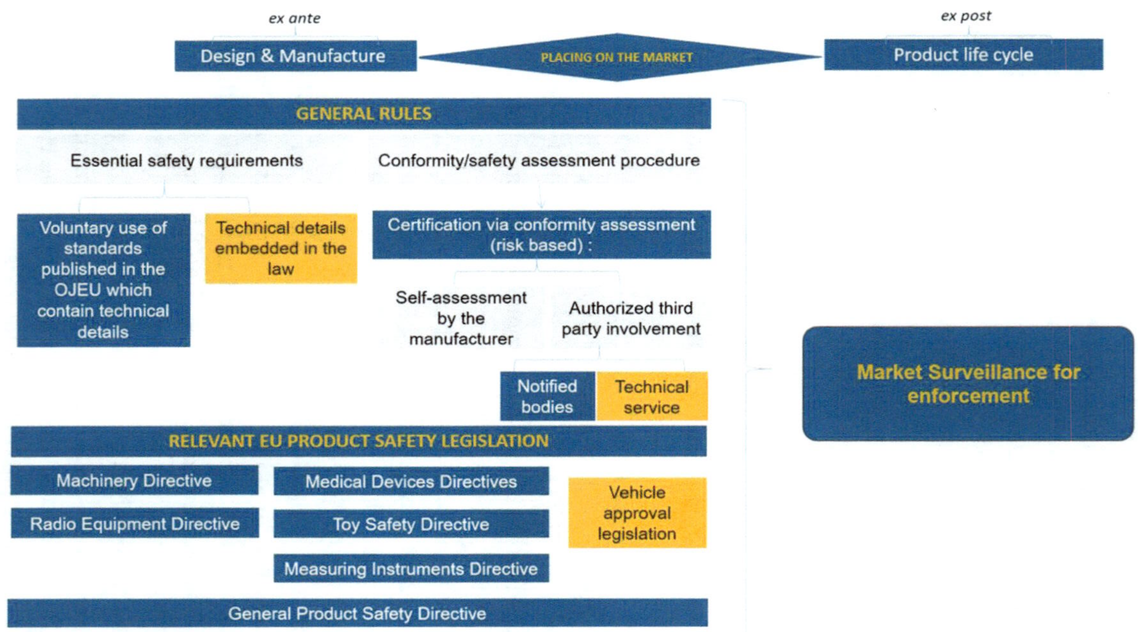

FIGURE 14.1 Current product safety legislation
SOURCE: EUROPEAN COMMISSION (2020, 5)

accidents. The second argument relates to injury prevention. By having to bear the accident costs with which an activity is associated, the producer has a strong incentive to take all possible precautions against a recurrence of the accident. Liability makes producers responsible for minimizing the potential risks posed to consumers by a product they are introducing into the market. Legal regulation should encourage manufacturers to become proactive about protecting customers from damage and improving the *ex ante* supervision of their own quality management systems (Winiger et al. 2018, 400–402; Leeuwen et al. 2015, 912). Thus, the companies that currently manufacture devices with AI are already subject to a well-developed doctrine of product liability (Asaro 2012, 170–76).

As recent research and the *Report on the Safety and Liability Implications of Artificial Intelligence, the Internet of Things and Robotics* (European Commission 2020) point out, in terms of liability issues, these emerging technologies share many interrelated characteristics, such as intelligence, autonomy, embodiment, complexity, connectivity, data dependency, opacity, and openness (see Table 14.1 for the details).

From these characteristics, it is apparent that the current legal framework for product liability is likely to become inadequate as commercially available AI machines become more sophisticated and autonomous (Asaro 2012, 242). Therefore, the authors of the "Civil Law Rules on Robotics" (European Parliament 2017) invited the European Commission to explore, analyze, and consider electronic personhood as a possible legal solution for autonomous robots. As evidenced by the European Parliament's 2017 resolution, the main reason behind this proposition is to introduce one more possible solution to the problem of establishing the legal accountability of artificially intelligent agents in torts and contracts. The document points out that in the case of autonomous robots, existing liability rules "would not make it possible to identify the party responsible for providing compensation and [require] that party to make good the damage it has caused" (European Parliament 2017, section AF).[2]

It is evident that new technologies pose risks that may not be covered only by civil or administrative means of law, as they potentially threaten such values as human life, health, and liberty, all of which are traditionally protected by criminal law. The question thus arises as to whether existing criminal law suffices and could be used as an instrument to protect society from AI, especially since traditionally criminal law is based on the guilt principle (negligence or

2 More about this proposition is presented in the chapter on electronic personhood.

TABLE 14.1 Characteristics of AI

Characteristics of AI	Description
Intelligence	"Intelligence" is hard to define. Attempts to do so often cause controversy. Intelligence has been defined in many ways: higher-level abilities (such as abstract reasoning, mental representation, problem solving, and decision making), the ability to learn, emotional knowledge, creativity, and adaptation to meet the demands of the environment effectively. Modern machines and ai systems can perceive analog signals that transmit information on the environment (much as humans do), learn from experience, and solve some problems. But up to now, there is no commonly accepted general theory of intelligence or standardized test of intelligence.
Autonomy	The most obvious feature of AI that distinguishes it from earlier technologies is its ability to act autonomously. Several notions of autonomy have been articulated in discussions of autonomous systems. Responsibility implies autonomy, but not inversely, so there can be systems that have degrees of technical autonomy without raising issues of responsibility. Agency is closely connected to qualities such as autonomy and embodiment. Autonomy requires automaticity and even goes beyond that, implying some degree of adaptability.
Embodiment	Embodiment is an important quality of many autonomous agents. It refers to the physical body that interacts with the surrounding environment. Pure software or "software agents" exist only in digital or cyber space (geographic position has no meaning in this instance). A physical body (e.g., sensors) may interact with the surrounding environment. Humans perceive the environment through analogous signals, and so must AI systems. A robot or machine that does not perceive its environment but acts according to a predefined plan or by remote control is not considered embodied or situated.

TABLE 14.1 Characteristics of AI (*cont.*)

Characteristics of AI	Description
Complexity, connectivity, and data dependency	These characteristics are reflected in both the plurality of economic operators involved in the supply chain and the multiplicity of components, parts, software, systems, or services that together form the new technological ecosystems (European Commission 2020, 2). The lines between the responsibilities of manufacturers/developers and of users are blurring (Asaro 2012, 174). Currently, there typically seems to be a shared or distributed responsibility between robot designers, engineers, programmers, manufacturers, investors, sellers, and users, because none of these agents can be identified as the ultimate source of action (World Commission 2017, 42). However, this is hardly the most efficient model to spur innovation or to provide the most just risk apportionment across society.
Openness and opacity	Products integrating AI are open to updates, upgrades, improving their own performance by learning from experience, and self-adaptation after they are placed on the market (European Commission 2020, 2). In other words, AI and other smart technologies use cognitive algorithms, which are programmed not merely to perform specific tasks but also to learn and further develop themselves in interaction with their environments. Given this complexity of the design, construction, and programming of AI devices, a central legal issue is to track the reasons behind all past actions and omissions (World Commission 2017, 6–7). Hence, there is an obvious tension between this "traceability" requirement and the development of robots with a high level of autonomy in decision making and advanced learning capabilities.

intentional fault), i.e., determining who is liable for damages caused by negligence or intentionally. Extensive scientific discussion is taking place, and it suggests "two possible answers available alternatively or conjunctively to address the insufficiency of civil law compensation to the victims of criminal AI behaviour: expanding the legal responsibility of the humans in charge of the AI systems, or providing for some remedies directed against system" (Lagioia and Sartor 2020, 459).

In the opinion of some scientists (Gordon 2021; Chesterman 2020; Lagioia and Sartor 2020), it is only a matter of time before AI systems becomes moral beings, in which event they could also become full subjects of criminal law.

14.5 Conclusions

This essay has first considered the issue of moral responsibility, explaining that this longstanding philosophical puzzle is far from resolved, which makes it all the more difficult to extend moral responsibility to the domain of AI. Nevertheless, it seems that some progress could be made by adopting compatibilist assumptions purely for practical purposes, although even then there will likely be cases when attributing moral responsibility will be impossible. Then, the focus shifted to legal responsibility arising from the characteristics of AI, which require new attitudes toward traditional liability rules. Existing EU member states' liability framework is built on Machinery and Product Liability Directives and on general rules of liability regimes, which do not always contain provisions explicitly addressing the new challenges and risks, since AI is a new technology characterized by such qualities as radical novelty, relatively fast growth, coherence, prominent impact, and uncertainty and ambiguity. Thus, the existing rules require revision. Smart technologies use cognitive algorithms, which are programmed to learn and to further develop themselves in interaction with their environments—another feature that complicates liability issues. As new technologies pose risks against which people are traditionally protected by criminal law but in which no human fault can be clearly established, the traditional model of criminal law should be reviewed as well.

Study Questions

1. Why is the notion of moral agency important in the context of moral responsibility?

2. Why is the question of free will relevant in debates about moral responsibility? What are the main established philosophical positions regarding free will?
3. What are some of the main aspects to consider regarding the attribution of moral responsibility to robots?
4. In what ways does AI complicate the question of attributing moral responsibility to humans?
5. What are the problematic characteristics of AI and other emerging technologies from a liability point of view?
6. How have existing European legal frameworks on liability and safety addressed the problematic issues raised by AI?
7. How does AI complicate the application of criminal liability? What solutions to this problem are possible?

References

Asaro, P. M. 2012. "A Body to Kick, but Still No Soul to Damn: Legal Perspectives on Robotics." In *Robot Ethics: the Ethical and Social Implications of Robotics, Intelligent Robotics, and Autonomous Agents,* edited by P. Lin, K. Abney, and G. A. Bekey, 169–86. MIT Press.

BEUC. 2017. *Review of Product Liability Rules.* https://www.beuc.eu/publications/beuc-x-2017-039_csc_review_of_product_liability_rules.pdf.

Carrier, R. 2005. *Sense and Goodness without God.* AuthorHouse.

Chesterman, S. 2020. "Artificial Intelligence and the Limits of Legal Personality." *International and Comparative Law Quarterly* 69(4): 819–44.

Dawkins, R. 1995. *River out of Eden.* Basic Books.

Docherty, B. 2015. "Mind the Gap: the Lack of Accountability for Killer Robots." *Human Rights Watch.* https://www.hrw.org/report/2015/04/09/mind-gap/lack-accountability-killer-robots.

European Commission. 2020. *Report on the Safety and Liability Implications of Artificial Intelligence, the Internet of Things and Robotics.* COM/2020/64 final.

European Parliament. 2017. *Civil Rules on Robotics. European Parliament Resolution of 16 February 2017 with recommendations to the Commission on Civil Law Rules on Robotics* (2015/2103(INL)). http://www.europarl.europa.eu/doceo/document/TA-8-2017-0051_EN.pdf.

Gordon, J.-S. 2021. "Artificial Moral and Legal Personhood." *AI & Society* 36: 457–71.

Gunkel, D. J. 2020. "Mind the Gap: Responsible Robotics and the Problem of Responsibility." *Ethics and Information Technology* 22(4): 307–20.

Himma, K. E. 2009. "Artificial Agency, Consciousness, and the Criteria for Moral Agency: What Properties Must an Artificial Agent Have to Be a Moral Agent?" *Ethics and Information Technology* 11(1): 19–29.

Lagioia, F., and G. Sartor. 2020. "AI Systems under Criminal Law: a Legal Analysis and a Regulatory Perspective." *Philosophy and Technology* 33: 433–65.

Leeuwen, V. B., and P. Verbruggen. 2015. "Resuscitating EU Product Liability Law?" *European Review of Private Law* 23(5): 899–915.

McKenna, M., and D. J. Coates. 2019. "Compatiblism." *Stanford Encyclopedia of Philosophy*. https://plato.stanford.edu/entries/compatibilism/.

Müller, V. C. 2020. "Ethics of Artificial Intelligence and Robotics." *Stanford Encyclopedia of Philosophy*. https://plato.stanford.edu/entries/ethics-ai/.

Rotolo, D., D. Hicks, and B. R. Martin. 2015. "What Is an Emerging Technology?" *Research Policy* 44(10): 1827–43.

Sparrow, R. 2007. "Killer Robots." *Journal of Applied Philosophy* 24(1): 62–77.

Sullins, J. P. 2011. "When Is a Robot a Moral Agent?" In *Machine Ethics*, edited by M. Anderson and S. L. Anderson, 151–61. Cambridge University Press.

Taddeo, M, and F. Luciano. 2018. "How AI Can Be a Force for Good." *Science* 361(6404): 751–52.

Talbert, M. 2019. "Moral Responsibility." *Stanford Encyclopedia of Philosophy*. https://plato.stanford.edu/entries/moral-responsibility/.

Tognazzini, N., and D. J. Coates. 2018. "Blame." *Stanford Encyclopedia of Philosophy*. https://plato.stanford.edu/entries/blame/.

Van Inwagen, P. 1983. *An Essay on Free Will*. Oxford University Press.

Wagenaar, W. A., and J. Groenewegen. 1987. "Accidents at Sea: Multiple Causes and Impossible Consequences." *International Journal of Man-Machine Studies* 27(5–6): 587–98.

Winiger, B., E. Karner, and K. Oliphant, eds. 2018. *Essential Cases on Misconduct: Digest of European Tort Law*, vol. 3. De Gruyter.

World Commission on the Ethics of Scientific Knowledge and Technology. 2017. Report of COMEST on Robotics Ethics. https://unesdoc.unesco.org/ark:/48223/pf0000253952.

Further Reading

Gruodytė, E., and P. Čerka. 2020. "Artificial Intelligence as a Subject of Criminal Law: Corporate Liability Model Perspective." In *Smart Technologies and Fundamental Rights*, edited by J.-S. Gordon, 260–81. Brill.

Kiršienė, J., E. Gruodytė, and D. Amilevičius. 2021. "From Computerised Thing to Digital Being: Mission (Im)possible?" *AI & Society* 35(4): 1–14.

O'Connor, T., and C. Franklin. 2021. "Free Will." *Stanford Encyclopedia of Philosophy*. https://plato.stanford.edu/archives/spr2021/entries/freewill/.

CHAPTER 15

Ethical and Legal Issues Related to Autonomous Vehicles

Sven Nyholm

15.1 Introduction

This chapter provides an overview of some of the most important emerging ethical and legal issues related to autonomous vehicles, also known as self-driving cars. Notably, automation in vehicles comes in different degrees and kinds, involving different forms of artificial intelligence (AI) (Nyholm and Smids 2020). Cars can be partially or fully automated. For the purposes of this chapter, however, the expression "self-driving car" will refer to any type of vehicle that either is fully automated or could operate in an autonomous mode in at least some traffic situations.

There are ethical questions related to the differences in levels and types of automation in cars. For example, are we expecting too much of human drivers if we require them to take over the vehicle's operation if the artificial intelligence in the car suddenly requests to hand control back to a human? In particular, is it reasonable to expect people to remain sufficiently alert at all times so that they can easily take over the steering or other driving tasks if necessary (Hevelke and Nida-Rümelin 2015)? Those are interesting questions. Here, however, I will not focus on such matters. Instead, I will discuss issues that arise during those times when the vehicle is operating in autonomous mode, regardless of whether it is possible to return control to a human occupant riding in the car.

When moral philosophers started investigating ethical issues related to self-driving cars around 2014, the discussion was exclusively about hypothetical thought experiments. If a self-driving car were involved in a crash and somebody was hurt, who should be held responsible? If the AI in the car had to react to a potential crash, what should the car do? Legal scholars had started thinking about such issues a little earlier than philosophers (e.g., Marchant and Lindor 2012; Peterson 2012). But those early articles in legal theory were also mostly about hypothetical scenarios.

In 2015, however, such scenarios began happening in real life (Nyholm and Smids 2020). In that year, there were about 20 small accidents involving

 | DOI:10.1163/9789004682900_019

experimental self-driving cars. No human beings were seriously injured. There were only some minor scratches on some of the cars. Mostly, what happened was that people in regular cars drove into experimental self-driving cars, typically because the self-driving cars were not behaving as the drivers in the other cars expected them to. For example, they accelerated more slowly than most human drivers do.

In those early accidents, human drivers were usually blamed. In 2016, however, for the first time, a self-driving car caused an accident (Nyholm 2018a). On Valentine's Day of that year, an experimental self-driving car operated by Google crashed into a bus, and Google had to admit that its car was at fault. Later that year, the first person died while riding in a self-driving car; a man was killed when his Tesla Model S car crashed into a truck while operating in autopilot mode. In 2018, for the first time, a human being was hit and killed by a self-driving car. The AI in an experimental car operated by Uber failed to recognize a human being crossing the road in time. The woman was first classified as a sign, then as a bike, and then reclassified as a human being. But by that point, it was too late. The car hit the woman, and she died on the way to the hospital.

Since then, we have seen an absolute explosion of philosophical articles about ethical issues related to self-driving cars. In the first few years after philosophers and legal scholars started writing about this topic, writing an overview of all existing articles was easy (see Nyholm 2018a; 2018b). Now that is becoming almost impossible, because so many scholars have written about self-driving cars. Accordingly, I will not try to summarize everything that has been discussed in academic philosophy and legal theory on the topic. It would not be possible to do so in a brief chapter. Instead, I will concentrate on some of the key issues that have received the most attention in recent years.

15.2 Safety and the Ethics of Experiments with Self-Driving Cars

The most important reason why people are excited about the prospect of self-driving cars concerns traffic safety. Eventually, it is hoped, self-driving cars will be much safer than regular cars. So far, however, this has not been proven in practice. This pattern already raises some interesting ethical questions.

To improve the safety of self-driving cars in a wide range of real-life traffic scenarios, it is necessary to experiment with self-driving cars in actual traffic. This involves imposing risks on people living in the communities where the experimental trips take place. As a result, a crucial ethical question arises. How much risk should we impose on people in this experimental stage to make sure that we will later save many lives in traffic accidents that will be avoided through developing very safe self-driving cars? After all, Elaine Herzberg, the woman killed by the self-driving car in the incident mentioned above, lost her life to an experimental vehicle. Should we tolerate such deaths now because of the greater number of lives that might later be saved if the technology industry is permitted to experiment with self-driving cars on public roads?

Philosophers Mark Howard and Robert Sparrow (2017) present an interesting claim about the ethics of risk and safety in the development of self-driving cars. They claim that as long as self-driving cars have not been proved to be safer than regular cars, it should be illegal to sell them. But once self-driving cars have been shown to be safer than regular cars, they continue, regular cars should be forbidden. If this argument is right, it suggests that society should accept the following general moral principle: if, in some risky domain of life, a safer alternative is introduced, then it is immoral to use the older, less safe alternative. Only the safest alternative should be permitted in a dangerous domain such as traffic.

But is this claim morally right? What if people who drive older, otherwise less safe cars take certain special safety precautions (Nyholm 2018b; Nyholm and Smids 2020)? For example, the legal requirements for getting a driver's license could be made much more stringent. Manually driven cars could be equipped with alcohol locks and speed-limiting technologies that would make it impossible to drive while drunk or faster than the speed limit. Could such steps adequately offset or compensate for the greater risks associated with manually driven cars? In general, when or if self-driving cars become much safer than regular cars, those who still wish to drive regular cars may need to come up with some strong justification as to why they should still be permitted to do so.

15.3 The Need for Ethics Programming and the Infamous Trolley Problem

We have noted that self-driving cars offer the promise of eventually becoming much safer than regular cars. Yet they cannot be 100 percent safe. Even the safest self-driving cars will sometimes crash. So we need to think about how to handle accident scenarios (Goodall 2014).

To return briefly to what I mentioned in the introduction, one possibility is that humans should always take over in crash scenarios. However, typical human reaction times are too slow. It won't always be possible for people to react in time. So automated cars must be programmed to respond to accident scenarios. Such programming might require making choices that impose serious risks on different people. In some situations, it is not possible to simply hit the brakes, and no option available to the car may be safe for everyone involved. Accordingly, the issue of what self-driving cars should do in situations where crashes are unavoidable is an inherently ethical problem. Therefore, some authors have suggested the need to equip self-driving cars with "ethics settings." For example, should the car always try to protect the people riding in the car, or should self-driving cars simply try to minimize overall harm when crashes are unavoidable (Goodall 2014; Nyholm 2018a)?

Imagine the following scenario. A self-driving car with five passengers suddenly detects a large obstacle on the road. Unless the car turns, the five passengers are likely to die. The only place to turn is onto a sidewalk. But a pedestrian is walking there. So the only way the car can save five people is by sacrificing one person. What should the car be programmed to do in such a situation?

Now consider an alternative scenario. In this case, only one person is in the automated car. Again, some large obstacle falls onto the road. And again, the car can save the passenger only by swerving onto the sidewalk. But this time, there are five pedestrians on the sidewalk. What should the car do now? Should it sacrifice the one passenger for the sake of the five?

These examples are similar to the so-called "trolley problem" (Nyholm and Smids 2016), a well-known thought experiment in which a trolley is about to hit five people on the tracks. You are standing next to a switch. If you pull the switch, the train will be redirected to a side track, where one person is located. Thus, to save the five, one person will have to be sacrificed. In another version of the problem, the only way to save the five on the tracks is to push a large and heavy person off a bridge and onto the train tracks in front of the trolley. The large person's weight will set off the automated brakes on the train before it hits the five. This would again kill one but save five. What should be done in these cases? The challenge of explaining and justifying differences in people's intuitions about such cases is encompassed in references to "the trolley problem" (Kamm 2015). There are many variations of this basic theme. Philosophers and psychologists have written extensively about trolley problems.

Many articles, in both the mass media and the academic literature, liken the ethics of self-driving cars to the trolley problem. Unfortunately, however, much of what philosophers and psychologists have written about the trolley problem is not helpful here (Hevelke and Nida-Rümelin 2015; Nyholm and Smids 2016). There are at least three reasons why.

First, in academic discussions of the trolley problem, we are asked to concentrate only on a very small set of situational considerations. In the real-world ethics of automated driving, in contrast, we must take as many considerations as possible into account. Second, in trolley problem discussions, we are typically asked to set aside questions of legal and moral responsibility. In the real-world ethics of automated driving, we cannot set these questions aside. Third, in trolley problem discussions, we assume that we know with certainty what the outcomes of different possible actions would be. In the real-world ethics of automated driving, we are dealing with risks and uncertainty.

For these reasons, the literature on the so-called trolley problem is less helpful than many people think in informing the ethics of automated driving. That is not to say that the literature on the trolley problem and the comparisons between trolley problem–inspired cases and the ethics of crashing self-driving cars are altogether irrelevant. If nothing else, it is at least useful to compare the ethics of self-driving cars with the trolley problem, because identifying key differences between the two can be a good way to clarify what matters most in the real-world ethics of self-driving cars.

15.4 Empirical Ethics

We will next explore so-called empirical ethics, which is an attempt to incorporate empirical investigation of ordinary people's intuitive attitudes and judgments into our ethical analysis. For example, we can study people's attitudes and intuitions by letting them make judgments about various real or simulated scenarios involving crashes of self-driving cars. We can then try to discern patterns in their judgments and intuitions. And we can try to incorporate our findings into ethical arguments. We could even claim that the law should track and align with people's common-sense views about what is right for self-driving cars to do.

Our topic here is automated driving and accident scenarios. Psychologists and behavioral economists have already started surveying ordinary people's intuitive opinions about how automated cars should handle crash scenarios. One interesting finding comes from interdisciplinary researchers at MIT in the United States (Bonnefon et al. 2016). They have found that when people are asked what kinds of accident algorithms they would like others to have, many say they want others to have cars programmed to minimize overall harm. However, when asked what accident programs they would like in their own self-driving cars, the responses seem to change. They don't want to be required to use or buy cars that are "altruistic" in the sense of being programmed to minimize overall harm. Instead, they prefer cars that would always try to save the people in the car, even if this decision does not minimize overall harm.

On the "moral machine" website also created by MIT researchers, one can explore numerous different dilemmas and cases and make intuitive judgments about them. For example, if a car would kill three grandmothers if it turns left or three children and two cats if it turns right, what should the car do? Or what if a car with a passenger in it can either go straight and crash into a wall, or turn and crash into a pedestrian who is crossing illegally despite a red light? What should the car do? People are invited to report their intuitions regarding dilemmas and forced choices such as these. Millions of people around the world have participated in this experiment. The researchers have collected these judgments and analyzed widely shared attitudes about moral dilemmas involving self-driving cars in accident situations (Awad et al. 2018).

Another interesting finding derived from this research is that depending on where people live in the world, they have slightly different attitudes about whose safety should be prioritized in imagined crash scenarios. In some parts of the world, participants were more likely to favor saving children at risk than older people at risk. In other areas, the opposite result was obtained. Similarly, in some parts of the world, the fact that somebody was breaking the traffic rules (e.g., crossing the street at a red light) was seen as weakening their right not to be hit by a self-driving car, whereas in other locations, that factor did not play a significant role in people's judgments. Several other fascinating cultural differences also emerged.

Is this survey-based empirical methodology a good basis for normative ethical and legal theories about crash scenarios? These findings are certainly very interesting. But there are some reasons to be skeptical (Nyholm 2018a). Here are three reasons.

First, people do not yet have much real-world experience of traffic involving self-driving cars. People's attitudes are likely to change once they acquire more experience of what it is like to be around self-driving cars. Thus, we should perhaps not put too much weight on people's current attitudes. Second, people's spontaneous gut reactions to hypothetical cases do not necessarily tell us anything about what sorts of arguments and reasons they might present to defend their intuitive judgments. In ethical and legal theorizing, we want to evaluate arguments, not just intuitive responses with no arguments or reasons to back them up. Third, people seem to have inconsistent attitudes. As I noted above, they want others to have harm-minimizing cars, but they want their own cars programmed to save themselves. Cars that minimize overall harm will sometimes save the car owner, but cars programmed to minimize overall harm may sometimes have to sacrifice the persons in the car.

In other words, people's attitudes and intuitions regarding automated driving and accident scenarios are certainly interesting to consider, but it is not clear that we can move smoothly from premises about people's attitudes to any solid conclusions about how best to deal with self-driving cars and accident scenarios. So again, it seems that we may need to look elsewhere in order to find more solid arguments.

15.5 Traditional Ethical Theories

We will next explore the option of applying traditional ethical theories from moral philosophy. Specifically, we will consider utilitarianism, Kantian ethics, and virtue ethics. Utilitarianism is the theory that we should always promote the overall good, by promoting everyone's happiness and well-being. Kantian ethics says we should adopt a set of basic principles we would be willing to accept as universal laws. Virtue ethics tells us that we should live our lives in ways that help us to exercise various virtues and excellences.

We can use these theories to explore the question of how self-driving cars should handle accident-scenarios (Gurney 2016). Perhaps we should have "utilitarian cars," or "Kantian cars" or "virtue-ethical cars." One initial problem worth noting here is that these ethical theories were originally developed with human moral agents in mind. That is, they were designed to address what humans should do, not what AI technologies should do. So it is not immediately obvious that we can simply transfer the moral principles that are supposed to guide human choices to the ethics of how self-driving cars should behave. In the end, it might be possible to specify clearly what principles of translation should be used when we export traditional theories about human-human interaction into the new domain of human-machine interaction. But we should be cognizant of the fact that this is a new form of ethics, where different rules and principles might apply.

With that cautionary note in mind, let us return to the choice among utilitarian, Kantian, and virtue-ethical approaches. Some philosophers will say that we need to make a choice here, and that we can use only one moral theory. But it is also possible that we should make use of all three moral theories. There is clearly something to learn from each one.

The lesson from utilitarianism (or consequentialism, more generally) might be that however cars are programmed to handle crash scenarios, we should think about this issue with our eyes on the greater good of society. We should reason carefully about what promotes overall well-being and other important human values.

The lesson from Kantian ethics could be that whatever rules we decide on should be universal in their application and respectful of everyone. For example, for the sake of fairness and equal treatment, people's cars should handle crash scenarios according to a shared set of rules that apply equally to everyone.

Lastly, consider virtue ethics. There are important virtues that people tend to exhibit in traffic. For example, people tend to conduct themselves in a fairly responsible way. Of course, there are many exceptions. But most people feel responsible and act responsibly when using very risky technologies such as motor vehicles. Will this still be the case when people start using self-driving cars?

Philosopher Mark Coeckelbergh (2016) has argued that people's tendency to feel a sense of responsibility when they use cars is influenced by the design and technology of the car. This observation is relevant from a virtue-ethical perspective. After all, being and feeling responsible is an important virtue. So a lesson we can distill from virtue ethics is that self-driving cars should be designed to make people who use such cars still feel responsible for what happens before, during, and after accidents. In general, it is important for emerging technologies powered by AI to be designed in such a way that they do not undermine our human capacities and tendencies to exhibit important virtues.

We do not yet have a good ethical theory of how automated cars should handle accident scenarios. But we do have a lot of materials to work with as we try to answer this question. We can learn important lessons from all the main traditional ethical theories. There are interesting results from "empirical ethics" that we should also take into account, and the discussion of trolley problems might also provide some interesting ideas. But there is more work to do here.

15.6 Moral and Legal Responsibility

As mentioned above, legal scholars started discussing crashes involving autonomous vehicles slightly earlier than moral philosophers did. Notably, the Anglophone legal literature has mostly focused on the American context. It has discussed such matters as how to extend American civil and criminal law to the issue of holding people or organizations responsible for crashes involving autonomous cars (e.g., Gurney 2016; Marchant and Lindor 2012; Peterson 2012; Ravid 2014). Accordingly, we need to be careful about generalizing the findings in the Anglophone legal literature to other contexts, other legal systems, or ethics more generally. Nevertheless, we can learn some interesting general lessons from the existing legal literature on this topic. Here are two such lessons.

First, the introduction of self-driving cars on public roads creates a sort of "existential crisis" within the domain of traffic (Nyholm 2018b). Self-driving cars are being introduced into society before we have clear ethical and legal frameworks guiding how to understand them and our relation to them. In other words, as more and more driving tasks are handed over to automated systems and as we move towards full automation, this development raises questions about how to understand the new role and responsibilities of the driver. It also raises questions about how to reinterpret the relation between the driver and their car.

Consider the role of the driver in a fully automated car with advanced AI. Is it now more like that of a manager, a supervisor, a commander, or what? Consider next the relation between a user of a self-driving car and the car itself. Is it more like the relation between an employer and an employee, a master and a slave, a superior and a subordinate, a principal and an agent, or what? The legal literature has usefully pointed out that we need to reconceptualize how we typically understand the relation between a user and a car. This can significantly affect how we view car users' legal and moral responsibilities.

A second key lesson from the legal literature is that when we reflect on responsibility for crashes involving self-driving cars, we should not forget that in ordinary life, what people do intentionally is not the only commonly recognized ground for attributing responsibility to them (Nyholm 2018b). We often also attribute responsibility for outcomes to people based on roles they perform (either professionally or privately) or rights they enjoy (such as ownership rights). For example, suppose that you own a dog that bites somebody. You might then be held both legally and morally responsible for the harm caused, even though your dog, and not you, bit the victim (Ravid 2014). In the same way, when we trace the legal and moral responsibility for outcomes caused by automated technologies with AI back to certain people, the right way to do this may sometimes not be via the most immediate, intentional actions of these people. It may rather be via the roles they play or the rights they enjoy in relation to the technologies in question.

In the introduction to this chapter, I mentioned that the ethics of self-driving cars has progressed from hypothetical thought experiments to discussing real-world accidents. In that context, I also mentioned the question of who should be held responsible when self-driving cars are involved in accidents. This has been a key issue in the real-world ethics of self-driving cars. So let us now briefly consider issues that arise in relation to responsibility and self-driving cars, both in the real world and in academic discussions (Marchant and Lindor 2012; Hevelke and Nida-Rümelin 2015; Nyholm 2018b).

Starting with the real-world cases mentioned earlier, Google has usually denied responsibility when its experimental self-driving cars have been involved in crashes. However, as mentioned above, there was one crash, on Valentine's Day 2016, when Google had to admit "partial responsibility" for its car crashing into a bus. Google promised that it would update the software of its cars so that they could better predict the behavior of buses (Nyholm 2018b).

In contrast, when a man died in a Tesla Model S car operating in autopilot mode later that same year, Tesla denied all legal and moral responsibility. It published a blog post expressing sympathy for the family of the dead man. But the company noted that as part of its user agreement, whoever uses Tesla's autopilot function must take responsibility for whatever problems might arise. At the same time, however, Tesla also said it would update the hardware in its cars, so that they would be better able to detect obstacles that it might be dangerous to crash into.

To some people, Google's response made more sense than Tesla's. Google assumed partial responsibility, and so it makes sense that it would also indicate plans to update the software. This is an interesting contrast to Tesla's response. Since Tesla stated that it would update its hardware, was that not an admission of blame for the crash? If Tesla was not to blame for the crash, why should Tesla need to update the technology in the car?

Some commentators have noted that it can seem unfair to blame human users of self-driving cars for accidents that their cars cause, even if those accidents involve harm to other people (Hevelke and Nida-Rümelin 2015). Users of self-driving cars who are lucky because their cars do not crash may not do anything different from unlucky users whose cars do cause accidents.

Why not always simply blame the companies building the self-driving cars? Some people who discuss this issue—both philosophers and lawyers—have worried that this might make car companies less motivated to create autonomous vehicles. (Marchant and Lindor 2012; Hevelke and Nida-Rümelin 2015). That would be a bad development, it has been suggested, since self-driving cars are thought to potentially have many benefits, in particular when it comes to increased traffic safety.

Another reason sometimes suggested as to why engineers and car designers should not be responsible for crashes involving self-driving cars is that they will not be able to reliably predict what these cars will do once they are out in traffic in the real world. When the vehicles are operating autonomously, the builders no longer control what they are doing. After all, they are self-driving cars, operating autonomously. So no human might have direct control over what the car is doing or the ability to fully predict what the AI in the car might decide is the best course of action in a particular traffic situation (Hevelke and Nida-Rümelin 2015).

Some philosophers who discuss issues like these worry that self-driving cars might give rise to what they call "responsibility gaps" and "retribution gaps" (Nyholm 2018b). This would mean that nobody can be sensibly blamed or justifiably punished when self-driving cars crash and people are harmed. If no human being is driving and the car is driving itself, how could any human being be blamed or punished for whatever harm the autonomous car might cause?

Do these worries about possible responsibility gaps and retribution gaps make sense? What should the law be? Indeed, it may be that the old ways in which we think about moral and legal responsibility for crashes involving cars with human drivers cannot be directly carried over to the new situation of crashes involving self-driving cars. Moreover, as many legal scholars contend, the old legal frameworks for assigning responsibility for car crashes may not work well in relation to self-driving cars. Our current traffic laws all assume that a human being is always driving the car (Gurney 2016).

However, there are ways to understand moral and legal responsibility that can be brought to bear on the issue of responsibility for crashes involving self-driving cars. I already noted above that we can think in terms of what roles and rights people have, and that this approach can ground moral and legal responsibilities. Other arguments can also be developed. For example, we could consider who benefits most from the presence of self-driving cars on the road. If a car company, for example, makes a lot of money by renting self-driving cars to people, then it might be fair to hold that company responsible for any accidents involving their lucrative cars.

Moreover, even if people may lack direct control over how self-driving cars behave on the road (since the cars are driving themselves!), people will still have indirect control over the cars' operation. Self-driving cars will be updated and maintained, and these updates and maintenance activities will be based on people's opinions about how self-driving cars should function (Nyholm 2018b). This degree of indirect control might be enough to justify making anyone in charge of updating and maintaining self-driving cars at least partly responsible for how the cars behave on the road.

However we decide regarding who should be held morally and legally responsible when self-driving cars cause harm, we should recognize that this might require some new thinking about car crashes and responsibility. Old ways of thinking about cars may not work in the same way when cars are driving themselves and the humans sitting in them are simply passengers. This is another key area where more work is needed from philosophers and legal scholars interested in our future world in which more and more AI technologies will take over tasks previously performed by humans, such as driving us around.

Study Questions

1. What is meant by "ethics settings" for accident scenarios? Why do some moral philosophers think that self-driving cars need to be equipped with such settings?
2. Can existing laws related to driving simply be carried over to the new situation of driving that involves self-driving cars? If not, why not?
3. What is meant by "the trolley problem"? Why might one be skeptical about comparing the philosophy of the trolley problem with real-world ethical and legal issues related to crashes involving self-driving cars?
4. What is "empirical ethics," and what challenges might be involved in trying to base ethical and legal reasoning about self-driving cars on the empirical findings associated with the well-known "moral machine" experiment?
5. In the text above, the traditional moral theories (utilitarianism, Kantianism, and virtue ethics) are related to the issue of how self-driving cars should be programmed to respond to accident scenarios. If you were to relate these traditional moral theories to the issue of who should be held legally and morally responsible in the case of a crash involving a self-driving car, how might you reason about that issue using the traditional moral theories?
6. What are responsibility gaps and retribution gaps? Why do some researchers studying autonomous driving worry that accidents involving self-driving cars might give rise to responsibility gaps and retribution gaps?

References

Awad, E., et al. 2018. "The Moral Machine Experiment." *Nature* 563: 59–64.

Bonnefon, J. F., A. Sharrif, and I. Rahwan. 2016. "The Social Dilemma of Autonomous Vehicles." *Science* 352(6293): 1573–76.

Coeckelbergh, M. 2016. "Responsibility and the Moral Phenomenology of Using Self-Driving Cars.", *Applied Artificial Intelligence* 30(8): 748–57.

Goodall, N. J. 2014. "Ethical Decision Making during Automated Vehicle Crashes." *Transportation Research Record: Journal of the Transportation Research Board* 2424(1): 58–65.

Gurney, J. 2016. "Crashing into the Unknown: an Examination of Crash-Optimization Algorithms through the Two Lanes of Ethics and Law." *Albany Law Review* 79(1): 183–267.

Hevelke, A., and J. Nida-Rümelin. 2015. "Responsibility for Crashes of Autonomous Vehicles: an Ethical Analysis." *Science and Engineering Ethics* 21(3): 619–30.

Kamm, F. 2015. *The Trolley Problem Mysteries.* Oxford University Press.

Marchant, G., and R. Lindor. 2012. "The Coming Collision between Autonomous Cars and the Liability System." *Santa Clara Legal Review* 52(4): 1321–40.

Nyholm, S. 2018a. "The Ethics of Crashes with Self-Driving Cars, A Roadmap I." *Philosophy Compass* 13(7): e12507.

Nyholm, S. 2018b. "The Ethics of Crashes with Self-Driving Cars, A Roadmap II." *Philosophy Compass* 13(7): e12506.

Nyholm, S., and J. Smids. 2016. "The Ethics of Accident-Algorithms for Self-Driving Cars: an Applied Trolley Problem?" *Ethical Theory and Moral Practice* 19(5): 1275–89.

Nyholm, S., and J. Smids. 2020. "Automated Cars Meet Human Drivers: Responsible Human-Robot Coordination and the Ethics of Mixed Traffic." *Ethics and Information Technology* 22(4): 335–44.

Peterson, R. W. 2012. "New Technology—Old Law: Autonomous Vehicles and California's Insurance Framework." *Santa Clara Law Review* 52: 101–53.

Ravid, O. 2014. "Don't Sue Me, I Was Just Lawfully Texting and Drunk When My Autonomous Car Crashed into You." *Southwest Law Review* 44(1): 175–207.

Sparrow, R., and M. Howard. 2017. "When Human Beings Are like Drunk Robots: Driverless Vehicles, Ethics, and the Future of Transport." *Transportation Research Part C* 80: 206–15.

Further Reading

Beiker, S. A. 2012. "Legal Aspects of Autonomous Driving." *Santa Clara Law Review* 52(4): 1145–56.

Gurney, J. K. 2013. "Sue My Car Not Me: Products Liability and Accidents Involving Autonomous Vehicles." *Journal of Law, Technology & Policy* 2: 247–77.

Gurney, J. K. 2015. "Driving into the Unknown: Examining the Crossroads of Criminal Law and Autonomous Vehicles." *Wake Forest Journal of Law and Policy* 5(2): 393–442.

Gurney, J. K. 2017. "Imputing Driverhood: Applying a Reasonable Driver Standard to Accidents Caused by Autonomous Vehicles." *In Robot Ethics 2.0: from Autonomous Vehicles to Artificial Intelligence,* edited by P. Lin, K. Abney, and R. Jenkins, 51–65. Oxford University Press.

Keeling, G. 2019. "Why Trolley Problems Matter for the Ethics of Automated Vehicles." *Science and Engineering Ethics* 26(1): 293–307.

Keeling, G., et al. 2019. "Four Perspectives on What Matters for the Ethics of Automated Vehicles." In *Road Vehicle Automation 6,* edited by G. Meyer and S. Beiker, 49–60. Springer.

Lin, P. 2015. "Why Ethics Matters for Autonomous Cars." In *Autonomous Driving: Technical, Legal and Social Aspects,* edited by M. Maurer et al., 69–85. Springer.

Nyholm, S. 2018. "Attributing Agency to Autonomous Systems: Reflections on Human-Robot Collaborations and Responsibility-Loci." *Science and Engineering Ethics* 24(4): 1201–19.

Santoni de Sio, F. 2017. "Killing by Autonomous Vehicles and the Legal Doctrine of Necessity." *Ethical Theory and Moral Practice* 20(2): 411–29.

Wolkenstein, A. 2018. "What Has the Trolley Dilemma Ever Done for Us (And What Will It Do in the Future)? On Some Recent Debates about the Ethics of Self-Driving Cars." *Ethics and Information Technology* 20: 163–73.

PART 4

Major Key Issues: Regulation and Standardization

Introduction to Part 4

In this part, we consider three closely related topics: legal regulation of autonomous machines, limits of legal automation, and responsible standardization.

The chapter on legal regulation of autonomous machines starts with a conceptual overview of the regulation phenomenon, briefly explaining three pillars of regulation that form a dynamic and complex legal system: rule of law, law of rules, and behavior. Next, this chapter introduces the concept of autonomous machines, focusing on the legal definition and characteristics that were developed in the European Union. It goes on to discuss why we need to regulate autonomous machines, providing a glimpse of general academic discourse on core threats to individual freedoms and rights, societal cohesion and harmony, employment and economic well-being, and trust in democracy, all of which are typically linked with developments in the realm of autonomous machinery. Finally, it reviews the key proposals for Europe that have been developed up to this time, including the Civil Law Rules on Robotics, proposed by the European Parliament in 2017; *Ethics Guidelines for Trustworthy AI*, proposed by the High-Level Expert Group on Artificial Intelligence (set up by the European Commission) in 2019; a report on liability for artificial intelligence and other emerging digital technologies, delivered by the Expert Group on Liability (also set up by the European Commission) in 2019; and finally, the Artificial Intelligence Act, a harmonized regulatory framework on AI, proposed in 2021 by the European Commission.

The chapter on limits of legal automation presents an overview of key concepts related to the automation of legal services. Technology can affect the work of courts and lawyers in two broad ways: it can improve, refine, streamline, optimize, and turbo-charge traditional ways of working (automation), and it can displace and revolutionize conventional working habits and bring radical change, enabling us to do new things rather than old things in new ways (transformation). Generally, automation is technologically simpler than transformation. But technologies that bring transformation are closely related to legal paradigm shifts and embody a longer-term approach. The explosive advance in artificial intelligence technologies has opened the door to forms of automation that can complete legal services much more cheaply and efficiently. The biggest pitfall is that people occasionally assume that because AI has successfully automated one complex task, it naturally can be used to automate nearly any other type of complex task. However, existing AI tends to be narrow in scope and tends to perform poorly in areas that are conceptual, abstract, value-laden, or open-ended, require common sense, or involve

 DOI:10.1163/9789004682900_020

engagement with the meaning of real-world humanistic concepts such as societal norms, social constructs, or social institutions.

The chapter on responsible standardization presents an overview of key concepts related to technology standardization. As the standardization of products and services has been acquiring a growing importance for businesses and policymakers due to the growing role of technologies and technology-based services in our societies, the intricate and tight dependencies between standards and the private and business affairs of people have given rise to a new rubric, *responsible standardization* (RS). RS addresses the question of whether and how standards development organizations and policymakers can ensure that technology and service standards are produced with responsibility toward the public, as opposed to the historically common practice according to which standards cater only to commercial or technological demands. This chapter explores the importance of standards and responsible standardization by asking simple questions and demonstrating examples of legitimacy, coerciveness, and vested commercial interests in the standards we use.

CHAPTER 16

Legal Regulation of Autonomous Machines

Paulius Astromskis

16.1 What Is Legal Regulation?

> Fundamental rights lie at the foundation of both international and EU human rights law and underpin the legally enforceable rights guaranteed by the EU Treaties and the EU Charter. Fundamental rights can however also be understood as reflecting special moral entitlements of all individuals arising by virtue of their humanity, regardless of their legally binding status.
>
> European Commission High-Level Expert Group on AI, 2019

On one hand, legal regulation may be taken to mean narrowly a legislative will ("law of rules"), employed on the assumption that individuals or organizations can be compelled by government to comply with prescribed behavior under penalty of sanctions or by the offer of rewards (Selznick 1985). Here, basic rationales for regulation relate to cases in which society does not affirm the outcome of certain behavior, whether it is a result of market failure or a collective sense of right and wrong (Harrison 2011). This regulation is supposed to increase public welfare by encouraging beneficial behaviors and discouraging detrimental ones through the use of positivistic legal norms (rulemaking) and their execution procedures (rule enforcement).

On the other hand, legal regulation can also be taken to mean broadly a right reason ("rule of law"),[1] employed on the assumption that there are legal norms that are (a) not legislated—for example, customary law,[2] which owes its positivity not to an act setting the norm but to common and continuous usage,[3]

1 The difference between "law of rules" and "rule of law" parallels what Germans would call *Gesetz* (i.e., the law as laid down and its formal rules) and *Recht*, which encompasses some claim to an ethical value, or in French between *loi* and *droit*, or in Lithuanian between *taisyklės* and *teisė*.

2 This typically refers to customs, traditions, or religion.

3 This term represents a "type (or form) of social regulation when impact on human behavior is being done by legal rules and principles" (Vaišvila 2004).

 | DOI:10.1163/9789004682900_021

or (b) legislated value statements, which are so abstract and indefinite in their limits that they cannot be considered positive in an ontological sense—such as, for example, the command to consider "good morals" (Kaufmann 1963), or principles of justice, reasonableness, and good faith.

Both approaches mentioned above indicate a form of behavioral control, through either externalized legislative will or internalized right reason. However, an extremely narrow approach to legal regulation may bring about a complete perversion of law, as was exposed in the Nuremberg trials.[4] The argument that we must abide even the basest statute, as long as it has been enacted with formal correctness, can no longer be considered after the experience of the Fascist and Communist dictatorships (Kaufmann 1963). But an extremely broad approach to legal regulation may also bring about a perversion of law as the courts, appealing to an alleged "spirit" of the law, may push aside a valid and sound legislative will that the courts perceive as blocking their path to a desired decision (Kaufmann 1963). In sum, extreme positivistic or naturalistic approaches are not desirable and should not be tolerated. The desired application and meaning of regulation should thus be within the efficient balance of the best from both worlds.

That having been said, an assumption may be made that behavior is regulated through the balance of interconnected formal rulemaking and rule enforcement institutions ("law of rules") and informal ones, namely customs, traditions, and religion ("rule of law"). Informal institutions reflect special moral entitlements and describe the ethical principles that must be observed to ensure fundamental human rights; therefore, they are the *foundation* of the legal system. Legislative, executive, and judicial branches of government (formal institutions) convert these moral entitlements and ethical principles into specific requirements that should be implemented, and therefore they are the *realization* of the legal system. Also, since legal regulation is a form of behavioral control, it should be constantly *assessed* in terms of compliance with foundational principles or specific requirements to operationalize the requirements and offer practical guidance where necessary.

These three pillars (rule of law, law of rules, and behavior) are interconnected and form a dynamic and complex legal system. Constantly evolving behavior demands regulatory oversight and tests the customary dogmas of moral

4 Notably, the Nuremberg defense of "superior orders" (*Befehl ist Befehldefense*) was grounded on the proposition that a person should not be held guilty for actions ordered by a superior official or authority). This defense was quashed by Nuremberg Principle IV: "The fact that a person acted pursuant to order of his Government or of a superior does not relieve him from responsibility under international law, provided a moral choice was in fact possible to him".

entitlements and ethical principles within these new contexts. Regulators, faced with new or emerging behaviors and accompanying legal omissions, will investigate the foundational mandate, accompanied by their common sense regarding right and wrong, before making a rulemaking decision. Also, foundations are constantly challenged as novel contexts are introduced for consideration. Presumably, this dynamically interconnected, tripartite system constantly adjusts toward an equilibrium point, where within the limits of rule of law, discovered legal gaps are filled by the law of rules, and thus the required behavior is internalized (Vaišvila 2004).

16.2 What Are Autonomous Machines?

> Whereas from Mary Shelley's Frankenstein's Monster to the classical myth of Pygmalion, through the story of Prague's Golem to the robot of Karel Čapek, who coined the word, people have fantasised about the possibility of building intelligent machines, more often than not androids with human features.
>
> European Parliament, 2017, preamble A

Up to now, artificial intelligence (AI) systems have been domain-specific, weak, or narrow, since current AI can only realize specific or given functions and cannot adapt to complex environments or constantly develop new functions, as humans can (Huang 2017). However, recent results on practically feasible computable variants of the old incomputable methods are reinvigorating the long-dormant field (Schmidhuber 2010). Disruptive technological developments and investments in artificial intelligence have soared, and countries across the globe are launching policies or plans to encourage AI-related research and development.[5] Shifts in technologies are projected to take society from robotic automation in closed-off, secure settings to autonomous robots in social and work environments, performing not just repetitive movements but characterized by flexibility, adaptability and learning (Rommetveit, van Dijk, and Gunnarsdóttir 2020).

A robot's autonomy can be defined as the ability to make decisions and implement them in the outside world, independently of external control or influence. This autonomy is of a purely technological nature, and its degree depends on how sophisticated a robot's interaction with its environment has

5 See the OECD AI Policy Observatory at https://www.oecd.ai/.

been designed to be (European Parliament 2017). Emerging new technologies increasingly perform tasks with less, or entirely without, human control or supervision. They are themselves capable of altering the initial algorithms due to self-learning capabilities that process external data collected in the course of the operation. The choice of such data and the degree of impact those data have on the outcome is constantly adjusted by the evolving algorithms themselves (European Commission, Expert Group on Liability 2019). However, although the autonomy of machines (in general) is rather clear, there is still no common, specific legal definition of these machines and their subcategories. The European Parliament (2017) called for such a definition by taking into consideration the following characteristics of an autonomous robot:

- acquires autonomy through sensors and/or by exchanging data with its environment (inter-connectivity) and analyzing the data;
- is self-learning (optional criterion);
- has physical support;
- adapts its behaviors and actions to its environment.

Autonomous machines promise greater efficiency in various domains: agriculture; the automobile industry; banking and financial technology; defense; education; energy; healthcare; manufacturing; marketing; media and entertainment; the public sector; space technology; security; virtual reality; and many others. Also, an unknown number of countries and industries are currently researching and developing lethal autonomous weapon systems, ranging from missiles capable of selective targeting to learning machines with cognitive skills to decide whom, when, and where to fight without human intervention (European Commission High-Level Expert Group on AI 2019). In other words, the scale, scope, and complexity of contemporary technological advancements are unlike anything humankind has experienced before (Schwab 2016).

16.3 Why Regulate Autonomous Machines?

> Whereas now that humankind stands on the threshold of an era when ever more sophisticated robots, bots, androids and other manifestations of artificial intelligence seem poised to unleash a new industrial revolution, which is likely to leave no stratum of society untouched, it is vitally important for the legislature to consider all its implications.
>
> European Parliament 2017, preamble B

The vision of creating autonomous machines has led to serious warnings that they could pose a significant existential risk to humanity due to a significant "control problem" (Bostrom 2002; 2014). Humans may be "locked out" of control where technological self-enhancement is no longer remotely understandable by even the most technically savvy humans (Torrance 2013). If these machines eventually reach a high enough level of development, they could start giving themselves new goals and building new artifacts to attain them, all independently of humans, who will become irrelevant at best or extinct at worst (Bostrom 2014). Bostrom (2003) illustrated these existential dangers with the famous Paperclip Maximizer thought experiment,[6] where the unforeseen outcome has been eloquently captured in this famous comment by Yudkowsky (2008): "The AI does not hate you, nor does it love you, but you are made out of atoms which it can use for something else." Scholars, novelists, and filmmakers have all considered the possibility that autonomous machines may take an evil turn (Westerlund 2020, citing Beltramini 2019).

This threat far exceeds the risks of climate change, overpopulation, and nuclear war (Bradley 2020; Yampolskiy and Fox 2013), and it contains features that make ordinary risk management ineffective (Bostrom 2002). Special attention is given to lethal autonomous weapon systems (European Commission High-Level Expert Group on AI 2019), which could lead to an uncontrollable arms race on a historically unprecedented level and create military contexts in which human control is almost entirely relinquished. Even in situations other than Terminator scenarios, competing organizations (firms or states) in the arms race may cut corners and compromise on safety standards (Armstrong, Bostrom, and Schulman 2016), thus resulting in poor-quality machines that do not take the interests of humans or the welfare of humanity into consideration (Bostrom 2017; Yudkowsky 2008). And there are ways to harm humans convincingly while mimicking respect of their rights (such as property inviolability), by manipulating them into making bad decisions and causing considerable damage to their well-being (Sotala and Yampolskiy 2015). Mere indifference to human values—including human survival—could be sufficient for autonomous machines to pose an existential threat (ibid). Misuse or overuse of AI could also lead to the detrimental effects of loss of human agency, devalued human skills, and an eroded potential for human determination (Floridi et al. 2018).

---

6 In this thought experiment, the premise is simple: the AI system is given a directive to maximize the production of paper clips. With no moral considerations, all obstacles are removed and all resources aligned to maximize the production of paper clips, regardless of the consequences (see Leahy 2019).

Autonomous machines may promise a success story of evolution and enhancement in all fields of human mental and physical activity. But they may also present a story of existential risk, about which we have been warned by thousands of opinion leaders in fields ranging "from economics, law and philosophy to computer security, formal methods and, of course, various branches of AI itself."[7] Indeed, today transhumanists, singularitarianists, cyberlibertarianists, extropianists, and transtopianists extol the benefits of technology, while technoantagonists describe technology as decidedly at odds with human well-being, thus opening human eyes to the possibility not only of technological utopias, but also of technological dystopias (Holowchak 2010).

Therefore already today, with the rising developments in AI, the threats to individual freedoms and rights, societal cohesion and harmony, employment and economic well-being, and trust in democracy are being ratcheted up (Arogyaswamy 2020). Advanced technologies can be very harmful if they are applied to people's lives without an understanding of the issues that may arise from introducing ever "smarter" technology, so their increasing adoption will raise new ethical, legal, and social issues (Westerlund 2020, citing Alsegier 2016; Veruggio and Operto 2006). Humans are fragile and delicate systems and AI can easily become the elephant in the crystal room; therefore, we need to ensure that technological developments will be at the service of the human project, not vice versa (Cath 2018).

Certainly, on one hand, issues related to regulation of the most sophisticated technologies might be analyzed through the lens of Frank H. Easterbrook's "The Law of the Horse" (1996), which assumes "that the best way to learn the law applicable to specialized endeavors is to study general rules," thereby neglecting the need for new specific regulations and fostering the application of old ones. And of course, the historical development of general rules and their application to various contexts cannot be ignored. However, legal systems tailored to regulate the "horse" issues, rather than those of autonomous machines, already cannot cope with the challenges posed by exponentially developing technologies (Appazov 2014). Therefore, the views of the opponents to this neglectful approach may be summarized by Lawrence Lessig's (1999) comment that the potential of the horse law to regulate most sophisticated autonomous machines seems to be overestimated. Moreover, assuming that the magnitude of harm resulting from underestimating the power of autonomous machines may be devastating, and that the probability of existential accidents cannot

7 Future of Life Institute, "Research Priorities for Robust and Beneficial Artificial Intelligence: An Open Letter," https://futureoflife.org/ai-open-letter.

be fully ruled out in advance, under the calculus of negligence,[8] insufficient regulatory attention to the phenomenon may constitute negligence.

The proposition that existing regulations will have to be changed to reflect new technological innovations was promoted by the Industrie 4.0 work group (Kagermann et al. 2013) and the RoboLaw research group (Palmerini 2014), and it is widely supported by various policy forums and initiatives, including the United Nations Centre on Artificial Intelligence and Robotics, the IEEE Global Initiative on Ethics of Autonomous and Intelligent Systems, the European Commission High-Level Expert Group on AI, and many others.[9] Indeed, scholars, organizations and policymakers have begun gravitating toward "artificial intelligence for social good," as a way to capture the ethos of all those who are involved at various levels in ensuring that AI can be used in a manner that would promote human self-actualization, increased agency, better social capabilities, greater societal cohesion, and overall flourishing (Mabaso 2021; Floridi et al. 2018).

However, a suitable way to comprehend and solve regulation problems has not yet been found (Kalanov 2016). A problem often underscored when we confront the relationship between technology and regulation is the slow pace of the law, in the sense that technological innovation outruns regulators' ability to intervene early enough upon the emergence of a new product (Palmerini et al. 2014). Lack of regulatory precedent, little established ethical guidance, and other ethical and social implications of introducing new technologies into mainstream society all constitute a very weighty issue that remains largely unresolved, even as the consequences of this interaction are already unfolding (Guihot et al. 2017).

But at the core of regulatory complexity is the paradox of freedom and control. More control means less freedom, and hence over-protection through over-regulation might arbitrarily stifle or diminish the value of welfare-enhancing innovations. On the other hand, too much liberalism and inadequate regulation may lead to a loss of trust between humans and machines, or to violations of fundamental human rights. Choosing south can be at the expense of north, while the obligation of legal regulators is to go both ways. Therefore, the main challenge for regulators is to balance freedom and control in a way that would maximize the overall well-being of individuals and society, thus promoting the benefits of AI and inhibiting the harmful effects (den Hertog 2010).

---

8 *United States v. Carroll Towing Co.*, 159 F.2d 169 (2d Cir. N.Y. 1947).

9 See for example the OECD AI Policy Observatory at https://www.oecd.ai/ and European Commission (2020).

16.4 What Are the Key Proposals for Europe?

> Whereas, notwithstanding the scope of the Directive 85/374/EEC, the current legal framework would not be sufficient to cover the damage caused by the new generation of robots, insofar as they can be equipped with adaptive and learning abilities entailing a certain degree of unpredictability in their behaviour, since these robots would autonomously learn from their own, variable experience and interact with their environment in a unique and unforeseeable manner.
>
> European Parliament 2017, preamble Z

The Civil Law Rules on Robotics, proposed by the European Parliament in 2017, specified key concerns and called on the European Commission to regulate the development of robotics and AI for civil use (European Parliament 2017). Alongside a call for definitions, as mentioned above, proposals were made regarding the registration of "smart robots," civil law liability, interoperability, access to code and intellectual property rights, and disclosure of the use of robots and AI by researchers and others. The European Parliament also proposed a Charter on Robotics, accompanied by a code of ethical conduct for robotics engineers, a code for research ethics committees, and licensing for designers and users. It even controversially proposed the possibility of "creating a specific legal status of electronic persons for the most sophisticated autonomous robots, responsible for making good any damage they may cause, and possibly applying electronic personality to cases where robots make autonomous decisions or otherwise interact with third parties independently" (European Parliament 2017).

The European Parliament has not provided any explanation or framework for the content of this new type of personhood, and thus, naturally, the idea was met with criticism by "artificial intelligence and robotics experts, industry leaders, [and] law, medical and ethics experts" (Open Letter to the European Commission: Artificial Intelligence and Robotics). Critics have argued that the idea of a legal status of "electronic person" for "autonomous," "unpredictable," and "self-learning" robots is "based on an overvaluation of the actual capabilities of even the most advanced robots, a superficial understanding of unpredictability and self-learning capacities, and a robot perception distorted by science fiction and a few recent sensational press announcements" (ibid). In addition to this technical perspective, experts note that "from an ethical and legal perspective, creating a legal personality for a robot is inappropriate whatever the legal status model" (ibid). However, the European Parliament has not suggested that robots should be treated like humans (Delvaux-Stehres

2018), nor did it suggest using any of the established models of legal status. Rather, it simply proposed studying, among other possibilities, the use of an e-personality, which would function a little bit like the legal personality of companies.

Ethics Guidelines for Trustworthy AI, proposed by the High-Level Expert Group on AI (set up by the European Commission in 2019), recognizes that it is important to build AI systems that are worthy of trust, since human beings will be able to confidently and fully reap their benefits only when the technology, including the processes and people behind the technology, is trustworthy. According to this proposal, "Trustworthy AI" has three components:

(1) it should be lawful, ensuring compliance with all applicable laws and regulations;
(2) it should be ethical, ensuring adherence to ethical principles and values; and
(3) it should be robust, both from a technical and social perspective, to ensure that, even with good intentions, AI systems do not cause any unintentional harm.

Each component is necessary but not sufficient to achieve Trustworthy AI; the components work in harmony and overlap in their operation. The High-Level Expert Group articulated fundamental rights and a corresponding set of ethical principles that are crucial in an AI context; listed seven key requirements that AI systems should meet to realize Trustworthy AI; and proposed technical and non-technical methods that can help with their implementation. Finally, the group provided a Trustworthy AI assessment list that can help in operationalizing the seven requirements, together with examples of beneficial opportunities and critical concerns raised by AI systems. Overall, the group specified a framework for Trustworthy AI (Figure 16.1) with key foundational, realization and assessment elements.

The ambition here is to help in securing the human flourishing of European citizens, both individually and collectively, and to create a culture of "Trustworthy AI for Europe," whereby the benefits of AI can be reaped by all in a manner that ensures respect for our foundational values—fundamental rights, democracy, and the rule of law (European Commission High-Level Expert Group on AI 2019). Notably, this framework of Trustworthy AI is silent on the previously proposed matter of electronic legal personhood for the most sophisticated autonomous machines, thus treating it as an advanced property consideration rather than a legal subject.

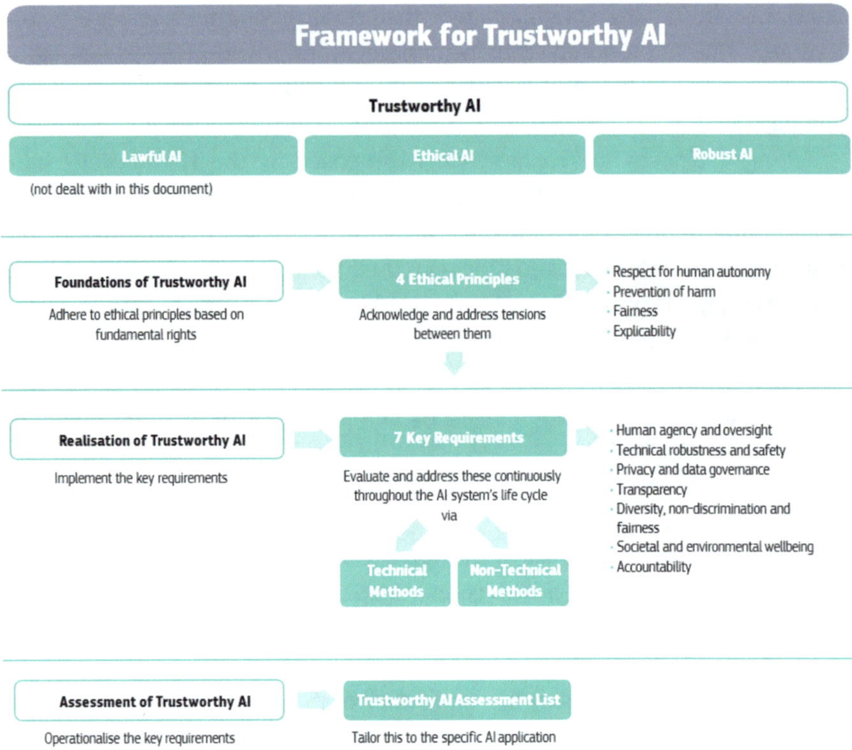

FIGURE 16.1 Framework for trustworthy AI

The report on "Liability for Artificial Intelligence and Other Emerging Digital Technologies" delivered by the Expert Group on Liability (also set up by the European Commission in 2019) addressed the issue of how liability regimes should be designed—and, where necessary, changed—to rise to the challenges that emerging digital technologies bring with them. It contained the following findings:

– A person operating a permissible technology that nevertheless carries an increased risk of harm to others, such as AI-driven robots in public spaces, should be subject to strict liability for damage resulting from its operation.
– In situations where a service provider ensuring the necessary technical framework has a higher degree of control than the owner or user of an actual product or service equipped with AI, this factor should be taken into account in determining who primarily operates the technology.
– A person using a technology that does not pose an increased risk of harm to others should still be required to abide by the duties to properly select,

operate, monitor, and maintain the technology in use and—failing that—should be liable for breach of such duties if at fault.

- A person using a technology that has a certain degree of autonomy should not be less accountable for any ensuing harm than if said harm had been caused by a human auxiliary.
- Manufacturers of products or digital content incorporating emerging digital technology should be liable for damage caused by defects in their products, even if the defect was caused by changes made to the product under the producer's control after it had been placed on the market.
- For situations exposing third parties to an increased risk of harm, compulsory liability insurance could give victims better access to compensation and protect potential tortfeasors against the risk of liability.
- Where a particular technology increases the difficulty of proving the existence of an element of liability beyond what can be reasonably expected, victims should be entitled to facilitation of proof.
- Emerging digital technologies should come with logging features, where appropriate in the circumstances, and failure to log, or to provide reasonable access to logged data, should result in a reversal of the burden of proof so as not to be to the detriment of the victim.
- The destruction of the victim's data should be regarded as damage, compensable under specific conditions.

Notably, this Expert Group also expressly concluded that it is not necessary to give devices or autonomous systems a legal personality, as the harm these may cause can and should be attributable to existing persons or bodies. This conclusion, coupled with the framework of Trustworthy AI and the subsequent Artificial Intelligence Act, clearly quashed the initial European Parliament proposal to regulate most sophisticated autonomous machines as persons rather than as things.

The Artificial Intelligence Act, as a harmonized regulatory framework on AI, was proposed in 2021 by the European Commission. It responded to calls for action contained in various AI-related European Parliament resolutions adopted in 2020, on ethics, liability, intellectual property, criminal matters , education, culture, and the audiovisual sector. The European Commission (2021a) recognized that the use of AI with its specific characteristics (e.g., opacity, complexity, dependency on data, and autonomous behavior) can adversely affect a number of fundamental rights enshrined in the EU Charter of Fundamental Rights, and therefore it set the following specific objectives for AI regulation:

- to ensure that AI systems placed on the Union market and used are safe and respect existing law on fundamental rights and Union values;

- to ensure legal certainty so as to facilitate investment and innovation in AI;
- to enhance governance and effective enforcement of existing law on fundamental rights and safety requirements applicable to AI systems; and
- to facilitate the development of a single market for lawful, safe, and trustworthy AI applications and prevent market fragmentation.

To achieve those objectives, this proposal presents a balanced and proportionate horizontal regulatory approach to AI that is limited to the minimum necessary requirements to address the risks and problems linked to AI, without unduly constraining or hindering technological development or otherwise disproportionately increasing the cost of placing AI solutions on the market. The European Commission (2021b) followed a risk-based approach and classified AI applications into the following categories:

- Unacceptable risk: AI systems considered a clear threat to the safety, livelihoods, and rights of people will be banned. This includes AI systems or applications that manipulate human behavior to circumvent users' free will (e.g., toys using voice assistants to encourage dangerous behavior by minors) and systems that allow "social scoring" by governments.
- High risk: AI systems identified as high-risk will be subject to strict obligations before they can be put on the market, including imperative requirements for adequate risk assessment and mitigation systems; high quality of the datasets; logging of activity to ensure traceability of results; detailed documentation; clear and adequate information to the user; appropriate human oversight measures to minimize risk; and high levels of robustness, security, and accuracy. High-risk AI systems, in this context, include AI technology used in these areas:
  - Critical infrastructures (e.g., transport) that could put the life and health of citizens at risk;
  - Educational or vocational training, including AI uses that may determine people's access to education or professional life course (e.g., scoring of exams);
  - Safety components of products (e.g., AI applications in robot-assisted surgery);
  - Employment, worker management, and access to self-employment (e.g., resume-sorting software for recruitment procedures);
  - Essential private and public services (e.g., credit scoring that may deny citizens the opportunity to obtain a loan);
  - Law enforcement that may interfere with people's fundamental rights (e.g., evaluation of the reliability of evidence);
  - Migration, asylum and border control management (e.g., verification of the authenticity of travel documents);

  - Administration of justice and democratic processes (e.g., applying the law to a concrete set of facts), and
  - Remote biometric identification systems.
- Limited risk: AI systems with specific transparency obligations. For example, when using AI systems such as chatbots, users should be aware that they are interacting with a machine so that they can make an informed decision whether to continue.
- Minimal risk: The proposal allows the free use of applications such as AI-enabled video games or spam filters. The vast majority of AI systems fall into this category. The draft regulation does not intervene here, as these AI systems present minimal or no risk to citizens' rights or safety.

In terms of governance, the European Commission has proposed that competent national market surveillance authorities should supervise the new rules, while the creation of a European Artificial Intelligence Board will facilitate their implementation, as well as driving the development of standards for AI. Additionally, voluntary codes of conduct are proposed for non-high-risk AI, along with regulatory sandboxes to facilitate responsible innovation (European Commission 2021b).

Study Questions

1. What are the core pillars of legal regulation?
2. What are autonomous machines?
3. Why is it important to regulate autonomous machines?
4. What are some of the key proposals for regulating autonomous machines in Europe?

References

Alsegier, R. A. 2016. "Roboethics: Sharing Our World with Humanlike Robots." *IEEE Potentials* 35(1): 24–28.

Armstrong S., N. Bostrom, and C. Schulman. 2016. "Racing to the Precipice: a Model of Artificial Intelligence Development." *AI & Society* 31: 201–6.

Arogyaswamy, B. 2020. "Big Tech and Societal Sustainability: an Ethical Framework." *AI & Society* 35: 829–40.

Appazov, A. 2014. "Legal Aspects of Cybersecurity." University of Copenhagen, Faculty of Law. https://www.justitsministeriet.dk/sites/default/files/media/Arbejdsomraader/Forskning/Forskningspuljen/Legal_Aspects_of_Cybersecurity.pdf.

Beltramini, E. 2019. "Evil and Roboethics in Management Studies." *AI & Society* 34: 921–29.

Bostrom, N. 2002. "Existential Risks: Analyzing Human Extinction Scenarios and Related Hazards." *Journal of Evolution and Technology* 9(1).

Bostrom, N. 2003. "Ethical Issues in Advanced Artificial Intelligence." Retrieved from https://nickbostrom.com/ethics/ai.html.

Bostrom, N. 2014. *Superintelligence: Paths, Dangers, Strategies*. Oxford University Press.

Bostrom, N. 2017. "Strategic Implications of Openness in AI Development." *Global Policy* 8(2): 1–14.

Bradley, P. 2020. "Risk Management Standards and the Active Management of Malicious Intent in Artificial Superintelligence." *AI & Society* 35: 319–28.

Cath, C., et al. 2018. "Artificial Intelligence and the 'Good Society': the US, EU, and UK Approach." *Science and Engineering Ethics* 24: 505–28.

Delvaux-Stehres, M. 2018. "There Is No Way a Robot Should be Treated like a Human Being." *Leaders League*. https://www.leadersleague.com/en/news/mady-delvaux-stehres-european-parliament-there-is-no-way-a-robot-should-be-treated-like-a-human-being.

den Hertog, J. A., 2010. "Review of Economic Theories of Regulation." Discussion Paper Series, No. 10–18. Utrecht School of Economics, Tjalling C. Koopmans Research Institute.

Easterbrook, F. H. 1996. "Cyberspace and the Law of the Horse." *University of Chicago Legal Forum* 1996: 207–16.

European Commission. 2019. "Liability for Artificial Intelligence and Other Emerging Digital Technologies." Expert Group on Liability and New Technologies.

European Commission. 2019. "Ethics Guidelines for Trustworthy AI." High-Level Expert Group on Artificial Intelligence.

European Commission. 2021a. *Proposal for a Regulation Laying Down Harmonised Rules on Artificial Intelligence (Artificial Intelligence Act)*. COM/2021/206 final.

European Commission. 2021b. "Europe Fit for the Digital Age: Commission Proposes New Rules and Actions for Excellence and Trust in Artificial Intelligence." Press release. https://ec.europa.eu/commission/presscorner/detail/en/ip_21_1682.

European Parliament. 2017. *Resolution with Recommendations to the Commission on Civil Law Rules on Robotics*. 2015/2103(INL).

European Parliament. 2020. *Artificial Intelligence in Criminal Law and Its Use by the Police and Judicial Authorities in Criminal Matters*. Draft report, 2020/2016(INI).

European Parliament. 2020. *Artificial Intelligence in Education, Culture and the Audiovisual Sector*. Draft report, 2020/2017(INI).

European Parliament. 2020. *Resolution on a Civil Liability Regime for Artificial Intelligence*. 2020/2014(INL).

European Parliament. 2020. *Resolution on a Framework of Ethical Aspects of Artificial Intelligence, Robotics and Related Technologies*, 2020/2012(INL).

European Parliament. 2020. *Resolution on Intellectual Property Rights for the Development of Artificial Intelligence Technologies*. 2020/2015(INI).

Floridi, L., et al. 2018. "AI4People—An Ethical Framework for a Good AI Society: Opportunities, Risks, Principles, and Recommendations." *Minds & Machines* 28: 689–707.

Guihot, M., et al. 2017. "Nudging Robots: Innovative Solutions to Regulate Artificial Intelligence." *Vanderbilt Journal of Entertainment & Technology* Law 20: 385–439.

Harrison, J. L. 2011. "Regulation, Deregulation, and Happiness." *Cardozo Law Review* 32: 2369–89.

Holowchak, M. 2010. "Technology and Freudian Discontent: Freud's 'Muffled' Meliorism and the Problem of Human Annihilation." *Sophia* 49: 95–111.

Huang, T. J. 2017. "Imitating the Brain with Neurocomputer a 'New' Way Towards Artificial General Intelligence." *International Journal of Automation and Computing* 14: 520–31.

Kagermann, H., et al. 2013. *Securing the Future of German Manufacturing Industry: Recommendations for Implementing the Strategic Initiative Industrie 4.0, Final Report of the Industrie 4.0 Working Group*. Forschungsunion im Stifterverband für die Deutsche Wirtschaft e.V.

Kalanov, T. 2016. "Man vs. Computer: Difference of the Essences. The Problem of the Scientific Creation." *International Journal of Contemporary Research and Review* 7(12): 20161–84.

Kaufmann, A. 1963. "The Ontological Structure of Law." *Natural Law Forum*, Paper 95. http://scholarship.law.nd.edu/nd_naturallaw_forum/95.

Leahy, S. M., et al. 2019. "The Digital Frontier: Envisioning Future Technologies Impact on the Classroom." *Futures* 113: 102422.

Lessig, L. 1999. "The Law of the Horse: What Cyberlaw Might Teach." *Harvard Law Review* 113(2): 501–49.

Mabaso, B. A. 2021. "Artificial Moral Agents Within an Ethos of AI4SG." *Philosophy & Technology* 34: 7–21.

"Open Letter to the European Commission: Artificial Intelligence and Robotics." http://www.robotics-openletter.eu.

Palmerini, E., et al. 2014. *Guidelines on Regulating Robotics, Report on Regulating Emerging Robotic Technologies in Europe: Robotics Facing Law and Ethics*. Guidelines on regulating robotics. RoboLaw deliverable D2.6, FP7-SiS project on regulating emerging robotic technologies in Europe: robotics facing law and ethics.

Rommetveit, K., N. van Dijk, and K. Gunnarsdóttir. 2020. "Make Way for the Robots! Human-and Machine-Centricity in Constituting a European Public–Private Partnership." *Minerva* 58: 47–69.

Schmidhuber, J. 2010. "The New AI is General and Mathematically Rigorous." *Frontiers of Electrical and Electronic Engineering in China* 5: 347–62.
Schwab K. 2016. "The Fourth Industrial Revolution: What It Means, How to Respond." World Economic Forum. https://www.weforum.org/agenda/2016/01/the-fourth-industrial-revolution-what-it-means-and-how-to-respond/.
Selznick, P. 1985. "Focusing Organisational Research on Regulation." In *Regulatory Policy and the Social Sciences*, edited by R. Noll, 363–67. University of California Press.
Sotala, K., and V. R. Yampolskiy. 2015. "Responses to Catastrophic AGI Risk: a Survey." *Physica Scripta* 90(1), 018001.
Torrance, S. 2013. "Artificial Agents and the Expanding Ethical Circle." *AI & Society* 28: 399–414.
Vaišvila, A. 2004. *Teisės teorija*. Justitia.
Veruggio, G., and F. Operto. 2006. "Roboethics: a Bottom-up Interdisciplinary Discourse in the Field of Applied Ethics in Robotics." *International Review of Information Ethics* 6.
Westerlund, M. 2020. "An Ethical Framework for Smart Robots." *Technology Innovation Management Review* 10(1): 35–44.
Yampolskiy, R., and J. Fox. 2013. "Safety Engineering for Artificial General Intelligence." *Topoi* 32: 217–26.
Yudkowsky, E., 2008. "Artificial Intelligence as a Positive and Negative Factor in Global Risk." In *Global Catastrophic Risks*, edited by N. Bostrom and M. N. Cirkovic, 308–45. Oxford University Press.

CHAPTER 17

Limits of Legal Automation

Darius Amilevičius

17.1 Legal Automation: Mission (Im)Possible?

Much has been written recently about artificial intelligence (AI) and law. One main goal of this chapter is to provide a realistic, demystified view of AI that is rooted in the actual capabilities of the technology, along with a high-level overview of AI and its use within law.

The technology of legal practice is changing rapidly. At its heart, "AI and law" involves the application of computer and mathematical techniques to make law more understandable, manageable, useful, accessible, or predictable. Pioneering researchers in the area of AI and law include Anne Gardner, L. Thorne McCarty, Kevin Ashley (Ashley 2017), Radboud Winkels, Market Sergot, Richard Susskind, Henry Prakken, Robert Kowalski, Trevor Bench-Capon, Edwina Rissland, Kincho Law, Karl Branting, Michael Genesereth, Roland Vogl, Bart Verheij, Guido Governatori, Giovanni Sartor, Ronald Stamper, Carole Hafner, Layman Allen, and many others. But since about 2000, the realm of AI and law has turned away from knowledge-representation techniques toward machine learning–based approaches, like the AI field more generally. One useful way of thinking about the use of AI within law today is to conceptually divide it into three categories of AI users: the administrators of law (i.e., those who create and apply the law, including judges, legislators, administrative officials, and police), the practitioners of law (i.e., those who use AI in legal practice, primarily attorneys), and those who are governed by law (i.e., the people, businesses, and organizations that must follow the law to achieve their ends) (Surden 2019).

But what is AI in the context of the relation to the practice of law? The literal meaning of the word *artificial* is synthetic, which often has a negative connotation of being an inferior substitute. However, artificial objects (e.g., flowers) can closely approximate their counterparts, and sometimes they can be advantageous because they have no maintenance requirements (as real flowers require sunshine and water). From a cognitive point of view, *intelligence* is the ability to learn from experience and to adapt to, shape, and select environments (Sternberg 2012). Defining the phrase "artificial intelligence" is problematic. For the purposes of this paper, Raphael's (1976) definition may be best,

 | DOI:10.1163/9789004682900_022

under which artificial intelligence is the science of making machines do things that would require intelligence if done by man.

Automation means full or partial replacement of human functions within some system of intent. According to one view, AI should have little bearing upon legal practice, because legal practice is thought to require advanced cognitive abilities and such higher-order cognition remains outside the capability of current AI technology. In fact, modern AI algorithms are unable to replicate most human intellectual abilities, falling far short in advanced cognitive processes—such as analogical reasoning—that are basic to legal practice. Although there is some truth to that view, its conclusion is overly broad. It overlooks a class of legal tasks for which current AI technology can still have an impact despite its technological inability to match human-level reasoning. Consider that outside the field of law, non-cognitive AI techniques have been successfully applied to tasks that were once thought to necessitate human intelligence—for example, language translation.

According to a second view, nowadays there may be a limited but not insignificant subset of legal tasks that can be partially automated using current AI techniques, despite AI's limitations relative to human cognition. The discussions surrounding AI and law are decidedly futurist in nature, because in most cases they are speculating about the effects of AI developments that do not currently exist and may never materialize. For futurists, legal processes are essentially algorithmic in nature: data (the facts) are transformed into outputs (a judgment or result) via the application of set rules (the law) (Pasquale 2019). Although such conversations have their place, they entail significant, sometimes unsupported assumptions about where the technology is headed. That speculative type of discussion often distracts from the important, though perhaps less exotic, law and policy issues actually raised by AI technology today (Surden 2019).

In the context of legal automation, it is very important to understand what today's AI technology is not. When many people hear the term "AI," they imagine current AI systems as thinking machines. However, today's AI systems are decidedly not intelligent thinking machines in any meaningful sense. Rather, they can produce useful, intelligent results without intelligence. These do so largely through heuristics—i.e., detecting patterns in data and using knowledge, rules, and information that have been specifically encoded by people into forms that can be processed by computers.

In addition, we must note that human natural language is often constitutive of law and legal judgments. Language does not merely represent one of many forms the law can take but is the only form capable of realizing foundational principles of the rule of law. Recognition of this power of language should guide the future of legal automation (Pasquale 2019). But at this time, natural language processing and understanding constitute one of the biggest obstacles for AI.

When attorneys are asked to use AI systems ethically, in fact several demands are being made of them, each of which requires regulation (including self-regulation) and technological capabilities of systems to be effective (Rogers and Bell 2019).

In sum, knowing the strengths and limits of current AI technologies is crucial to understanding AI's place within law. It helps users gain a realistic understanding of where AI is likely to impact the practice and administration of law and, just as importantly, where it is not.

17.2 Today's Legal Automation Systems: Intelligent Results without Intelligence

As a result of extensive private-sector and university research, AI-enabled computer systems have slowly begun to make their way into various facets of the legal system. Currently, AI is neither magic nor intelligent in the human-cognitive sense of the word. Current AI technologies produce intelligent results without intelligence by harnessing patterns, rules, and heuristic proxies that allow them to make useful decisions in certain, narrow contexts. Today's AI is not very good at dealing with abstractions, understanding meaning, transferring knowledge from one activity to another, or handling completely unstructured or open-ended tasks. Most tasks where AI has proven successful (e.g., chess, credit card fraud, tumor detection) involve highly structured areas with clear right and wrong answers and strong underlying patterns that can be algorithmically detected.

17.2.1 *Machine or Deep Learning and Its Application to Law*

Machine learning (ML) refers to a subfield of computer science concerned with computer programs that can learn from experience and thus improve their performance over time (Russel and Norwig 2021). The idea that computers are "learning" is largely a metaphor and does not imply that computer systems are artificially replicating the advanced cognitive systems thought to be involved in human learning (Witten et al. 2011). Commonly, ML algorithms are used to detect patterns in data so as to automate complex tasks or make predictions. They are closely associated with the larger enterprise known as predictive analytics, as researchers often employ ML methods to analyze existing data and predict the likelihood of uncertain outcomes. In high-level terms,

ML is a subset of AI that is capable of solving tasks that are not feasible or too cumbersome with "traditional" programming languages.

Despite the variety of ML algorithms, the data are arguably more important than the selected algorithm. Many issues can arise with data, such as insufficient data, poor quality of data, incorrect data, missing data, irrelevant data, and duplicate data values (Campesato 2020). ML can be divided into the following types: (1) *supervised learning* (relying on lots of labeled data produced manually by humans), (2) *semi-supervised learning* (lots of partially labeled data), (3) *unsupervised learning* (lots of unlabeled data, no human participation), and 4) *reinforcement learning* (trial, feedback, and improvement). According to Andrew Ng, nowadays "99% of all ML is supervised."

One important subfield of ML is deep learning (DL), which focuses on neural networks and algorithms for training neural networks. DL comprises many types of neural networks. A DL model requires at least two hidden layers in a neural network; very deep learning involves neural networks with at least ten hidden layers. Currently, DL can surpass humans in some image classification and other tasks. DL introduces deep neural networks with new algorithms and new architectures (e.g., convolutional neural networks, recurrent neural networks, and long short-term memory networks).

DL focuses on finding patterns in datasets, but generalizing those results is a more difficult task. Some initiatives have attempted to explain more fully the outcomes of neural networks, but such work is still in its infancy (see the next subsection). Although deep learning is powerful and has produced impressive results in many fields, some important ongoing challenges are being explored, including (1) bias in algorithms, (2) susceptibility to adversarial attacks, (3) limited ability to generalize, (4) lack of explainability, and (5) DL algorithms' ability to determine correlation but not causality (Campesato 2020).

In a recent interview, Geoffrey Hinton[1] has expressed the opinion that state-of-the-art DL technologies will ultimately be able to do everything, but only after quite a few conceptual breakthroughs. For example, in 2017 Ashish Vaswani et al. (Vaswani et al. 2017) introduced transformers, which derive really good vectors representing word meanings. It was a conceptual breakthrough. We need a bunch more breakthroughs like that one. But we also need a massive increase in scale. The human brain has about 100 trillion parameters,

---

1 Geoffrey Honton is one of the so-called "godfathers" of AI. For his foundational contributions to the field, Hinton won the Turing Award, alongside fellow AI pioneers Yann LeCun and Yoshua Bengio. His opinion is taken from a recent interview (MIT, 2020); see https://www.technologyreview.com/2020/11/03/1011616/ai-godfather-geoffrey-hinton-deep-learning-will-do-everything/.

or synapses. What we now call a really big model, such as GPT-3 (Brown et al. 2020), has 175 billion (making it a thousand times smaller than the brain). Common sense is the next big capability to tackle. Models such as GPT-3, which generates wonderful text, must understand a lot to generate that text, but it's not quite clear how much it actually understands.

If performing well, ML algorithms may produce automated results that approximate those that a similarly situated person would have made. ML is thus often considered a branch of AI, since a high-performing algorithm may produce automated results that appear "intelligent." Because ML has been successfully employed in a number of complex areas previously considered exclusively in the domain of human intelligence, the question arises as to what extent these techniques might be applied within the practice of law.

A subset of legal tasks often performed manually today by attorneys are potentially partially automatable with techniques such as ML, provided that the limitations are understood and accounted for. I say "partially" because often the goal of such automation is not to replace an attorney but, rather, to act as a complement. The ML algorithms do not and cannot take over such crucial tasks as determining whether certain ambiguous documents are relevant under uncertain law, or whether they will have significant strategic value in litigation. Rather, in many cases, the algorithms can reliably filter out large but probably irrelevant swaths of documents so that the attorney does not have to waste limited cognitive resources analyzing them. Additionally, these algorithms can highlight certain potentially relevant documents for increased attention.

ML algorithms are better suited for some tasks than for others. By generalizing about the type of tasks that ML algorithms perform particularly well, we can define where such algorithms could impact legal practice. Likely areas include (1) legal prediction, (2) finding hidden relationships in data, (3) judicial decisions and data relationships, and (4) document classification and clustering (Surden 2014).

In sum, AI techniques—especially ML—have been successfully applied to problems that had traditionally been believed to require human cognition. But since current AI technology cannot match the abstract analysis and higher-order cognitive abilities routinely displayed by trained attorneys, current AI techniques may have little impact upon law, barring significant technological advances. On the other hand, statistical and other heuristic-based assessments of data can sometimes produce automated results in complex tasks that, while possibly less accurate than results produced by human cognitive processes, can be sufficiently accurate for certain purposes that do not demand extremely high levels of precision and accuracy.

17.2.2 *From Black Box Models to White Box Models*

From a legal standpoint, AI remains a form of automatic processing of data. As such, just like any other method that processes data automatically, AI must follow the rules established by the international community, which compel AI designers to explain how decisions are reached. Explainable AI (XAI) has become a legal obligation, because XAI must be not only for developers, but for users too. The legal problem of AI worsens because to function effectively, an algorithm requires huge volumes of data. Collecting data requires access to networks, emails, text messages, social networks, hard disks, and more. Designers and developers need to add ethical rules to AI algorithms so that technological development will not be slowed down by regulations and fines.

Algorithm explainability began with the first complex machines in the 1940s, starting with the Turing machine. Alan Turing himself struggled to explain how the intelligence of his machine solved encryption problems. In today's era of AI, accurately interpreting and communicating trustworthy AI findings are crucial skills to master. The results of ML models can often prove difficult and sometimes impossible to explain, so both users and developers face challenges when asked to explain how and why an AI decision was made. The AI designer cannot possibly create a single explainable AI solution for the hundreds of ML and DL models.

European and U.S. law has established a risk of litigation when results cannot be explained, but developers deal with overwhelming amounts of data and results in real-life implementations, making it nearly impossible to find explanations without the proper tools. The exponential progress of AI, including rule-based expert systems, ML algorithms, and DL, has led to the most complex algorithms in history. The difficulty of explaining AI (i.e., making it understandable and plain) has grown proportionally to the progress made.

Interpreting tells the meaning of something. AI literature often refers to a black box, or a system whose internal workings are hidden and not understood. A black-box AI model takes an input, runs one or several algorithms, and produces an output that might work but remains obscure. But there is another formal definition of a black box that contradicts the first one. This second definition describes the flight recorder in an aircraft. In this case, the black box records all the information in real time so that a team of experts can analyze the timeline of a given flight in minute detail. In other words, it contains detailed information. Similarly, in computer systems, a log file records events, messages between systems, and any other type of information the designers of a system saw fit to include in the process. As such, the log file is the approximate equivalent of an aircraft flight recorder. To avoid confusion, when a log file or any other means of recording or extracting information is referred to, we commonly use the term *white box.*

Once a user or developer has access to the information of a white box model, he or she will need to explain and interpret the data provided. To illustrate XAI, let's suppose that some virus has infected the patient. Both the health AI program and the doctor have made a mistake. The error made by AI has gone undetected, since the AI algorithm has run with perfect accuracy. The critical issue for the AI specialists resides in the fact that at first, the doctor does not trust AI or any other system to make life-or-death decisions. A doctor needs to be able to trust the XAI system enough to let it help with a decision. And this constitutes the heart of XAI—if an algorithm runs with perfect accuracy but does not provide the diagnosis that will save a patient's life, the prediction is either a false positive or a false negative. XAI goes beyond theoretical AI and puts the human user at the center of the process, forcing humans to get involved in the field the dataset was built for (Rothman 2020).

In sum, machines compute, but humans construe. Machines can outperform humans in many fields, but humans can reduce machines to dust with ethics. Machine intelligence takes raw data, makes sense of it, and can produce predictions. Humans take raw data, interpret it, and make careful decisions to avoid conflicts. Everything goes well as long as these two forms of intelligence converge. When they collide, the machine, or rather its owner, will have a tremendous price to pay.

17.2.3 *Logical Rules and Knowledge Representation*

Another major branch of AI is representation of logical rules and knowledge. Representation of the law in computer programs is not a new idea. There can be implicit or explicit representation of the law. The latter is preferable, because it allows the representation to be assessed for accuracy and can provide some justification for the conclusions the system produces (Bench-Capon 1991).

The goal behind this area of AI is to model real-world phenomena or processes in a form that computers can use, typically for the purpose of automation. Often, this involves programmers providing a computer with a series of rules that represent the underlying logic and knowledge of whatever activity the programmers are trying to model and automate. Knowledge representation has a long and distinguished history in the field of AI research and has contributed to many so-called expert systems. Typically, system designers try to translate experts' knowledge into a series of formal rules and structures that a computer can process.

To create a tax preparation system, for example, software developers, in consultation with tax attorneys and other experts in personal income tax laws, translate the meaning and logic of tax provisions into a set of comparable formal rules that a computer can process. These methods based on knowledge, logic, and rules involve a top-down approach to computation—that is, programmers must explicitly provide the computer with all its operating and decision rules ahead of time. This is in contrast to the bottom-up ML approach, where the computer algorithm organically determines its operating rules on its own. Although they have not made as large an impact as ML systems, there is a power in this explicit, top-down knowledge representation.

Once rules have been represented in a computer programming language, a computer can manipulate them in deductive chains to reach nonobvious conclusions about the world. Additionally, knowledge-based AI systems can harness the power of computing to reveal hard-to-detect details—such as contradictions—embedded in systems that a human would not be able to discern (Surden 2019).

As noted above, the knowledge base originates from the expert system or knowledge-based system, which was first developed by AI researchers. A knowledge-based system consists of two components: a knowledge base and an inference engine. The inference engine represents logical assertions and conditions about the world. The first knowledge-based systems represented facts about the world as simple assertions in a flat database and used rules to reason regarding these assertions. With the evolution of database systems and information extraction techniques, knowledge bases have become larger and more dynamic, able to manage both structured and non-structured data in various domains. They enable data to be linked between sources and to be understood by computers so that they can perform sophisticated tasks on behalf of humans. The knowledge base is one of the most essential components in realizing the idea of a semantic system. It has recently received much research attention as a resource for providing knowledge, an auxiliary tool for facilitating the work of search engines, and an expert system to support decision making in various domains (Zhang and Sheng 2018).

Knowledge-and rules-based AI systems, in the right setting, can be very powerful tools. The idea of creating legal knowledge bases, or more generally knowledge-based systems, is not new. Legal knowledge bases have been developed in the past for diverse tasks including citation analysis, e-governance, criminal law analysis, and legal advice systems. However, the scope of these tasks has mostly been confined within a single document and, in some cases, to small databases, so as to understand the provisions of a particular law, the argumentation structure of a particular legal case, or the logical reasoning of a particular court procedure.

Nowadays, an approach to constructing a logically sound legal knowledge base that allows for large-scale analyses has emerged. In Europe, the OPENLAWS.eu Consortium is developing an open platform where laws, cases, and legal literature from all member states will be publicly available. Gupta et al. (2017) have applied this approach to a corpus of over 1.1 million judicial records from Henan, China to build a legal knowledge base of Chinese judicial documents for large-scale analytics.

17.2.4 *Hybrid Systems*

As noted above, there are, at a high level, two broad ways to program computer systems to perform AI tasks. The first approach involves ML, where systems rely on algorithms to detect patterns in data that can be harnessed to make intelligent decisions. The second approach involves knowledge representation and logical rules, in which explicit facts and rules about some activity are explicitly programmed into software, harnessing the knowledge of domain experts about how some system or activity operates. Both AI approaches can be effective depending on the domain, and some AI systems actually are combinations of multiple techniques.

ML–Knowledge Representation Hybrid Systems. Many modern AI systems are hybrids of these two approaches. For example, self-driving cars operate using trained ML systems that help them drive. The system learns to drive itself through a repeated training process, by which it automatically infers appropriate driving behavior. However, much of the behavior of the self-driving car also involves explicit rules and knowledge representation. In many autonomous vehicle projects, humans have hand-coded a series of rules, based on their knowledge of driving, that represent generally appropriate behavior. For example, the behavior that one should generally stop at a stop sign is likely to be hand-coded. In addition, human coders manually update features on maps, such as identifying stop signs. A complex AI system such as a self-driving vehicle must rely upon a mix of AI technologies, including ML models as well as hand-coded knowledge-representation rules about the world. The larger point is that humans need not think of AI systems as exclusively involving one approach or another; often, they are a mixture of the two.

Human-AI System Hybrids and Humans in the Loop. Most ML models rely on data prepared by humans. But the interaction between humans and machines doesn't stop there. The most powerful systems are set up to allow both sides to interact continuously through a mechanism commonly referred to as "humans in the loop" or HITL.

Many real-world applications such as military planning problems, supply and logistics, vehicle routing, production planning, manufacturing, and health care planning systems require taking action in time-critical situations. The command and control of these complex, dynamic systems often requires integrating human operators into the decision-making process. Successful system performance then depends on the effectiveness and efficiency of human–computer interactions and the timeliness of the resulting output. Many successful contemporary AI systems are not fully autonomous but, rather, involve hybrids of computer and human decision making.

A fully autonomous system makes all important decisions about its own activity. Delays and failures in making decisions are often expensive in terms of money, system performance, and sometimes even human lives. Both humans and computer algorithms have strengths and limitations, and their strengths can be integrated through a joint cognitive problem-solving approach. Human cognitive skills are limited when voluminous data must be interpreted and analyzed, whereas computer algorithms can fail when heuristic or intuitive knowledge about the system is required. A hybrid solution can thus improve the system's overall performance. The primary benefit of an integrated human–machine system is to increase the effectiveness of decision makers in situations where the computer can support and enhance human judgment (Ganapathy et al. 2011). The system will defer to a human to make a difficult judgment or assessment that remains outside the system's capability or for which a computer decision is deemed societally inappropriate.

A self-driving vehicle driving autonomously may not know what to do if, for instance, a police vehicle temporarily reroutes vehicles onto a sidewalk. One popular approach in self-driving cars is known as "remote assistant." When a self-driving vehicle encounters a situation where it doesn't know what to do, it can essentially call for help to a call center staffed by people. The staff can respond by taking remote control of the vehicle, steering it around the difficult situation, and then returning it to autonomous mode once things appear normal.

The more general point here is that many complex AI systems will not be fully autonomous but will keep humans in the loop for particularly difficult judgments or assessments beyond state-of-the-art AI. For this reason, partially autonomous, human-in-the-loop systems are nowadays common in the legal domain (Surden 2019).

17.3 A Brief Overview of the Actual Market Situation of AI in Law and Legal Practice

The idea that technology can support better access to legal services and contribute to the provision of legal services is non-controversial. In many areas of human activity, technological advances have made goods and services cheaper and more accessible. In the legal space, especially for eDiscovery, components such as linguistic intelligence, content classification, emotional intelligence, and behavioral intelligence now are used by legal teams to mine data for patters and anomalies, map custodian relationships and conversations, autonomously classify millions of documents, and target incidents at the source. But the use of legal AI software goes beyond eDiscovery. Legal professionals at in-house legal departments, law firms, and alternative legal service providers use AI tools to help with case outcome predictions, due diligence, contract review, contract management, and non-disclosure agreements. Nowadays, legal AI software is not man against machine. Rather, today's real-world AI solutions help attorneys and allied professionals accomplish data analysis and review at a level beyond human capacities.

Based on recent surveys and assessment of companies in the field and their offerings, current applications of legal AI software appear to fall in five major categories.

1. Legal case management software, which covers workflow management, billing and invoicing, and reporting and analytics. Legal case management software has many benefits for law firms and solo attorneys: (a) increasing revenue by making it easier to track billable hours, ensuring that attorneys get paid for every minute they spend on case work; (b) streamlining time-consuming processes; (c) managing deadlines; and (d) making better decisions. One recent survey identified a list of 25 especially popular companies.[2]
2. Due diligence. The due diligence process assesses a legal situation and is required to intelligently advise clients on what their options are and what actions they should take. Doing extensive due diligence can positively impact long-term shareholder returns, but the process can also be very time-consuming and tedious. Moreover, lawyers are prone to mistakes and inaccuracy when doing spot checks. In 2021, the top picks in this group (among 35 candidates) were Kira Systems (https://kirasystems.com) and Leverton (https://leverton.ai).

2 https://www.capterra.com/legal-case-management-software/.

3. Prediction technology, in which an AI software generates results that forecast the outcome of litigation. The leaders in 2021 (again among 35 candidates) were Intraspexion (www.intraspexion.com), which searches for high-risk documents and displays them according to the level of risk that the AI has determined; Ravel Law (http://ravellaw.com), able to identify outcomes based on relevant case law, judge rulings, and referenced language from more than 400 courts; and (c) Lex Machina (https://lex machina.com), with a variety of features that assist lawyers in their legal strategy.
4. Legal analytics. Case documents and docket entries provide supplementary insights during litigation. Current AI tools claim to be able to extract key data points from these documents to support arguments. Lawyers can use data points from past case law, win/loss rates, and a judge's history to identify trends and patterns. In 2021, the leaders among the 35 competitors in this set were Lex Machina and Ravel Law.
5. Document automation. Law firms use software templates to create completed documents based on data input. Many software companies in this field claim that the final document, which could take days if drafted manually, can be generated in a matter of minutes. As of 2021, the most popular of the 35 companies in this space were Neota Logic System, with its software PerfectNDA (www.neotalogic.com/solution/perfectnda/), and TrademarkNow (www.trademarknow.com).

Among the dozens of AI legal technology companies and applications, there remain many looming questions with respect to adoption. Replacing the role of human legal experts, for now, is clearly controversial. The main formal objection is that it is simply not possible to automate the intellectual activities central to resolving legal questions. Moreover, the legal profession has long relied on maximizing billable hours. For this reason, merely eliminating manual (even boring) tasks will probably not be a strong enough factor to drive AI adoption. Rather, the pressure to adopt AI will likely come from peer pressure. Firms with no ability to automate may find themselves relatively overpriced for legal services that other firms have largely automated away.[3]

3 https://emerj.com/ai-sector-overviews/ai-in-law-legal-practice-current-applications/.

17.4 Conclusion

Understanding the technology allows attorneys and lawyers to see why AI tends to be useful for certain types of tasks and not others. This knowledge is important to inform a critical evaluation of where AI is or is not likely to impact law for the foreseeable future. People occasionally assume that because AI has successfully automated one complex task, it can naturally be used to automate nearly any other type of complex task. However, existing AI tends to be narrowly tailored for specific types of tasks with particular characteristics. It is a mistake, for example, to assume that just because AI successfully beat a grandmaster in the game of Go—a famously difficult game—the same technology will lead to the automation of creative legal argumentation or problem solving.

Current AI technology tends to work best in situations characterized by underlying patterns, unambiguous rules, definitive right answers, and semi-formal or formal structures that make up the process. By contrast, AI tends to perform poorly, or not at all, in areas that are conceptual, abstract, value-laden, open-ended, policy-or judgment-oriented; require common sense or intuition; involve persuasion or arbitrary conversation; or involve engagement with the meaning of real-world humanistic concepts, such as societal norms, social constructs, or social institutions.

Study Questions

1. Is legal automation a "mission possible" in the near future?
2. Does moral and ethical regulation have an impact on the development of AI technologies and their application in the legal domain?
3. What limitations do machine learning and deep learning have regarding their potentially vast application in the practice of law?
4. What impact would a biased dataset have on the performance quality of a deep learning system?
5. How do you understand the concept of a "human in the loop"?

References

Ashley, K. 2017. *Artificial Intelligence and Legal Analytics: New Tools for Law Practice in the Digital Age*. Cambridge University Press.

Brown, T. B., et al. 2020. "Language Models Are Few-Shot Learners." https://arxiv.org/pdf/2005.14165.pdf.

Bench-Capon T., ed. 1991. *Knowledge-Based Systems and Legal Applications*. London: Academic Press.

Campesato, O. 2020. *Artificial Intelligence, Machine Learning, and Deep Learning*. Mercury Learning.

Ganapathy, S., et al. 2011. "Interactive Model-Based Decision Making for Time-Critical Vehicle Routing." In *Human-in-the-Loop Simulations*, edited by L. Rothrock and S. Narayanan, 203–20. Springer.

Gupta, A., et al. 2017. "Toward Building a Legal Knowledge-Base of Chinese Judicial Documents for Large-Scale Analytics." *International Conference on Legal Knowledge and Information Systems* (JURIX 2017: the Thirtieth Annual Conference): 135–44.

Pasquale, F. 2019. "A Rule of Persons, Not Machines: the Limits of Legal Automation." *George Washington Law* Review 87(1): 1–54.

Raphael, B. 1976. *The Thinking Computer: Mind Inside Matter*. W. H. Freeman.

Rogers, J., and F. Bell. 2019. "The Ethical AI Lawyer: What Is Required of Lawyers When They Use Automated Systems?" *Law, Technology and Humans* 1(1): 80–99.

Rothman, D. 2020. *Hands-On Explainable AI (XAI) with Python*. Packt Publishing Ltd.

Russell, S., and P. Norvig. 2021. *Artificial Intelligence: a Modern Approach*. Pearson.

Sternberg, R. 2012. "Intelligence." *WIREs Cognitive Science* 3(5): 501–11.

Surden, H. 2014. "Machine Learning and Law." *Washington Law Review* 89(1): 87–114.

Surden, H. 2019. "Artificial Intelligence and Law: an Overview." *Georgia State University Review* 35(4). https://readingroom.law.gsu.edu/gsulr/vol35/iss4/8.

Vaswani, A., et al. 2017. *Attention Is All You Need*. https://arxiv.org/pdf/1706.03762.pdf.

Witten, I., et al. 2011. *Data Mining: Practical Machine Learning Tools and Techniques*. Elsevier.

Zhang, W., and Q. Sheng. 2018. *Managing Data from Knowledge Bases: Querying and Extraction*. Springer.

CHAPTER 18

Responsible Standardization

Vladislav V. Fomin

18.1 Introduction

> Until the 1980s standards setting had been primarily an internal matter for firms or the domain of private sector technical bodies at the national level. Each country produced its own standards without much regard for what others were doing. International standards were few and far between, prescribing specifications for widely used products such as thickness of credit cards (0.76 mm), the sensitivity of photographic film (ISO ratings), the dimensions of freight containers, the thread pitch of screws, and the reference temperature for measurements of industrial length.
>
> MATTLI AND BÜTHE 2003, 1

What is standardization, what makes it responsible or irresponsible, and why is the topic of standardization of interest to students outside engineering disciplines?

The growing academic interest in standardization is related to global economic and societal developments in general, and to the expanding role of technologies in business and private life in particular. As news and policy headlines sparkle with such terms as the fourth Industrial Revolution, and as the EU and national leaders promote versatile initiatives on digitization of services, including science fiction echoing "RoboLaw," it becomes difficult to underestimate the importance of technology to the operation of our society. In most cases, the technologies we use are the product of standardization processes, due to how national and international markets are organized. For instance, if a company is intending to sell a technology product internally in its national market or to export it, a number of certifications will be required to make sure that it meets certain safety, technology, environmental, or other standards (Hesser et al. 2006).

For virtually any product to enter a national or international market, the product must meet certain safety, technology, health, environmental, usability, or other standards. Consider how hotels are rated as having up to five "stars" as an assessment of quality. That is an everyday example of how standards are applied.

 | DOI:10.1163/9789004682900_023

> Do a simple experiment to see how many products you use on a daily basis claim to adhere to standards. Flip over any electronic gadget you use to study or work—a keyboard, a laptop, a tablet device, or a phone charger. You will see a series of pictograms on the back side of the device: CE, PCT, FCC, ULL, and maybe others. These all signal that the product has been certified according to the relevant standards, where the letters correspond to certain organizations responsible for the product certification. In many cases, those organizations decide whether the product can be sold in the specific market, depending on whether it meets the standard's requirements.

Although the standardization of products and services is a largely unknown topic to most laypeople, this issue has been acquiring greater importance for scholars and policymakers due to the growing role of technologies and technology-based services in our societies and the intricate and tight dependencies they introduce with the lives, private and business affairs, and well-being of people around the world. As one example of standardization efforts designed to support well-being, we could cite the already-mentioned Robolaw, which deals with the introduction of artificial intelligence (AI) in judicial systems. The rubrics of cyber-physical systems (European Commission 2013) also exemplify the introduction of technologies into people's lives as part of rehabilitation, assisted living, prosthetics, and so on. In recognition of this growing importance of standards, the European Commission has been launching various activities.

Why and how can the growing importance of technologies in our lives be a proxy for the importance of the topic of standards and standardization in such disciplines as law, ethics, health, and business? Why has the European Commission been introducing various initiatives focused on building expert knowledge on standardization, including the program to launch Europe-wide education on the topic (European Commission 2017)? To answer these questions, let's examine what is understood by standards and standardization and what implications those phenomena have for citizens, companies, and markets.

18.2 What Are a Standard and Standardization?

There are many definitions of the word "standard," and different types of standards can be distinguished. A technical standard is an established norm or requirement related to technical systems. It is usually defined in a document as a set of specifications that manufacturers must adhere to. The word "standard" can also refer to methods, processes, and practices, in which case the word "norm" can be used instead.

Among the most familiar general public standards are A4 (in Europe) and Letter (in the U.S.) office paper sizes. The standard prescribes specific characteristics (the dimensions) of the sheet of paper, but it does not prescribe the manufacturing method. A standard can also do the opposite, i.e., prescribing a method for doing something without imposing any specific characteristics of the product subject to that method. As an example, consider environmental testing standards for detecting the presence of harmful substances in the air. Standardization, then, in general terms, can be defined as the process of making a standard.

The importance of standards and standardization for scholars and practitioners in different domains can be demonstrated by asking simple questions about the legitimacy, coerciveness, and unbiased nature of standards we use:

- Who has defined the safety and health norms for the products we use?
- Is it compulsory for the manufacturers of the products to follow the safety, health, or environmental standards defined for the specific products they produce and sell?
- Can a nationally adopted standard (e.g., in the health or education domain) be based on technologies that are subject to royalty payments? If so, who has to pay the intellectual property (IP) or patent royalties, and to whom?
- Who can participate in the process of standard development? Can a participant in a standardization process promote his or her own proprietary interests at the expense of, for example, national or societal interests?

These questions lay the groundwork for a discussion of responsible standardization. Let us explore these concepts in more detail.

18.2.1 *The Issues of Legitimacy, Coerciveness, and "Bias-Free" Standardization*

Who defines what health or safety standards the products we use must adhere to? Let's take a look at one product likely to gain prominence in the near future: automated and semi-automated vehicles. If you were to trust your vehicle to drive you home from a party, would it make a difference whether the lane keeping assistance system (LKAS) in your car conformed to international safety standards?

Standards typically originate from standard setting organizations (SSOs, also referred to as standard development organizations or SDOs) or industry consortia, where interested stakeholders develop a standard through specified consensus mechanisms. Standards developed and released by formal bodies such as the International Standards Organisation (ISO) are referred to as *de jure* standards, meaning that they come from a recognized legal entity (hence "de jure" or according to the law) and that the development of the standard took place according to the specified rules for reaching consensus.

The International Standards Organisation (ISO) is an independent, non-governmental international organization with a membership of 165 national standards bodies. Established in 1946, ISO brings together experts to share knowledge and develop voluntary, consensus-based, market-relevant international standards that support innovation and provide solutions to global challenges.

Go to www.iso.org and look for this particular standard: "ISO 11270:2014. Intelligent transport systems—Lane keeping assistance systems (LKAS)—Performance requirements and test procedures." If you scroll down the page, you can find a "Buy" button to purchase the technical documentation describing all the features of LKAS. Further down, you can learn that the standard was developed in the Technical Committee (TC) ISO/TC 204. If you click on the committee number, you can find more information on the scope and mission of the TC, its chairman, the work groups (WGs) in the TC, and the tasks assigned to each WG.

Now go to the website of Tesla, the leader in the electric car market. You have likely heard that Tesla cars have a semi-or fully automated autopilot driving mode. Try to find information on which technology safety standards the Tesla LKAS system conforms to.

If you had to choose between two very similar cars with a semi-or fully automatic autopilot function, would you choose the one with an LKAS system that conforms to the international ISO standard or the one that conforms to a proprietary standard of the manufacturer? Any ISO standard can be purchased online for a small fee so that you can study it in detail. Could you obtain similar access to a proprietary manufacturer's standard?

De facto standards can be released by industry consortia or by any kind of organization. When a proprietary standard developed by a single company becomes widely used, it begins to be referred to as a *de facto* standard, even though we cannot know whether or not it was developed through a consensus mechanism.

"De jure" is often (and in my view quite misleadingly) associated with the mandatory nature of a standard—i.e., when the use of a standard is required by law. However, *de jure* standards are not mandatory by definition. For example, national authorities can set compulsory *de facto* or *de jure* standards that local market players must adhere to. Automotive vehicle crash safety standards are an example of a mandatory *de jure* standard. An example of a mandatory *de facto* standard could be the adoption of Adobe's PDF (portable document format) in national e-government initiatives prior to 2005. In other words, prior to 2005, many national governments identified PDF as a document type that must be used in citizen-to-government (C2G) or government-to-government (G2G) electronic document exchanges.

A headline in the *Detroit News* on January 14, 2021 read, "Self-Driving Vehicles Allowed to Skip Some Crash Safety Standards under New Rule." The news report explained, "The Trump administration issued final rules Thursday that will allow self-driving vehicle manufacturers to skip certain federal crash safety requirements in vehicles that aren't designed to carry people." This report indicates that there are federal requirements for crash safety standards, that they are compulsory for automotive vehicle manufacturers, and that they were made non-compulsory for the manufacturers of self-driving vehicles.

Although the news report tells us about the coerciveness of the crash safety standards, it is silent on the origin of those standards—whether they were developed by SSO, an industry consortium, or some expert group led by the responsible committee of the federal government. Or were they perhaps simply passed on to the federal government from Tesla? Would the federal mandate to use Tesla proprietary crash safety standards be legitimate if the standards were intended to ensure the safety of all cars, drivers, and passengers on U.S. roads?

In 2005, the popular PDF document format changed its legal status from *de facto* to *de jure* by virtue of being released as ISO standard 19005–1:2005. This move by the Adobe corporation was prompted by many national governments' reluctance to mandate the use of a proprietary standard. Microsoft Office document formats (DOC, XLS, PPT) present a similar case. Originally developed as proprietary company products, those document formats attained global acceptance—i.e., they became *de facto* standards—and were passed on to formal SSOs only later to obtain the status of a *de jure* standard.

Rents and economies of scale associated with standards establish the significance of standardization in the development of national industries, compelling national governments to promote and protect the interests of local firms in the international standardization arena (Su and Fomin 2010). At the same time, the lack of standards or the existence of unfavorable standards is likely to create obstacles for market development and exports.

Reflecting on the history of Adobe PDF and Microsoft DOC document formats acquiring *de jure* status, do you think Adobe and Microsoft benefited from promoting their proprietary technologies to this status, given the compulsory status of those standards in e-government initiatives across the globe?

More often than not, the developers of standards receive substantial direct or indirect rents, usually due to the intellectual property rights or patents associated with the standard. When proprietary standards become a public good, as can be said of these document formats in the context of e-society rhetoric, can we say that the national governments that mandated the use of those standards were free of economic or political bias in making their decision?

18.2.2 *Is Today's Standardization Responsible?*

Departing from the historical view of standards as purely technological artifacts and standardization as the business of engineers, the topic of *responsible standardization* (RS) has been growing in importance recently (Jakobs 2020). RS calls for recognition of the fact that standards must not only deliver on the technical expectations of the handful of engineers participating in the standard's development process, but must also meet societal needs and follow the ethical norms of users of the technologies (Gordon and Fomin 2019), who are often completely ignorant regarding the standards, the standardization process, and the implications for products that support people's everyday lives.

The meaning of the term "responsible" in the context of standardization can be best explained as responsibility toward the public (Preston and Post 1975), an idea that became popularized in the early 2000s in business and academic domains under the tag of "corporate social responsibility" (Sen and Bhattacharya 2001).

To answer the question of whether a standardization process has indeed been designed to be responsible to the public, one must examine how standards are developed. Although most of the 100,000 or so standards in use today were and continue to be produced by formal SDOs, among which the largest number pertain to the already-mentioned ISO, International Electrotechnical Committee (IEC), and International Telecommunications Union (ITU), hundreds of consortia are also developing international standards. Among the best-known ones are the World Wide Web Consortium (W3C), overseeing development of Web standards; the 3rd Generation Partnership Project (3GPP), overseeing strategic coordination of mobile telecommunications standards bodies; and the Internet Engineering Task Force (IETF), which oversees the development of technical standards for the Internet.

The differences between different SDOs and industrial standards consortia are found in the rules for and fees of membership, the technology domains concerned, and the status of the standards produced, among other factors. What the two types of standards development have in common is that the development process is based on specified consensus mechanisms.

Thus, the answer to the question of responsible standardization to public can be pursued by answering another question: how is the public interest reflected or represented in the consensus mechanisms through which the standards come to be established?

Whereas industrial consortia standardization is obviously driven by corporate interests of the involved companies, one might expect the international standards development organizations to be free from or less affected by corporate interests and more focused on the interests of the public domain. Unfortunately, this is not the case.

One important organizational characteristic of international formal standards development is that international SDOs are the venue where representatives of National Standardization Organizations (NSOs) meet to engage in standards development. ISO, for example, has 157 national members, while the IEC has 72. In the United States, the situation is different, as the American National Standardization Institute (ANSI), which functions as the country's national standards oversight organization, has accredited more than 250 standards organizations that do most of the actual work.

On one hand, NSOs rely on the input of national stakeholders, which opens the door for representation of the public interest in the standardization process at the national level. However, international standards are developed at the international level, where work is organized in technical committees (TCs) and working groups (WGs), members of which (by the rules of SDO) cannot represent the interests of any particular national stakeholder (see Figure 18.1). NSO-nominated members to the international SDO's committees represent their *country's* interests in standardization decision making and act in their *personal capacity* in standard specifications development (for a detailed overview of the standardization process, see Bousquet et al. 2009).

The lack of representation of public interests is further aggravated by the very low level of public awareness regarding where the standards come from and how their development can be influenced. This situation has been described as a "blurred standardisation landscape," due to the lack of tools or methods for "seeing through" the process, let alone ensuring the incorporation of public concerns or ethical issues in standard development.

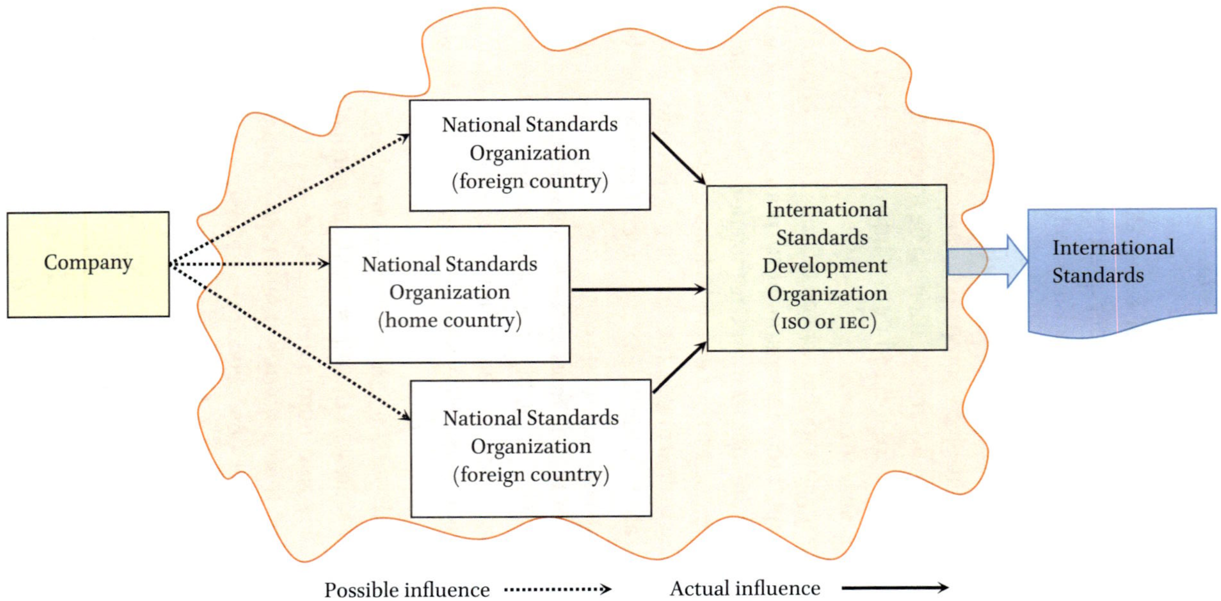

FIGURE 18.1 The process flow in the development of international standards
ADOPTED FROM BOUSQUET ET AL. (2011)

In response to the growing demand for corporate social responsibility in the early 2000s, the major SDOs have published codes of ethics (ISO 2004; ITU 2011) for their standard development processes. This move, however, has not resulted in any visible shift toward ethical standards or toward greater public visibility and awareness of standardization processes. Besides, even technically optimal standards developed according to a code of ethics may be misused by the general public, due to their lack of understanding of technology's inherently social and moral dimensions. One recent example is the "Dieselgate" scandal in the United States, in which environmental standards for carbon dioxide emissions designed to protect the public interest were intentionally bypassed by the trickery of a major car manufacturer seeking to gain a larger market share.

18.2.3 *Can Standardization Be Made More Responsible?*

Can standardization be made more responsible to the public if the development of standards is enriched by representation of the interests of traditionally excluded groups and stakeholders, such as consumers and impartial experts? Should the process of developing standards be left up to the market? In cases where standards have direct implications for people's well-being or even their very lives, can governments intervene in the standardization process by imposing certain ethical norms or requirements?

Although international standardization has existed for more than 150 years, during which it did not require any particular regulatory intervention, let alone ethical considerations, the advent of the new socio-technical paradigm established by the use of intelligent technologies, the Internet of Things (IoT), and other developments calls for closer examination of the problem.

Taking the discussion of legal rights for intelligent robots (IRs) as an example (Gordon 2020a and 2020b), once IRs have reached a certain level of rationality and autonomy (see the European Parliament's Resolution on Civil Law Rules on Robotics 2017), the discourse on implementing proper ethical standards to protect intelligent artificial beings should not take place solely in the free-market economy. One should instead see international governing institutions influencing standards development to avoid sole reliance on the corporate interests of the participating stakeholders.

On the other hand, governments traditionally have had no will, interest, nor budget for significant action in the standardization domain (Fomin et al. 2008, 470). With this backdrop, a possible way forward may be found in developing some type of interfacing model, according to which the government establishes ethical norms to be met in the application of standardized technologies within society and SDOs are obligated to adhere to these norms when developing technical standards.

18.3 Responsible Standardization for AI

AI has been recently enjoying a massive rise in popularity and has received considerable attention from scholars and the government for its ability to automate decisions that have traditionally been made by human experts. Smart systems, deploying AI-based technologies in medicine, law, engineering, and other domains, will eventually become ubiquitous, raising all sorts of associated ethical issues (primarily, though by no means exclusively, related to privacy and information security). These systems will be based on international standards, as discussed above. Shaping these standards so as to incorporate ethical aspects is the most effective (and possibly only) way to integrate these aspects into the systems that will eventually be implemented. This can be achieved only if all stakeholders (including, among others, societal groups, researchers, and policymakers) have the opportunity to be heard in the process. Accordingly, this requires cooperation between scientific research, society, and policymaking.

In the EU, we have seen a number of initiatives aimed at establishing this form of cooperation, such as the call for inclusiveness of the European Standardization System. While not directly related to standardization, a few initiatives to mention are the High-Level Expert Group on Artificial Intelligence, the European Ethical Charter on the Use of Artificial Intelligence in Judicial Systems and Their Environment (CEPEJ), and the 2021 Artificial Intelligence Act (EUROPEAN COMMISSION 2021).

Advances in the development of AI and its application to societal-level tasks and problems (such as RoboLaw, cyber-human systems, and automated driving) call for research that can contribute to developing a system of standard categories of levels of automation for managerial or user decision making, taking into account the risks and uncertainties involved in the AI context. Such a system could follow the example and success of ISO management system standards (MSSs), as described in the text box below.

Future research must juxtapose traditional decision-making tasks and categories with regard to technology use and interaction with technology-based services alongside the possibilities that new services and products deliver. It must carefully examine the risks and uncertainties involved, review business trends with regard to AI application, determine an appropriate regulatory system, and suggest what measures can and must be implemented in forthcoming standards for AI and AI-based services, so as to ensure that technology serves society responsibly.

Management System Standards (MSSs) developed by ISO have achieved truly global successes in a number of domains, starting with the quality management ISO 9001 series and continuing with the environmental management ISO 14001 series, the information security management systems (ISMS) ISO 27001 series, and others. The ISO website explains that MSSs "help organizations improve their performance by specifying repeatable steps that organizations consciously implement to achieve their goals and objectives, and to create an organizational culture that reflexively engages in a continuous cycle of self-evaluation, correction and improvement of operations and processes through heightened employee awareness and management leadership and commitment." For more information, see https://www.iso.org/management-system-standards.html.

18.4 Conclusions

The goal of responsible standardization is to incorporate ethical issues into the standardization of intelligent technologies and systems that will define modern life for future societies. To this end, we have reviewed (1) the concept and role of standardization, and the mechanisms for developing standards; (2) the concept of responsible standardization and ways of making standardization more responsive to societal needs; and (3) the concept and role of AI and other smart technologies in contemporary societal and technological development. Better understanding of those concepts and topics will facilitate more responsible standardization in the future. Knowledge of the advantages and risks of AI-based technologies, on one hand, and greater possibilities for participation in the standard-setting process (especially by traditionally underrepresented public stakeholders, such as end users, NGOs, and unions), on the other hand, can establish a foundation for more active and more critical societal involvement with the technological realities of our world.

Study Questions

1. What is meant by the term "standard"?

2. What types of standards can be distinguished based on their origin, level of coercion, and legal status?
3. Where do the majority of global standards come from?
4. What characteristics of the standardization process contribute to a standard being considered "responsible"?
5. What are the challenges on the road to establishing responsible standardization as a consistent practice?

References

Bousquet, F., V. V. Fomin, and D. Drillon. 2009. "Standardization: a Major Tool for Competitive Intelligence." *Proceedings of the 14th EURAS Workshop on Standardisation, Wissenschaftsverlag Mainz in Aachen*, 27–36.

Bousquet, F., V. V. Fomin, and D. Drillon. 2011. "Anticipatory Standards Development and Competitive Intelligence." *International Journal of Business Intelligence Research* 2: 16–30.

European Commission. 2013. *Cyber-Physical Systems: Uplifting Europe's Innovation Capacity* (p. ec.europa.eu/digital-agenda/en/cyber-physical-systems-1). Unit A3-DG CONNECT, Communications Networks, Content & Technology Directorate-General.

European Commission. 2017. *European Market Needs for Education in Standardisation/ Standardisation-related Competence*. Directorate-General for Internal Market, Industry, Entrepreneurship and SMEs (European Commission). https://op.europa.eu/en/publication-detail/-/publication/c013b068-e084-11e7-9749-01aa75ed71a1.

European Commission. 2021. *Proposal for a Regulation laying down harmonised rules on artificial intelligence* (*Artificial Intelligence Act*) (COM/2021/206 final). Commission to the European Parliament. https://digital-strategy.ec.europa.eu/en/library/proposal-regulation-laying-down-harmonised-rules-artificial-intelligence-artificial-intelligence.

Fomin, V. V., M. K. Pedersen, and H. J. de Vries. 2008. "Open Standards and Government Policy: Results of a Delphi Survey." *Communications of the Association for Information Systems* 22: 459–84.

Gordon, J.-S. 2020a. "Building Moral Robots: Ethical Pitfalls and Challenges." *Science and Engineering Ethics* 26(1): 141–57.

Gordon, J.-S. 2020b. "What Do We Owe to Intelligent Robots?" *AI & Society* 35(1): 209–23.

Gordon, J.-S., and V. V. Fomin. 2019. "Ethics and Standardization." In *Corporate Standardization Management and Innovation*, edited by K. Jakobs, 177–92. IGI Global.

Hesser, W., H. J. Vries, and A. Feilzer. 2006. *Standardisation in Companies and Markets*. Helmut Schmidt University Germany. http://www.asia-link-standardisation.de/index.php?section=project⊂=econtent.

ISO. 2004. *ISO Code of Ethics*. ISO. https://www.iso.org/publication/PUB100011.html.

ITU. 2011. *ITU Code of Ethics*. ITU. https://www.itu.int/en/general-secretariat/Documents/ethics/SO-2011-002-en.pdf.

Jakobs, K. 2020. "Responsibility by Design?! On the Standardisation of 'Smart' Systems." In *Smart Technologies and Fundamental Rights*, edited by J.-S. Gordon, 285–315. Brill.

Mattli, W., and Büthe, T. 2003. "Setting International Standards. Technological Rationality or Primacy of Power?" *World Politics* 56: 1–42.

Preston, L. E., and J. E. Post. 1975. *Private Management and Public Policy: the Principle of Public Responsibility*. Prentice-Hall.

Sen, S., and C. Bhattacharya. 2001. "Does Doing Good Always Lead to Doing Better? Consumer Reactions to Corporate Social Responsibility." *Journal of Marketing Research* 38(2): 225–43.

Su, J., and V. V. Fomin. 2010. "Balancing Public and Private Interests in ICT Standardization: the Case of AVS Codec." *What Kind of Information Society? Governance, Virtuality, Surveillance, Sustainability, Resilience* 328/2010: 64–72.

PART 5

Education

Introduction to Part 5

Education has been recognized as a human right in many national constitutions and at the European and international levels. Under European Union law and international agreements, states bear an obligation to realize the right to education, which entails important positive duties. Amongst others, states are urged to improve all aspects of the quality of education, to ensure that recognized and measurable learning outcomes are achieved, to build up knowledge on the use of information and communication technologies in education, and to emphasize the development of quality indicators and monitoring instruments (Commission on Human Rights 2002).

The Commentary on Article 14 of the Charter of Fundamental Rights of the European Union (CFR), which explains the scope of the right to education, suggests that the form and content of teaching must be acceptable, relevant, culturally appropriate, of good quality, and adaptable to the needs of students and changing societies (EU Network of Independent Experts on Fundamental Rights 2006). Providing citizens with access to quality education is considered an absolute priority, one that can be achieved only with strong national legal and policy frameworks that set the conditions for the delivery and sustainability of high-quality and relevant education (UNESCO 2014).

Quality and relevance in education are relative matters, not static concepts. They require continuous evaluation and adjustment to the changing knowledge requirements of society. European policy on education plays a significant role in the determination of what constitutes educational quality and relevance. Although sometimes criticized for driving the education sector toward more commercialization and commodification, such as through stressing cooperation with industry and competitive funding (Gideon 2015; Beech 2013), European policy on education is recognized as a powerful tool that highly influences national education systems. Despite its character as soft law, it certainly has changed and is still changing the landscape of European education and, hence, deserves considerable attention.

In recent years, EU policies have increasingly focused on digitalization as a crucial component of future education. They introduced the concept of "fit for the digital age" (Council of the European Union 2017a) and strongly urged the teaching of digital skills and competencies to all people, through all stages of education and life. The EU member states have communicated their interest in building a digital Europe and to providing the "best education and training" (Council of the European Union 2017b). Digital technologies in education are

 | DOI:10.1163/9789004682900_024

recognized as tools to achieve better quality in teaching and learning and to acquire essential skills and competencies.

Early EU policies on education, which originated from the Lisbon European Council of 2000, mostly covered infrastructure-related considerations, such as student-to-computer ratios and broadband access (Conrads et al. 2017). In the next few years, additional elements such as teacher training, competence building, and content development were included (Conrads et al. 2017). By 2011, all European countries had national policies for information and communication technology (ICT) in education (European Commission 2011a). Emerging technologies also played a crucial role in the development of open and distance education, which widened access and participation in education by means of flexible learning opportunities and have become an increasingly important part of the European lifelong learning strategy. Based on the concept of distance education, massive open online courses (MOOCs) are probably the most germane example of how digital technologies are transforming the education landscape (European Training Foundation 2018). Today, much more advanced and complex technologies have entered the field of education, such as artificial intelligence (AI), learning analytics, data mining, and machine learning, all of which bring revolutionary opportunities in education and promise to augment and enhance human capabilities.

CHAPTER 19

The Right to Education

Aušrinė Pasvenskienė and Paulius Astromskis

19.1 The Scope of the Right to Education

The right to work is closely related to the right to education. As Brynjolfsson and McAfee observed, "Technological progress is going to leave behind some people, perhaps even a lot of people, as it races ahead. ... There's never been a better time to be a worker with special skills or the right education because these people can use technology to create and capture value. However, there's never been a worse time to be a worker with only 'ordinary' skills and abilities to offer, because computers, robots, and other digital technologies are acquiring these skills and abilities at an extraordinary rate" (European Parliamentary Research Service 2020).

The right to education has many facets and has thus far eluded precise definition. One of the more widely accepted and cited definitions describes it as "the right of access to the knowledge and training which are necessary to full development as an individual and as a citizen."[1] It is a guarantee of and a vehicle for the implementation and respect of other inalienable human rights and freedoms, by providing individuals with the means to obtain knowledge and skills. It has a solid foundation in several universal and regional human rights instruments.[2] The content of the right to education can be mapped by analyzing different international and regional instruments that address the topic. Although the provisions of the CFR and the European Convention on Human Rights (ECHR) do not explicitly mention the exact content of fundamental rights, their very essence may be found in the case law of the European Court of Human Rights (ECtHR) and the Court of Justice of the EU (CJEU).

The right to education creates complex and diverse obligations and responsibilities for various stakeholders. The primary responsibility of states is to guarantee the right to education for everyone living in their territory and subject

1 UN Doc. E/CN.4/SR.226, at 14 (May 4, 1951).

2 This right can be found in Article 26 of the Universal Declaration on Human Rights, Article 2 of the First Protocol of the European Convention on Human Rights and Fundamental Freedoms, the UNESCO Convention against Discrimination in Education and the International Covenant on Economic, Social and Cultural Rights, among others.

 | DOI:10.1163/9789004682900_025

to their jurisdiction. They have a duty to provide an educational system that respects the right to education and to abstain from any actions that may hinder or restrict access to education. States must also guarantee universal access to basic education and to the acquisition of relevant knowledge, skills, and competencies, as well as the quality and standards of instruction (Singh 2013).

The Commission on Human Rights acknowledged that recognizing a right does not mean that states can fulfill the related obligations immediately, but only depending on "the relative magnitude of the problems of each country and the means at its disposal."[3] Moreover, the clause in article 13 of the International Covenant on Economic, Social and Cultural Rights (ICESCR), "with a view to achieving the full realization of this right," reflects the progressive nature of this obligation, as it is unrealistic to expect states to be able to realize the full scope of the right to education immediately (Coomans 2004). In addition, the term "to respect" is understood as containing both a negative obligation not to interfere and a positive obligation to actively respect individual convictions (EU Network of Independent Experts on Fundamental Rights 2006).

In international documents, the right to education is usually seen from two perspectives. On one hand, it requires the state to take positive measures to make education available and accessible. On the other hand, it grants individuals the personal freedom to choose an education according to one's philosophical and religious beliefs, implying negative obligations for the state. Although its extent depends largely on how each state gives shape to the vague contours of the right to education, as articulated in international law, and on the specific conditions prevalent in a given country, all forms and levels of education must demonstrate four essential and interrelated features: *availability*, *accessibility*, *acceptability*, and *adaptability* (UN CESCR 1999), or the so-called 4A's framework. These four internationally recognized principles were developed by former UN Special Rapporteur on the Right to Education Katarina Tomaševski, and they are regularly used to evaluate whether a specific education system is compatible with universally applied international standards of education, as well as to construe the content of the right to education in a particular country. In relation to article 13(2) of the ICESCR, states are obliged to respect, protect, and fulfill all four elements of the right to education.

Conceptually, the principles of availability and accessibility are related to the right to education, whereas acceptability and adaptability refer to rights *in* education. The principle of availability obligates states to establish education

3 UN Doc. E/CN.4/AC.14/SR.1, at 14 (May 17, 1951).

institutions and programs in sufficient quantity, to allocate funds to enable their proper functioning, and to ensure that sufficient human resources are provided for their operation (including not just teachers but also proper training of teachers). The extent of availability depends on several factors, including the development context in which educational institutions operate. The standard of availability in a particular country can range from elementary infrastructure (including buildings, sanitation facilities, safe drinking water, and basic teaching materials) to well-equipped libraries, computer facilities, and smart technologies.

The second principle, accessibility, concerns states' obligation to ensure access to compulsory education. It comprises three overlapping dimensions: non-discrimination, physical accessibility, and economic accessibility (UN CESCR 1999). Non-discrimination requires education to be accessible to all, especially vulnerable groups. Physical accessibility guarantees education within safe physical reach, either by attendance at some reasonably convenient geographic location or via modern technology, such as distance learning (ibid). Economic accessibility requires education to be affordable for all.

The realization of the principle of accessibility is relevant within the context of open and distance education and is intertwined with the very idea of lifelong learning. Open and distance education is a medium through which education can be provided to adult learners, those in remote areas, excluded learners with specific needs, people with disabilities, and other marginalized or disadvantaged groups. Open education also allows diverse learners and knowledge seekers, most importantly non-privileged and underrepresented ones, to access free, digitally enabled learning materials and experiences (Lambert 2018). In addition, Tait argues that open and distance universities have produced changes in the higher education system in terms of quality and innovation (Tait 2008) and may contribute to equality among human beings, inclusion, social justice, and economic development (Tait 2013). Modern debate on a social justice–oriented definition of open education suggests a shift from what openness might look like toward whom the openness should ultimately serve, along with how openness might achieve greater educational and societal equality (Lambert 2018).

The rapid growth of open and distance education has increasingly contributed to achieving the commitment of the Education 2030 Framework for Action to promote quality lifelong education for all, in all settings and in all levels of education. It highlights the importance of harnessing technologies to fulfill the right to education. At the same time, it is equally important to acknowledge that open education technologies require an ethical and responsible approach, as "open" does not necessarily relate to the quality of material or its ethical nature. Archer and Prinsloo (2017) note that open educational resources, as technology, not only represent a disruption in access to knowledge but are also products of a changing society. Their use creates a burden to ensure that the technology is harnessed in a responsible and ethical manner.

The third principle, acceptability, concerns the recognition of subjective rights of children, the guarantee of minimum standards of quality, safety, and health, and respect for diversity, such as by providing instruction in an appropriate language (Tomaševski 2001). This principle stipulates that the education available to and accessible by citizens must also be of good quality. States' obligation to provide quality education for all is grounded in many international and regional human rights treaties, as well as in most domestic legal systems through national constitutions and legislation. Moreover, UN Sustainable Development Goal 4 reinforces the states' commitments to ensuring quality education. This principle further requires an acceptable form and substance of education, including curricula and teaching methodologies (Abidjan Principles 2019). This means that evaluating the role of digital technologies in education is of great importance. Often recognized as a driver of quality assurance and improvement in education, digital technologies may also be seen as a major contributor to the fulfillment of the right to education.

Finally, adaptability means that the content and process of learning must be flexible, adapted to the needs of changing societies and communities, and compatible with the needs of learners within their diverse social and cultural settings (UN CESCR 1999). The usual approach to ensuring adaptability is to review the content and process of education from the learners' viewpoint to consider whether their interests are treated as a priority (Tomaševski 2001). That implies providing relevant content and using relevant teaching and learning methods in education, as well as providing skills that are determined by the learner's future needs.

Recognition of internet access as a new human right and its implications for exercising the right to education represents a great example of adapting education to the needs of changing societies and widening access to education. When addressing the issues involved in safeguarding the right to education, the CESCR Committee highlighted the need to expand internet access and to educate people on the use of new technologies and the internet (CESCR Committee 2012). In 2019 High Court of Kerala (India) went even further. Taking into consideration technological advancement and its growing importance in everyday life, it decided that "the right to have access to Internet becomes the part of right to education" (Faheema Shirin RK vs State of Kerala 2019).[4] The court emphasized that access to information on the internet facilitates vast opportunities for affordable and inclusive education and the promotion of the right to education. It also underscored the need to promote digital literacy as a necessary contributor to high-quality education, since it affects the enjoyment of the right to education (ibid). Thus, we can conclude that digital technologies play an increasingly important role in the full realization of the right to education.

In addition to the 4A's, the prohibition of all forms of discrimination is seen as a cornerstone in the protection of the right to education. The principle of non-discrimination prohibits not only direct discrimination but also all indirect forms of discrimination that by the application of other criteria of differentiation, lead in fact to the same result.[5] States are obligated to ensure that everyone has equal access to quality, inclusive education, without any discrimination on any ground, and to organize their education systems so as to prevent discrimination (Abidjan Principles 2019). Therefore, there is an even greater need to analyze the types and the uses of digital technologies in education, as growing evidence suggests that decisions made by algorithms may be discriminatory. The use of digital technologies may both create discrimination and exacerbate existing discrimination and inequality. The state must address any situation that breaches the rights of equality and non-discrimination with regard to the right to education, including disparities in educational opportunities or outcomes (ibid). It is essential to tackle both the positive effects and the potential risks of digital technologies in education in order to guarantee the protection of the right to education. The following section discusses different roles of digital technologies in education and their effects on the right to education.

19.2 Education Policies

EU policies have paid increasing attention to constructing a flexible educational landscape that equips learners with necessary specific and general skills at all stages so that they can tackle the challenges of a modern workplace (European Commission 2015; 2017a; 2017c; 2018a). They contribute to spreading the message and explaining why European education systems need

4 Kerala High Court, W.P(C), No. 19716/2019-L.

5 Bressol and Others Case C-73/08, ECLI:EU:C:2010:181.

transformation and the application of modern and innovative education models that employ digital technologies.

Most education policies view innovation as the most important driver of global economic growth (European Commission 2017a). Unpreparedness for the future digital transformation may result in lost opportunities for social and economic growth (European Commission 2018). Commonly, universities are seen as the key institutions for disseminating knowledge and performing research, and thus they are expected to fulfill the increasing demand for economic, cultural, and technological development. However, technology-driven policies predicated mainly on enabling economic success have been criticized by some authors as "a techno-centric, utopian and economic driven mind-set" (Zhao et al. 2006, 674; see also Selwyn 2012). One major concern is that education policies should be inspired by a more human perspective, since education systems are complex and since adapting to emerging economic needs is a long process that requires considerable readjustment by both education programs and individuals.

Twenty years ago, the Lisbon Strategy identified education institutions as key players in innovation and technology development (Lisbon European Council 2000), and this message was echoed ten years later in the Europe 2020 document (European Commission 2010a). Since 2015, the Digital Single Market Strategy has been a leading driver of the Europe 2020 strategy, aiming at better access to online goods and services for consumers and businesses, as well as appropriate conditions for digital networks and services to flourish and maximize the growth potential of Europe's digital economy (European Commission 2015). Stressing the need to change the way in which education and training systems adapt to the digital revolution, this strategy encouraged EU member states to tackle the lack of essential digital skills among Europeans.

Economic development and better education quality both increase employability. Employment opportunities are consistently a top priority in a wide range of EU policies and strategies (European Commission 2017a, 2017b, 2017c), and education systems are expected to facilitate the entry of young people into the labor market. Analysts say that the so-called fourth industrial revolution will result in a digital transformation of our economies and societies, fundamentally modifying how we live, work, and relate to one another (Schwab 2016; G20 Digital Economy Ministerial Declaration 2017; European Commission 2018).

Furthermore, digital skills and competencies have become essential not only to comply with new labor market requirements but also to keep up with daily routines, regardless of the profession. An inclusive Digital Single Market (European Commission 2015) demands specific skills to take part in e-services, e-government, e-justice, e-health, e-energy, e-finances, e-transport, and so on. Since 2006, digital competency has been listed among eight key competencies for lifelong learning (European Parliament and Council of the European Union 2006). In 2018, the definition of digital competencies was widened to cover emerging issues such as programming, cybersecurity, intellectual property, robotics, and AI (European Parliament and Council of the European Union 2018).

Digital competency and the application of digital tools in education have been spotlighted in a series of communications on education (European Commission 2011b; 2015; 2016a; 2017a; 2017b). These documents recognize that education can highly benefit from innovation and digital technologies in the following areas: improving learning outcomes, increasing accessibility of education, ensuring personalized teaching, enhancing equity, and improving efficiency (European Commission 2018b). EU documents identify three priorities: (1) making better use of digital technology for teaching and learning, (2) developing relevant digital competencies and skills for the digital transformation, and (3) improving education through better data analysis and foresight (ibid). The use of AI applications, robotics, cloud computing, blockchain, and learning analytics pilots in education is recognized as a possible enabler of the positive advancement of education systems (ibid).

Among other opportunities for and in education, digital technologies help to improve quality and access in education and to develop more flexible learning environments. Not only are they an enriching tool for more effective teaching and learning practices, but they also contribute to reducing social barriers to education (European Commission 2012). Guaranteeing equal access to high-quality, inclusive education for all students, including students with disabilities or other special needs, from poorer households, and from disadvantaged socio-economic backgrounds, is considered a key value by the EU (Council of the European Union 2018). Sustainable Development Goal (SDG) 4 within UNESCO's 2030 Agenda aims to "ensure inclusive and equitable quality education and promote lifelong learning opportunities for all." UNESCO has also suggested that the systematic integration of digital technologies can make a significant contribution to the implementation of SDG 4. A special role is given to AI, which is expected to accelerate the delivery of open and flexible education systems that enable equitable and quality learning opportunities (UNESCO 2019). AI can be particularly beneficial in the areas of education management information systems, empowering teaching and learning, learning assessments, identifying current and future skill needs, and the adoption of intelligent platforms and data-based learning analytics in lifelong learning systems (ibid). AI applications in education also support human interaction and collaboration between teachers and learners as the core of education, underscoring the fact that AI and machines are complementary tools intended to enrich the educational process, not to replace teachers. In other words, AI applications in education should be human-centered. Moreover, they must also be free from bias, promote gender equality, and ensure data privacy and security as well as ethical and responsible use.

Special attention should be given to open and distance education because the EU has a longstanding interest in widening access to education. Emerging technologies serve as a tool to deliver greater flexibility in teaching and learning, making distance education an alternative for those who cannot or do not want to experience on-campus education. Open and distance education has become an important element of lifelong learning, which is emphasized as a key policy objective in the Europe 2020 strategy and the Bologna Process. Therefore, traditional face-to-face learning is increasingly provided alongside alternative forms of delivery, including distance, blended, or e-learning. Although open education resources and MOOCs are often regarded with skepticism by quality assurance and accreditation bodies (UNESCO 2020), many positive developments have occurred in this area and have contributed to the realization of the right to education.

The increasing attention and support devoted to digital technologies in EU education policies affirms the need to readjust and exploit the full potential of these technologies (G20 Digital Economy Ministerial Declaration 2017) and to ensure a right to technologically enhanced education. Nevertheless, the implementation of such right remains vague as there is no clarity or precision as to what, how, and to what extent digital technologies are selected, realized, and monitored by educational institutions. Given this situation, education policies must be assessed and applied attentively.

Although learners need to develop the skills that markets require,[6] technological development in higher education institutions has proceeded at a relatively slow pace. These institutions in general still remain rather conservative, resistant to change, and reluctant to innovate (Rafael et al. 2017; OECD 2016).

---

6 The learners are expected to acquire much deeper technological knowledge and skills than just the basics. Digital competence entails the "confident, critical and responsible use of, and engagement with, digital technologies for learning, at work, and for participation in society." It involves "information and data literacy, communication and collaboration, media literacy, digital content creation (including programming), safety (including digital well-being and competences related to cybersecurity), intellectual property related questions, problem solving and critical thinking" (Council of the European Union 2018).

Different reasons for resistance to technological innovation can be observed. Unwillingness to engage with technological change may be a result of a lack of knowledge, skills, technical support, and financial support, all of which are necessary to modernize the form and substance of educational processes. Education institutions often lack the capacity to harness technological potential. Some support comes from multiple EU initiatives (European Commission 2016b; 2010b; 2010c) under the policy umbrella of the Europe 2020 strategy (European Commission 2010a), which encourages member states to tackle the lack of essential digital skills among European citizens.

The classical notion of the right to education justifies this unwillingness to tackle the opportunities and challenges presented by technological developments as a resistance to overly specialized and overly technology-oriented education. Delbrück notes that the idea of education is not limited only to "technical" aspects of learning skills crucial in a modern civilized society, but rather that it embodies a wider meaning, i.e., "the intellectual, spiritual, and emotional development of the human being, of his or her intellectual, spiritual, and emotional potential" (Delbrück 1992, 94; in German this process and state are referred to as *Bildung*). Education in the sense of *Bildung* necessitates an understanding of the world and discovery of personal identity as a human being (ibid).

The conservative *Bildungs*-approach to education is a possible reflection of a consensus that education must empower the human being to be a part of society and to develop personality and identity. This original academic tradition of liberal arts and sciences education aimed at imparting general knowledge, but not at serving societal and economic development. Early European universities focused on the education of the whole person. However, the spread of the Humboldtian tradition of the scientific disciplines resulted in the narrowing of areas of study (Van der Wende 2011). The later re-emergence of liberal arts education in Europe, which started around two decades ago, called for diversity, flexibility, and interdisciplinarity in education to address the downside of excessive specialization (ibid). Accordingly, that allows justifying application of digital technologies in education not as an element of specialized education but rather as one supporting a multidisciplinary and flexible approach in education.

It can also be argued that the application of innovative technologies in legal education could risk making education too narrow and specialized, with a potential accompanying loss of human values. However, one cannot support complete ignorance of technological expansion and the opportunities it offers. Thus, if a fair balance and diversity of competencies (i.e., creativity, reasoning, critical thinking, and entrepreneurial skills; European

Commission 2017d, 2017e), including the skills that machines cannot replace (European Commission 2018b, 2019)—the so-called uniquely human skills (Microsoft 2018)—and responsible and critical application of new technologies (European Commission High-Level Expert Group on Artificial Intelligence 2019) are preserved, the right to education will be guaranteed.

Legal education must respond to technological growth in all of its structural areas: developing specific courses, adapting all educational contexts, applying it in legal curricula, and designing study programs. If not, future legal professionals may face difficulties in finding the right place in the labor market, along with limitations of their right to work.

The IEEE Global Initiative (2019) recommended ensuring that workers can improve their adaptability to rapid technological change by providing them with adequate training programs. Those training programs could be available to any worker, with a special attention to low-skilled members of the workforce. They could be private (sponsored by the employer) or public (offered freely through specific public channels and policies), and they should be available while workers are between jobs or still employed. They should also ensure that not only workers whose jobs are directly affected benefit from training programs, but also any employee in the company, so that everyone has the chance to keep up with technical changes (i.e., the training should be not only reactive but also preventive). Thus, every company should increase its investment in the internal training of its workforce based on the profitability gains realized through automation. The public sector could facilitate such initiatives by sharing in investment in such training programs through tax incentives.

The High-Level Expert Group on AI (2019) also suggested that ensuring Trustworthy AI requires us to build and maintain an ethical culture and mindset through public debate, education, and practical learning. According to these experts, communication, education, and training play an important role, both to ensure that knowledge of the potential impact of AI systems is widespread and to make people aware that they can participate in shaping technology development within society. Therefore, governments, industry leaders, educational institutions, and unions face a responsibility to bring citizens into the new digital era and ensure they have the right skills to fill future jobs. As for AI issues in the workforce, the EU White Paper on AI (2020a) called for underpinning the European approach to AI with a strong focus on skills to fill competence shortages. The European Commission undertook to present a reinforcement of the Skills Agenda, aiming to ensure that everyone in Europe can benefit from the digital transformation of the EU economy. Also, it seeks to establish and support, through the advanced skills pillar of the Digital Europe Programme, networks of leading universities and higher education institutes to attract the best professors and scientists and offer world-leading master's degree programs in AI.

Moreover, one of the policy initiatives identified in the EU national strategies on AI is on human capital, with the goal of fostering the educational development of people in using and developing AI solutions. It includes aspects of formal education and training (e.g., reforms of educational systems to include AI courses and programs), vocational and continuing learning (e.g., training the existing workforce to obtain AI-related skills and competencies), and labor market intelligence and needs (e.g., identifying forthcoming skill needs due to changes in technology developments) (European Commission 2020b).

19.3 Technology Policies

The importance of digital technologies in education has also been reflected in a number of technology-specific policy papers discussing the benefits and possible impact of AI, automation, and robotics in education. Research centers and academia are seen as vital players in providing the necessary education and skills in a world where tasks are increasingly performed by intelligent systems. The idea of a substantial transformation of education systems from preschool to higher education can be traced in all relevant documents and policies. Not surprisingly, the EU has declared the modernization of education to be "a priority for governments" in the Digital Single Market Strategy (European Commission 2018).

AI and robotics are considered of strategic importance in EU technology policies, which advocate for a significant increase in technology-related subjects at every level of education. These policies also call for teaching on the conscious, responsible, and well-informed use of digital technologies (European Commission High-Level Expert Group on Artificial Intelligence 2019). Clearly, education institutions cannot implement these far-reaching and fundamental changes alone. The EU has called for a wide-ranging and long-term action plan with a multidisciplinary approach and various stakeholders involved, including education and training institutions, social partners, and business (ibid). This major technological impact not only poses significant challenges for education systems but could possibly disturb the fundamental principles of higher education—namely, institutional autonomy and academic freedom.

Not surprisingly, AI-enabled developments in education have grabbed the interest of a multitude of stakeholders. The anticipated restructuring of future labor markets adds to the pressure to rethink current educational models, as digital skills are recognized as a necessity for "all levels of learners" and "in all age groups" (European Parliament 2017). Future employment growth in occupations that rely, or will rely more heavily, on digital technologies such as robotics and machine learning require reflection even now on the future direction of education. Education and training systems are expected to guarantee that managers, developers, users, and employers are aware of and trained in "trustworthy" (i.e., lawful, ethical, and robust) AI (European Commission High-Level Expert Group on Artificial Intelligence 2019). Policies also advocate for the analysis and monitoring of labor market transformations to identify the fields in which jobs are being created or where they will be lost as a result of the increased use of robots (European Parliament 2017).

EU policies on robotics and AI have additional concerns besides the obvious need for improved digital skills. Maintaining a human-centered and inclusive approach to AI is emphasized as a cornerstone (European Commission High-Level Expert Group on Artificial Intelligence 2019). EU policies also stress those skills that cannot be replaced by a machine, such as critical thinking, creativity, and management and social skills. Interdisciplinarity and ethics (European Commission 2018b) in the development and use of new technologies are considered indispensable features. EU member states are encouraged to educate and inform individuals on the opportunities and challenges inherent in AI and digital literacy through all levels of education systems: primary, secondary, tertiary, and beyond. Understanding AI systems is considered crucial for all citizens. Besides a basic understanding of machine learning and reasoning, at least a basic knowledge of data protection, personal data management, the implications of digital tracking, the importance of fairness, and the explainability, transparency, and robustness of AI systems will be required (European Commission High-Level Expert Group on Artificial Intelligence 2019). Moreover, citizens will need sufficient information on how AI works and on its potential impacts so as to make informed decisions on whether to develop, use, or invest in an AI system or simply to perceive how they can participate in shaping this transformative societal development (European Commission High-Level Expert Group on Artificial Intelligence 2018). Therefore, the need to understand liability issues and the legal responsibility of automated systems also becomes crucial (European Parliament 2017). Finally, existing technology policies reflect the values commonly established in education documents, such as inclusive and non-discriminatory use of AI, the involvement of people of diverse backgrounds and people with disabilities in the development of AI (European Commission 2018b), and increasing women's participation in science and technology (European Commission High-Level Expert Group on Artificial Intelligence 2019).

The analysis of policies on educational technology provided here reveals a clear awareness of the urgent need to modernize existing education systems. To fulfill the growing, evolving expectations for future graduates and labor markets, education systems must take dramatic steps now. Education institutions have always been key contributors to economic development, but today universities, together with policymakers and many components of the public and private sectors, are involved in even more complex and globalized economies, seeking to develop a suitably skilled labor force, and generating, applying, and communicating new ideas and innovations.

As noted above, the expectations articulated by education policy and the reality of current education systems do not match. One possible way to encourage faster change in education systems would be a universal agreement that the thoroughgoing integration of technology is essential to ensure the fundamental right to education. That step would impose a duty on the state and education institutions to promote, support, and realize technological advancement in education through positive actions.

CHAPTER 20

Educational Technologies

Aušrinė Pasvenskienė and Paulius Astromskis

Although some countries are still struggling to ensure minimum educational standards, others are seeking to modernize their education systems and to continuously improve the quality of education. Education is not a static commodity and cannot be considered in isolation from its greater purpose (UNESCO 2007). People have not only a right to quality education, which is a foundation for social cohesion and an open society, but also a right to be equipped with the skills and knowledge that will ensure their personal, professional, and social development and employability throughout their lives. Future jobs will go to those who "embrace the technology, not those that resist it" (Microsoft 2018).

On one hand, digital innovations could be seen as just another in a long list of requirements that education systems are expected to fulfill, along with addressing the implications of "changing labor markets, technological advances, urbanization, migration, political instability, environmental degradation, natural hazards and disasters, competition for natural resources, demographic challenges, increasing global unemployment, persistent poverty, widening inequality and expanding threats to peace and safety" (UNESCO 2015). On the other hand, modern technology developments are something very different, unprecedented, and still not completely understandable, a feature that introduces significant opportunities and poses a number of challenges, risks, and threats. Some authors argue that contemporary education models will be swept away by the fourth education revolution and that barely a single facet of education will remain untouched by such phenomena as AI, augmented reality, and virtual reality (Seldon and Abidoye 2018).

We know that education is poised for significant disruption; we just don't know when it will happen (Navitas Ventures 2019). In higher education alone, UNESCO predicts a shortage of almost 100 million seats by 2025, creating enormous challenges and opportunities for governments and education institutions around the world (ibid). Solving these enormous challenges calls for the use of educational technologies to increase the accessibility of education and thus support the right to education.

The European Commission (2020a) promises that its updated Digital Education Action Plan will help to make better use of data and AI-based technologies such as learning and predictive analytics, with the aim of improving

 | DOI:10.1163/9789004682900_026

education and training systems and making them fit for the digital age. The European Commission's High-Level Expert Group on Artificial Intelligence (2019) also suggests that trustworthy AI technologies could assist in more accurately forecasting which jobs and professions will be disrupted by technology, which new roles will be created, and which skills will be needed. This could help governments, unions, and industry to plan the retaining of workers in new skills, and it could also give citizens who may fear redundancy a path of development into a new role. In addition, AI can be a great tool to fight education inequalities and create personalized and adaptable education programs that could help everyone acquire new qualifications, skills, and competencies in accordance with their own ability to learn, and it could increase both the learning speed and the quality of education, all the way from primary school to the university level.

Global EdTech Landscape 3.0 (Navitas Ventures 2019) mapped $50 billion of investment in 15,000 education innovation and technology teams around the world. They have clustered educational technologies into eight groups, as shown below in Table 20.1.

Currently, almost half of the EU population lacks basic digital skills (European Commission 2016b). EU policies highlight the need to equip European citizens with digital skills and competencies and therefore require education systems to adapt to technological change and development. However, various surveys have shown that to keep up with the digital economy, simply improving digital literacy is not enough, as technology constantly advances. The World Economic Forum (2016) suggests that almost half of subject knowledge acquired by first-year students in a four-year technical degree program will be outdated before the student graduates. A World Bank report (2019) projects that a large percentage of children entering primary school in 2018 will work in occupations that do not yet exist. In the face of rapidly changing technologies, other skills become increasingly vital along with digital skills and competencies, such as cognitive skills (critical thinking, problem solving, reasoning), socio-behavioral skills (curiosity, creativity), entrepreneurial skills, and adaptability to changing environments. All these skills can facilitate adaptability to and the ability to advance technological change (Levin 2012); they are sometimes referred to as "uniquely human skills" (Microsoft 2018).

Because digital skills and competencies are now considered necessary not only in the workplace but also in all phases of everyday life, constant technological advancement requires education systems to enable learners to retrain in new skills, to learn and relearn, and to permanently readjust their skills. Such skill development is a matter of lifelong learning. Accordingly, today's integrated, technology-driven economies are increasingly valuing tertiary

TABLE 20.1 Educational technologies in eight groups

Create	Building a digital curriculum	Digital tools allow teachers to design interactive online course programs, with premade courses and custom bundles of tech tools to support specific curriculum aspects, such as STEM. K-12 teachers are sharing lesson plans and class activities.
	Transforming publishing and research	Various providers can now create, publish, and distribute verified, credible knowledge and ideas, and incumbent publishers are diversifying into new fields. For research academics, this area of transformation is seeing the emergence of new social networks for researchers, new models for submitting papers, and new discovery systems for academic research.
	Courseware of the future	For all education providers, whether in K-12 or higher education, this is an opportunity to digitize learning content and create adaptive materials to personalize instruction—potentially transforming learners' skill and knowledge acquisition and their ability to retain, recall, and apply knowledge in different situations. This will help people achieve deeper engagement with topics and see connections across subject boundaries.
Manage	Improving operational efficiency	Technology can be a powerful tool to relieve the burden of manual processes. New educational technology providers are challenging incumbent enterprise management systems, providing tailored solutions for specific education needs such as class planning, enrollment, or degree accreditation.
	Improving student management	These management platforms can remove friction from the entire student learning journey and use rich data analytics to improve student outcomes and retention.

TABLE 20.1 Educational technologies in eight groups (*cont.*)

	Staff recruitment and development	Technology has changed the way all organizations identify, recruit, and develop their talent, and education is no exception. From managing relief teachers in schools to attracting global academic talent, new platforms are replacing traditional paper-based programs. Technology is also expanding access to scalable professional development for educators.
Discover	Making admissions easier	By reducing paperwork and streamlining the enrollment process, technology can improve the student (or parent) experience and reduce the time required to process applications. This also has implications for international agents, as AI chatbots can effectively guide a student through the process.
	New international pathways	College preparation and pathway programs provide greater access to traditional education programs, and they will increasingly be delivered through multiple channels. Admissions consultants and mentors, such as MBA coaches, could also scale their services via video and other advice or tutoring platforms.
	Student financing	Removing a roadblock for some prospective students, new platforms make it easier to find and apply for alternative funding sources, from student loans to grants and scholarships. Technology tools can also help providers digitize forms and match verified details for financial aid or grant approval. With increasing concern around affordability and return on investment (particularly in the United States, where a lot of the educational technology funding is directed), this is an interesting cluster to watch.

TABLE 20.1 Educational technologies in eight groups (*cont.*)

Connect	Shifts in learning management systems	Incumbent learning management systems (LMSs) such as Moodle and Blackboard have made great inroads in both K-12 and higher education, but the market is turning toward open application programming interfaces (APIs) to create interoperable systems.
	Learning becomes social	Other platforms are emerging to connect students and teachers through virtual meetups, offering the potential to bring together alumni, parents, and other stakeholders.
Experience	Getting the basics right	New tools are making it easier (and more fun) to get the foundations in place, including math, science, and literacy. Pop quizzes are more engaging (and interactive) in a digital dimension.
	Immersive classroom technology	Different skills are absorbed and retained more effectively in different ways. For specialized skills such as coding or robotics, students (including young children) are using tech platforms to learn through play and, in the process, acquiring valuable life skills.
	Virtual and augmented reality	Virtual reality (VR) technology is still emerging, but educators are already using it to share 360-degree video tours, including virtual excursions. Augmented reality (AR) is gaining traction as a way of gamifying learning and bringing science to life.
Learn	Open or proprietary online platforms	Massive open online courses (MOOCs) have evolved from free programs to paid courses and branded credentials. They have also expanded into other languages and regions. Some platforms here are directories of available courses; we define these as "open." Others create, brand, and deliver their own

TABLE 20.1 Educational technologies in eight groups (*cont.*)

		material; we consider these "proprietary." In both cases, specialized skills, including language and workplace training, are being delivered.
	On-demand skills training	Private training can now happen at scale, and vocational skills such as coding and programming are now available through intensive boot camp programs. These have shifted from in-person to online delivery (or a combination of the two).
	In-person teaching can also be innovative	New learning models can still be face-to-face in nature; many educators are flipping traditional teaching practices with highly personalized instruction.
	Language connects students beyond borders	Language learning platforms are increasingly interactive and scalable, replicating the traditional "teach yourself" model via apps or providing guided language tutoring through video conferencing. Some interesting global players are emerging here, particularly in Asia and Latin America.
Credential	Scalable test preparation	Online tutoring platforms are flourishing. They help students prepare for study in another language, or for specific tests such as the SAT and GMAT. Online videos and adaptive questions and course materials can help students improve.
	New testing techniques	Alternatives to incumbent language tests such as the IELTS are already emerging, using technology to measure skills and capabilities. These assessment platforms can also help education providers assess course or scholarship applications and help

TABLE 20.1 Educational technologies in eight groups (*cont.*)

		human resource departments to identify and evaluate new talent.
	Unlocking the value of credentials	This area also forces institutions to rethink the traditional currency of their programs. New platforms are emerging to store and share digital certificates and diplomas, as well as providing flexible "micro-credentials." Both formal and informal sources of knowledge may be recognized in future credentials—from watching podcasts to on-the-job experience.
Advance	Identifying graduate talent	From internships to graduate recruitment programs, new technology provides real-time "job boards," industry-focused networking platforms, and innovative project-based internships to bridge the gap between study and work experience. New assessment tools also enable remote graduate testing, so that potential skills gaps can be identified and addressed.
	A lifetime of careers, not a career for life	The traditional resume and interview process is also being reconceived, along with further workplace education in an age that demands lifelong skills development. This will impact career centers and coaching, as well as industry talent assessment and recruitment agencies.

SOURCE: GLOBAL EDTECH LANDSCAPE 3.0 (NAVITAS VENTURES 2019

education and also recognizing lifelong, ongoing learning as essential for everyone to cope with current and future developments. More and more learning will occur in the work context and will be based on individual ambitions (European Commission 2018c). EU member states are urged to adapt their education systems to the new demands for skills, which require reforms at all levels, from primary school to tertiary education.

As part of developing digital competency, it is crucial to take into account aspects of education about digital technologies themselves—e.g., digital safety, management of digital identities, data protection, perception of risks in the online environment, and responsible, critical, ethical, and safe engagement in the digital world. Easy access and daily exposure to digital data carry threats along with increased opportunities. Reports have shown that young people do not develop sophisticated digital skills just by using digital devices (Fraillon et al. 2018). We must thus adopt and promote standards of legal and ethical behavior related to privacy and data protection and must teach learners to engage positively and competently with the digital environment (Li et al. 2019).

To succeed and prosper in a digital society and overcome digital risks, people need both to seize the opportunities offered by digital evolution and to identify and respond competently to the challenges of the digital environment. New technologies put fundamental rights at risk. Automated information filtering mechanisms, driverless cars and other means of transportation, and aggregated personalized news services replace humans as decision makers and can adversely affect human decisions. Automated decision making can also lead to exclusion and discrimination when certain services are offered to some and not to others (Peters 2018). For this reason, all learners must have a basic understanding of digital technology concepts (including AI and robotics) so that they can engage effectively and critically with technological systems. Learners must know how and where their data are used and understand when they are vulnerable. They should also have the ability and skills to evaluate the risks and report problems that arise.

Just as education systems are encouraged to modernize teaching and learning and to integrate digital technologies in education, they are also expected to educate about the opportunities and challenges of digital technologies. Educators should equip future citizens and professionals with values and ethics, highlighting the intangible benefits for society of character traits such as concern for the common good, trust building, and thoughtful deliberation (Philbeck et al. 2018). Therefore, raising awareness of the ethical and human rights issues surrounding the potential impact of digital technologies on society is crucial.

Benedek and Kettemann (2013) argued that the digital dimension of the right to education includes the right to use the internet for education and the right to be educated about the internet. Today's much wider spread of digital technologies requires wider knowledge of their possible uses and awareness of potential threats. That kind of education serves as a precondition, first for appropriate implementation of the right to education and second for exercising a number of other related human rights, such as the right to freedom of expression, the right to family life and privacy, and the right to work.

Therefore, it could be argued that to enable more effective and efficient application of digital technologies in education, a greater contribution from policymakers is needed. Currently, most European countries have strategies in place for digital education, either specifically or within a broader strategy that incorporates elements of digital education (European Commission/EACEA/Eurydice 2019). Despite this, the preceding analysis has demonstrated that too often technology initiatives have failed to deliver the expected value or to deliver positive impacts. It would be unreasonable simply to expect teachers, lecturers, and education leaders to fully understand and grasp how digital technology can support positive change, especially considering the continuous changes in digital technologies, which make it rather difficult for teachers to keep their knowledge updated (Bower 2016).

Therefore, the strategies should address the complexity of challenges. Skilled and confident staff should be a priority in order to ensure efficient application of digital technologies in education. Equally important, we must know what technologies to select so as to achieve the needs of an education institution; thus, it is important to establish standards and apply certain measures to identify the most promising and trusted products. National education strategies and policies requiring education institutions to have their own digital education plans would also contribute to greater quality in digital education and would allow more flexibility. Tsai and Gasevic (2017) emphasize the lack of institutional policies developed specifically to guide the practice of learning analytics, taking into consideration an individual institution's own cultural, economic, political, and technical context, as one of the biggest challenges. The importance of institutional policies is also highlighted by the rapidity of technological developments, which requires systematic follow-up because strategic objectives become outdated very quickly. Policymakers should devote special attention to the development and application of more complex, AI-based technologies, as they present both major opportunities and potential risks yet still lack a comprehensive governance framework. All necessary measures must be taken to identify and prevent discriminatory practices. Ethicists urge establishing *ex ante* conformity assessments for AI technologies sold to European consumers (Coeckelbergh and Metzinger 2020). Hengstler et al. (2016) argue that before a technology is used, it must be certificated and approved, and policies must be established to govern it. Education institutions should also be required to ensure continuous and appropriate monitoring and evaluation systems, which are also not a widespread practice at this time (European Commission/EACEA/Eurydice (2019).

We can conclude that the current wave of technological progress implies a right to technologically enhanced education, fulfillment of which obligates the state to take positive actions to ensure efficient, effective, and high-quality use of digital technologies.

Study Questions

1. What does the right to education entail?
2. What obligations and responsibilities does the right to education create for the state?
3. Why is the application of digital technologies important in education?
4. What are the risks of the application of digital technologies in education?
5. What challenges do education systems face in ensuring the proper application of digital technologies in education?

References

Abidjan Principles. 2019. *On the Human Rights Obligations of States to Provide Public Education and to Regulate Private Involvement in Education*. https://www.abidjanprinciples.org/.

Archer, E., and P. Prinsloo. 2017. "Some Exploratory Thoughts on Openness and an Ethics of Care." In *Ethics in Higher Education: Values-Driven Leaders for the Future*, edited by D. Singh and C. Stückelberger, 273–85. Globethics.net.

Beech, D. J. 2013. *The European Research Area: beyond Market Politics. Europe of Knowledge*. https://era.ideasoneurope.eu/2013/10/05/the-european-research-area-beyond-market-politics/.

Benedek, W., and M. C. Kettemann. 2013. *Freedom of Expression and the Internet*. Council of Europe Publishing.

Bower, M. 2016. "Deriving a Typology of Web 2.0 Learning Technologies: Deriving a Typology of Web 2 Learning Technologies." *British Journal of Educational Technology* 47(4): 763–77.

CESCR Committee. 2012. *Concluding observations: Ecuador. E/C.12/ECU/CO/3*. https://www.refworld.org/docid/52d551274.html.

Coeckelbergh, M., and T. Metzinger. 2020. "Europe Needs More Guts When It Comes to AI Ethics." Tagesspiegel Background. https://background.tagesspiegel.de/digitalisierung/europe-needs-more-guts-when-it-comes-to-ai-ethics.

Commission on Human Rights. 2002. *Report on the Fifty-Eighth Session, Economic and Social Council, United Nations*. https://undocs.org/pdf?symbol=en/E/CN.4/2002/200.

Conrads, J., et al. 2017. "Digital Education Policies in Europe and Beyond: Key Design Principles for More Effective Policies." In *Publications Office of the European Union*, edited by C. Redecker et al. Publications Office of the European Union, Luxembourg.

Coomans, F. 2004. "Exploring the Normative Content of the Right to Education as a Human Right: Recent Approaches." *Persona y Derecho* 50: 61–100.

Council of the European Union. 2017a. *Conclusions EUCO 14/17*. https://www.consilium.europa.eu/media/21620/19-euco-final-conclusions-en.pdf.

Council of the European Union. 2017b. *The Rome Declaration*. https://www.consilium.europa.eu/en/press/press-releases/2017/03/25/rome-declaration/pdf.

Council of the European Union. 2018. *Council Recommendation on Promoting Common Values, Inclusive Education, and the European Dimension of Teaching 2018/C 195/01*. https://eur-lex.europa.eu/legal-content/EN/TXT/?uri=CELEX%3A32018H0607%2801%29.

Delbrück, J. 1992. "The Right to Education as an International Human Right." *German Yearbook of International Law* 35: 92.

EU Network of Independent Experts on Fundamental Rights. 2006. *Commentary on the EU Charter: Article 14: the Right to Education*. https://www.right-to-education.org/resource/commentary-eu-charter-article-14-right-education.

European Commission. 2010a. *Europe 2020: a Strategy for Smart, Sustainable and Inclusive Growth*. COM/2010/2020 final. http://eur-lex.europa.eu/LexUriServ/LexUriServ.do?uri=COM:2010:2020:FIN:EN:PDF.

European Commission. 2010b. *Communication from the Commission to the European Parliament, the Council, the European Economic and Social Committee and the Committee of the Regions Youth on the Move. An Initiative to Unleash the Potential of Young People to Achieve Smart, Sustainable and Inclusive Growth in the European Union*. COM/2010/477 final. https://europa.eu/youthonthemove/docs/communication/youth-on-the-move_EN.pdf.

European Commission. 2010c. *Communication from the Commission to the European Parliament, the Council, the European Economic and Social Committee and the Committee of the Regions on a Digital Agenda for Europe*. COM/2010/245 final. https://eur-lex.europa.eu/LexUriServ/LexUriServ.do?uri=COM:2010:0245:FIN:EN:PDF.

European Commission. 2011a. *Key Data on Learning and Innovation through ICT at School in Europe 2011*. European Commission. https://data.europa.eu/doi/10.2797/61068.

European Commission. 2011b. *Communication from the Commission to the European Parliament, the Council, the European Economic and Social Committee and the Committee of the Regions on Supporting Growth and Jobs—An Agenda for the*

Modernization of Europe's Higher education Systems. COM/2011/0567 final. https://eur-lex.europa.eu/legal-content/EN/TXT/?uri=celex:52011DC0567.

European Commission. 2012. *Communication from the Commission to the European Parliament, the Council, the European Economic and Social Committee and the Committee of the Regions on Rethinking Education: Investing in Skills for Better Socio-economic Outcomes.* COM/2012/0669 final. https://eur-lex.europa.eu/legal-content/EN/TXT/HTML/?uri=CELEX:52012DC0669&from=FR.

European Commission. 2015. *Communication from the Commission to the European Parliament, the Council, the European Economic and Social Committee and the Committee of the Regions on a Digital Single Market Strategy for Europe.* COM/2015/192 final. https://eur-lex.europa.eu/legal-content/EN/TXT/?uri=celex%3A52015DC0192.

European Commission. 2016a. *Communication from the Commission to the European Parliament, the Council, the European Economic and Social Committee and the Committee of the Regions on improving and modernizing education.* COM/2016/0941 final. https://eur-lex.europa.eu/legal-content/EN/TXT/?uri=CELEX%3A52016DC0941.

European Commission. 2016b. *Communication from the Commission to the European Parliament, the Council, the European Economic and Social Committee and the Committee of the Regions on a new Skills Agenda for Europe: Working Together to Strengthen Human Capital, Employability and Competitiveness.* COM/2016/0381 final. https://eur-lex.europa.eu/legal-content/EN/TXT/?uri=CELEX:52016DC0381.

European Commission. 2017a. *Communication from the Commission to the European Parliament, the Council, the European Economic and Social Committee and the Committee of the Regions on a Renewed EU Agenda for Higher Education.* COM/2017/0247 final. https://eur-lex.europa.eu/legal-content/EN/TXT/?uri=CELEX%3A52017DC0247.

European Commission. 2017b. *Communication from the Commission to the European Parliament, the Council, the European Economic and Social Committee and the Committee of the Regions on Strengthening European Identity through Education and Culture.* COM/2017/673 final. https://ec.europa.eu/commission/sites/beta-political/files/communication-strengthening-european-identity-education-culture_en.pdf.

European Commission. 2017c. *A Concept Paper on Digitisation, Employability and Inclusiveness: the Role of Europe.* http://ec.europa.eu/newsroom/document.cfm?doc_id=44515.

European Commission. 2017d. *European Commission Reflection Paper on Harnessing Globalization.* COM/2017/240 final. https://eur-lex.europa.eu/legal-content/EN/TXT/?uri=COM%3A2017%3A240%3AFIN.

European Commission. 2017e. *European Commission Reflection Paper on the Social Dimension of Europe* COM/2017/206 final. https://eur-lex.europa.eu/resource.html?uri=cellar:cea6403b-2b4c-11e7-9412-01aa75ed71a1.0017.02/DOC_1&format=PDF.

European Commission. 2018a. *Communication from the Commission to the European Parliament, the Council, the European Economic and Social Committee and the Committee of the Digital Education Action Plan.* COM/2018/022 final. https://eur-lex.europa.eu/legal-content/EN/TXT/?uri=COM:2018:22:FIN.

European Commission. 2018b. *Communication from the Commission to the European Parliament, the Council, the European Economic and Social Committee and the Committee of the Regions on Artificial Intelligence for Europe.* COM/2018/237 final. https://ec.europa.eu/digital-single-market/en/news/communication-artificial-intelligence-europe.

European Commission. 2018c. *Communication from the Commission to the European Parliament, the Council, the European Economic and Social Committee and the Committee of the Regions Coordinated Plan on Artificial Intelligence.* COM/2018/795 final. https://eur-lex.europa.eu/legal-content/EN/TXT/?uri=COM:2018:795:FIN.

European Commission. 2019. *Communication from the Commission to the European Parliament, the Council, the European Economic and Social Committee and the Committee of the Regions: Building Trust in Human-Centric Artificial Intelligence* COM/2019/168 final. https://eur-lex.europa.eu/legal-content/EN/TXT/?uri=COM:2019:0168:FIN.

European Commission. 2020a. *White Paper on Artificial Intelligence: a European Approach to Excellence and Trust.* https://commission.europa.eu/system/files/2020-02/commission-white-paper-artificial-intelligence-feb2020_en.pdf.

European Commission. 2020b. *National Strategies on Artificial Intelligence: a European Perspective in 2019.* https://publications.jrc.ec.europa.eu/repository/handle/JRC119974.

European Commission High-Level Expert Group on Artificial Intelligence. 2018. *Draft Ethics Guidelines for Trustworthy AI.* https://ec.europa.eu/digital-single-market/en/news/ethics-guidelines-trustworthy-ai.

European Commission High-Level Expert Group on Artificial Intelligence. 2019. *Ethics Guidelines for Trustworthy AI.* https://ec.europa.eu/digital-single-market/en/news/ethics-guidelines-trustworthy-ai.

European Commission/EACEA/Eurydice. 2019. *Digital Education at School in Europe: Eurydice Report.* https://eacea.ec.europa.eu/national-policies/eurydice/sites/eurydice/files/en_digital_education_n.pdf.

European Parliament. 2017. *Resolution with Recommendations to the Commission on Civil Law Rules on Robotics.* 2015/2103(INL). https://eur-lex.europa.eu/legal-content/EN/TXT/?uri=CELEX%3A52017IP0051.

European Parliament and Council of the European Union. 2006. *Recommendation 2006/962/EC on Key Competences for Lifelong Learning.* https://eur-lex.europa.eu/legal-content/EN/TXT/?uri=CELEX%3A32006H0962.

European Parliament and Council of the European Union. 2018. *Recommendation 2018/C 189/01 on Key Competences for Lifelong Learning.* https://eur-lex.europa.eu/legal-content/EN/TXT/PDF/?uri=CELEX:32018H0604(01)&from=EN.

European Parliamentary Research Service. 2020. *The Ethics of Artificial Intelligence.* https://www.europarl.europa.eu/RegData/etudes/STUD/2020/634452/EPRS_STU(2020)634452_EN.pdf.

European Training Foundation. 2018. *Digital Skills and Competence, and Digital and Online Learning.* https://www.etf.europa.eu/sites/default/files/2018-10/DSC%20and%20DOL_0.pdf.

Fraillon, J., et al. 2018. *Preparing for Life in a Digital World: IEA International Computer and Information Literacy Study 2018.* IEA International Association for the Evaluation of Educational Achievement. https://doi.org/10.1007/978-3-030-38781-5.

G20 Digital Economy Ministerial Declaration. 2017. *Shaping Digitalisation for an Interconnected World.* https://unctad.org/meetings/en/Contribution/dtl_eWeek2017c02-G20_en.pdf.

Gideon, A. 2015. "The Position of Higher Education Institutions in a Changing European Context: an EU Law Perspective." *Journal of Common Market Studies* 53(5): 1045–60.

Hengstler, M., E. Enkel, and S. Duelli. 2016. "Applied Artificial Intelligence and Trust—The Case of Autonomous Vehicles and Medical Assistance Devices." *Technological Forecasting and Social Change* 105: 105–20.

IEEE Global Initiative on Ethics of Autonomous and Intelligent Systems. 2019. *Ethically Aligned Design: Vision for Prioritizing Human Well-being with Autonomous and Intelligent Systems.* https://standards.ieee.org/content/dam/ieee-standards/standards/web/documents/other/ead_v2.pdf.

Lambert, S. R. 2018. "Changing Our (Dis)Course: a Distinctive Social Justice Aligned Definition of Open Education." *Journal of Learning for Development* 5(3): 225–44.

Levin, H. M. 2012. *The Importance of Educational Adaptability: Invitational Research Symposium on Technology Enhanced Assessments.* https://www.ets.org/Media/Research/pdf/session5-levin-paper-tea2012.pdf.

Li, H., L. Yu, and W. He. 2019. "The Impact of GDPR on Global Technology Development." *Journal of Global Information Technology Management.* https://doi.org/10.1080/1097198X.2019.1569186.

Lisbon European Council. 2000. *Presidency Conclusions.* http://www.europarl.europa.eu/summits/lis1_en.htm.

Microsoft. 2018. *Future Computed: Artificial Intelligence and Its Role in Society.* https://blogs.microsoft.com/uploads/2018/02/The-Future-Computed_2.8.18.pdf.

Navitas Ventures. 2019. *Global EdTech Landscape 3.0*. https://learningandteaching-navitas.com/events/edtech-sector-landscape-3/.

OECD. 2016. *Innovating Education and Educating for Innovation: the Power of Digital Technologies and Skills*. OECD Publishing, Paris, https://doi.org/10.1787/9789264265097-en.

Peters, M. 2018. *Artificial Intelligence, What's New?* European Commission. https://ec.europa.eu/digital-single-market/en/blogposts/artificial-intelligence-whats-new.

Philbeck, T. H., N. Davis, and A. M. Engtoft Larsen. 2018. *Values, Ethics and Innovation: Rethinking Technological Development in the Fourth Industrial Revolution*. World Economic Forum. http://www3.weforum.org/docs/WEF_WP_Values_Ethics_Innovation_2018.pdf.

Schwab, K. 2016. *The Fourth Industrial Revolution: What it Means, How to Respond.* World Economic Forum. www.weforum.org/agenda/2016/01/the-fourth-industrial-revolution-what-it-means-and-how-to-respond/.

Seldon, A., and O. Abidoye. 2018. *The Fourth Education Revolution: Will Artificial Intelligence Liberate or Infantilise Humanity*? University of Buckingham Press.

Selwyn, N. 2012. *Education in a Digital World: Global Perspectives on Technology and Education*. Routledge.

Singh, K. 2013. *Justiciability of the Right to Education: Report of the Special Rapporteur on the Right to Education.* UN General Assembly. https://www.ohchr.org/Documents/HRBodies/HRCouncil/RegularSession/Session23/A.HRC.23.35_en.pdf.

Tait, A. 2008. "What Are Open Universities for?" *Open Learning: the Journal of Open, Distance and e-Learning* 23(2): 85–93.

Tait, A. 2013. "Distance and E-Learning, Social Justice, and Development: the Relevance of Capability Approaches to the Mission of Open Universities." *International Review of Research in Open and Distributed Learning* 14(4).

Tomaševski, K. 2001. *Human Rights Obligations: Making Education Available, Accessible, Acceptable and Adaptable*. Right to Education Primers, no. 3. http://biblioteca.clacso.edu.ar/gsdl/collect/ar/ar-033/index/assoc/D599.dir/11.pdf.

Tsai, Y. S., and D. Gasevic. 2017. "Learning Analytics in Higher Education—Challenges and Policies: a Review of Eight Learning Analytics Policies." *Proceedings of the Seventh International Learning Analytics & Knowledge Conference, Vancouver, Canada*, 233–42.

UN Committee on Economic, Social and Cultural Rights (CESCR). 1999. *General Comment No. 13: the Right to Education* (Article 13 of the Covenant). http://www.refworld.org/docid/4538838c22.html.

UNESCO. 2007. *A Human Rights–Based Approach to Education for All*. https://www.unicef.org/publications/files/A_Human_Rights_Based_Approach_to_Education_for_All.pdf.

UNESCO. 2014. *The Right to Education: Law and Policy Review Guidelines.* https://unesdoc.unesco.org/ark:/48223/pf0000228491.

UNESCO. 2015. *Education 2030: Incheon Declaration and Framework for Action for the implementation of Sustainable Development Goal 4: Ensure Inclusive and Equitable Quality Education and Promote Lifelong Learning Opportunities for All.* https://unesdoc.unesco.org/ark:/48223/pf0000245656.

UNESCO. 2019. *Beijing Consensus on Artificial Intelligence and Education.* https://unesdoc.unesco.org/ark:/48223/pf0000368303?fbclid=IwAR1socBC65LI4AkGLGkIbod2tBhtZRTo2dxZ_6jzw_XtQDPhl-iS4HxRcBY.

Van der Wende, M. 2011. "The Emergence of Liberal Arts and Sciences Education in Europe: a Comparative Perspective." *Higher Education Policy* 24: 233–53.

World Bank. 2019. *World Development Report 2019: the Changing Nature of Work.* World Bank. https://www.worldbank.org/en/publication/wdr2019.

World Economic Forum. 2016. *The Future of Jobs Report.* http://reports.weforum.org/future-of-jobs-2016/skills-stability/.

Zhao Y., J. Lei, and P. F. Conway. 2006. "Global Perspective on Political Definitions of E-learning: Commonalities and Differences in National Educational Technology Strategy Discourses." In *The International Handbook of Virtual Learning Environments*, edited by J. Weiss et al., 673–97. Springer.

PART 6

Appendices

APPENDIX 1

Guidelines for Regulation of Information Technologies

Vladislav V. Fomin and Darius Amilevičius

A1.1 Primacy of Human Beings

Two primary drivers of the deployment of computational systems from the invention of computers to the present time were the automation of tasks and the introduction (or expansion) of control of tasks where humans could not have complete or sufficient control.

With the advances in technologies, both the complexity and range of tasks that can be performed by IT have been steadily increasing, resulting in the increasing reliance of society and business on sophisticated technological tools for communication, transport, information processing, health, education, assisted living, and in many other areas. IT capabilities exceed the speed and precision of human actions and reactions in such areas as computation, memory, and perception. In a complex and globalized society of increasingly interconnected actors, robotization transcends human physical and cognitive limits in decision-making and regulation processes.

Where people seek to exercise control over their environment through the introduction of IT tools, they need to confer power on technological artifacts, such as artificial intelligence (AI). This requires accepting that, because of the increased autonomy and agency of such entities, human action is limited. At the same time, actions over which humans have control increase. This gives rise to a paradox: the more human power over the environment increases thanks to machines, the more human beings are deprived of agency and control.

The EC High-Level Expert Group on AI has been working on issues and challenges related to this paradox, aiming to define an ethical and legal framework for the design, production, use, and governance of AI and to illuminate issues specific to each category of stakeholders (e.g., AI developer, private user, public sector), as different situations raise different challenges. The group's resulting document on "Ethics Guidelines for Trustworthy AI" revealed the increasing number of urgent and complex moral questions in this domain.

The paramount challenge for the deployment of AI systems remains: systems executing massive and complex tasks that could not be controlled without

 | DOI:10.1163/9789004682900_027

the use of AI still require human oversight, as the responsibility for those systems rests with humans.

A1.2 Algorithm Fairness

One of the most important subjects in the field of AI, perhaps the most important of all, is fairness. AI is moving beyond "nice-to-have" and becoming an essential part of modern digital systems. As humans rely more and more on AI for decisions, it becomes absolutely essential to ensure that those decisions are made ethically and free from unjust biases. Any decision-making system can exhibit bias toward certain factors and thus needs to be evaluated for fairness.

Fairness is a generic concept not restricted to AI. Because there is no single, global definition of fairness, it's important to thoughtfully consider what fairness means in the specific context of a use case. One of the major challenges in making algorithms fair lies in deciding what fairness actually means. Trying to understand what fairness means, and when a particular approach is the right one to use, is a major area of ongoing research. In general terms, fairness is the impartial and just treatment or behavior without favoritism or discrimination. The legal definition of fairness concerns avoiding the disparate treatment of and disparate impact on certain groups based on protected attributes like gender, race, religion, color, age, and more. But for digital technologies, fair AI requires a mathematical fairness definition.

AI Fairness isn't just an ethical or legal issue. It's important to remember that fairness in AI starts and ends with people. First, one needs to understand where and how bias can creep into AI systems. Bias can make its way into an AI system at any point in the development life cycle, from the diversity of the team building the system, to the way in which researchers collect and label data, to the choice of dataset or objective function, to name just a few possibilities. In general terms, there are two main sources of unfairness in AI system: (1) bias in the data that systems learn from; (2) how the algorithms are designed, because machine learning algorithms generally rely on correlational rather than causal relationships.

To build a trustworthy AI system, researchers must follow the six tenets of fair data, reproducibility, privacy, accountability, technical robustness and safety, and transparency.

A1.2.1 *Fair Data*

An AI model is only as good as the data it was trained on. Training data serve as the foundation of AI solutions everywhere and can make or break their success. There are two main sources of bias in this regard:

- A training dataset could have societal and historical bias baked into the data. One commonly referenced example is the gender bias learned through an AI approach called natural language processing (NLP). NLP is designed to understand human language, but to learn human language, it needs a lot of training data—a dataset the size of, say, all of Wikipedia or Google News. There's just one problem: all those data and all those articles and pages were created by humans, with all of our imperfections and bias written in. A training dataset must be clean, representative, and thoroughly described by its authors.
- Confirmation bias occurs when we collect data specifically with a predetermined assumption in mind—for example, if we want to prove that a treatment works for a disease and only collect samples where it has worked.

Main points to achieve these goals are good data management, clear data, and a proper data management policy.

A1.2.2 *Reproducibility*

Although reproducibility is a cornerstone of science, the surveys have confirmed that the current documentation practices at top AI conferences render most of the reported research results irreproducible (this is called the "reproducibility crisis"). This inability to reproduce results affects the trustworthiness of science. To ensure high trustworthiness of AI and machine learning, research measures must be taken to increase their reproducibility. Reproducibility in empirical AI research refers to the ability of an independent research team to produce the same results using the same AI method, based on the documentation provided by the original research team.

Main points to achieve this goal are moving from alchemy to science, stretching the limits of inference, and better documentation and traceability.

A1.2.3 *Privacy*

The basic definition of privacy is having the power to seclude oneself, or information about oneself, so as to limit the influence others can have on our behavior. Privacy has been traditionally recognized as a prerequisite for the exercise of human rights such as the freedom of expressions, the freedom of association, and the freedom of choice.

Privacy is a fundamental right particularly affected by AI systems. AI offers the ability to gather, analyze, and combine vast quantities of data from different sources, thus increasing the information-gathering capabilities of social actors who use this technology. The potential impact of AI on privacy is immense, and therefore it is imperative to raise awareness about these issues. Prevention of harm to privacy also necessitates adequate data governance that covers the quality and integrity of the data used, its relevance in light of the domain in which the AI systems will be deployed, its access protocols, and processing of data in a manner that protects privacy.

Main points to achieve this goal are privacy and data protection, quality and integrity of data, and access to data.

A1.2.4 *Algorithm Accountability*

Accountability refers to being answerable to somebody else and being obligated to explain and justify action and inaction. The same kind of opacity (sometimes called "black box") with which AI systems are designed and deployed creates the appearance of an absence of human control and responsibility and can bring the systems into conflict with important societal values. Algorithm accountability requires putting mechanisms in place to ensure responsibility and accountability for AI systems and their outcomes, both before and after their development, deployment, and use. Although regulation is not necessarily a popular topic when it comes to technological innovation, we must remember that when black-box algorithmic systems get assimilated into the private and the public sectors, they permeate the justice system, education, law enforcement, and many other important areas of society.

Main points to achieve this goal include model certification, third-party independent ongoing testing of model performance, the use of models that provide audit trails of their decision making, and algorithmic impact assessments prior to public-sector deployment.

A1.2.5 *Technical Robustness and Safety*

A crucial component of achieving trustworthy AI is technical robustness, which is closely linked to the principle of prevention of harm. Technical robustness requires that AI systems be developed with a preventative approach to risks and in a manner such that they can reliably behave as intended while minimizing unintentional and unexpected harm and preventing unacceptable harm. This should also apply to potential changes in their operating environment or the presence of other agents (human and artificial) that may interact with the system in an adversarial manner. In addition, the physical and mental integrity of humans should be ensured.

Main points to achieve this goal are having a fallback plan and general safety, accuracy, reliability, and reproducibility.

A1.2.6 *Algorithm Transparency*

An algorithm is a self-contained, step-by-step set of operations that computers and other "smart" devices carry out to perform calculation, data processing, and automated reasoning tasks.

Increasingly, algorithmic IT systems implement institutional decision making with far-reaching impacts, including their applications for education, access to credit, healthcare, and employment. The ubiquity of and reliance on algorithmic systems in our everyday lives raises a number of questions on how the systems are designed and implemented in the context of preventing error and bias in critical tasks. At the same time, there is also growing evidence that some algorithms and analytics can be opaque, making it impossible to determine when their outputs are biased or erroneous.

Computational models can be distorted as a result of biases contained in their input data and/or their algorithms. Algorithms and the decisions they yield can be opaque because of many factors, including technical (explainability, comprehensibility), economic (intellectual property protection, the cost of providing transparency), and social (privacy) ones. Even well-engineered computer systems can produce unexplained outcomes or errors, either because of the erroneous algorithmic logic or because the conditions of their use change, invalidating assumptions on which the original analytics were based.

The issue of non-transparency of algorithmic systems is associated with numerous risks in automated decision making related to discrimination against individuals. Developers of IT systems should plan and construct analytical systems that adhere to accepted ethical and oversight standards when algorithms are used to make automated decisions or as input in decisions made by people.

The Association for Computer Machinery (ACM) has developed a set of principles intended to support the benefits of algorithmic decision making while addressing the aforementioned concerns of algorithmic opacity. The seven ACM Principles for Algorithmic Transparency and Accountability (see https://www.acm.org/binaries/content/assets/public-policy/2017_usacm_statement_algorithms.pdf for a comprehensive description) are awareness; access and redress; accountability; explanation; data provenance; auditability; and validation and testing.

A1.3 Regulation

The increasing scope and depth of deployment of IT in organizations and society contributes to the growing importance of addressing the issues of social control of and by technology.

Regulation through IT concerns new forms and arenas of regulation enacted through innovative IT solutions (often called "RegTech"). These technologies are driving changes in the ways in which regulators seek to supervise and monitor business and societal conduct, as well as how business and society comply with laws and regulations. These technologies, which are increasingly implicated in regulatory practices, include new forms of real-time big-data analytics, machine learning and other AI techniques, use of blockchains and distributed ledgers, Internet of Things solutions, and natural language processing techniques.

Regulation of IT becomes increasingly challenging with IT's growing ubiquity and complexity. It must encompass the pervasive effects of such popular IT platforms as Google, Amazon, and Facebook with respect to privacy, competition and information veracity, insurance, health and safety policies (such as those related to autonomous cars), and so on.

There are growing demands to regulate various IT solutions and to increase the regulatory powers of governments related to IT uses, sometimes through introducing entirely new regulatory frameworks and bodies.

The topic of regulation of and through IT is related to topics of standardization and algorithm transparency, among others. Specifically in the context of AI, the development and deployment of AI systems require larger regulatory and technological frameworks and standards to establish trust in the governance principles and the results produced by the systems.

A1.4 Standardization

The growing academic interest in standardization is related to global economic and societal developments in general, and to the role of technologies in business and private life in particular. EU and national leaders have promoted versatile initiatives on the digitization of services, on such topics as the knowledge society in general and "RoboLaw" in particular.

The technology we use, in most cases, is the product of standardization process due to the ways in which national and international markets are organized. Whether a company intends to sell a technology product internally in its national market, to export it to a foreign market, or to import a technology product, a number of certifications will be required to ensure that it meets safety, technology, environmental, or other standards.

With the growing ubiquity of and reliance on technologies, there is an increasing call for "responsible standardization," according to which technology standards are expected to incorporate ethical norms and principles in how they are designed, built, and implemented. To this end, the following topics gain importance for research and education: (1) the concept and role of standardization, and the mechanisms for developing standards; (2) the concept of responsible standardization and ways of making standardization more responsive to societal needs; and (3) the concept and role of AI and other smart technologies within contemporary societal and technological development.

In the context of AI, the concept of standardisation gains importance against the backdrop of the opacity or transparency of AI algorithmic logic. Processes that are opaque to human observers must be made compatible with rule-based systems with which humans have traditionally worked, so as to enable reflective analysis and explicability. Here, standards are needed for training data and for how to use AI in organizations (the level of decision making, the level of autonomy, the responsibilities and risks, etc.).

A1.5 Assessment of AI Systems

When one is using an AI system, it's important to understand who is responsible if the system fails, as the problem may lie in a number of areas. AI assessment lists apply particularly to AI systems that directly interact with users, and they are primarily addressed to developers and deployers of AI systems. Given the application-specific nature of AI systems, the assessment list will need to be tailored to the specific use case and context in which the system operates. The assessment list and governance structure must be developed in close collaboration with stakeholders across the public and private sectors. The European Commission believes that a given AI application should generally be considered high-risk in light of what is at stake, considering whether both the sector and the intended use involve significant risks, in particular from the viewpoint of the protection of safety, consumer rights, and fundamental rights. When the AI application is employed in a sector where, given the characteristics of the activities typically undertaken, significant risks can be expected to occur, there must be a strict procedure for assessing the AI system. Such sectors include healthcare, transport, and energy, among others.

Artificial intelligence is in its very early stages of pursuing successful adoption in both the private and public sectors. For the most part, it remains a complex technology that requires skills and technical knowledge that are not required for most other IT procurement decisions. For that reason, it is important to have proper policy and procedures in place and to assess the value of AI-related products carefully. The guidelines discussed above should be useful for private-and public-sectors policymakers with no or limited AI knowledge to help them make an initial assessment of a particular situation.

APPENDIX 2

Guidelines for Regulation of Robotics

John-Stewart Gordon and Kęstutis Mosakas

A2.1 Welfare

The development and use of AI systems should be conducive to the welfare of humanity, sentient beings, and the natural environment. AI systems should improve rather than hinder the living conditions as well as the physical and mental well-being of humans (including future generations) and sentient life in general. They should also contribute to preserving the integrity of the natural environment and ecosystems. The welfare benefits of the development and use of different AI systems should constantly be weighed against the costs, such as the potential harm involved, the resources required for the utilization of AI systems, and the conflicts of interest that may arise. The promotion of welfare through AI requires sustainability, strategic planning, and the consideration of interests of all relevant parties impacted by AI.

A2.2 Autonomy and Control

AI systems should be developed with respect for human autonomy and should not directly or indirectly impose certain decisions or life choices on individuals. A system specifically developed to assist a human user should be made in a way that would allow the user to have an appropriate degree of control over it without impinging on their freedom to choose. Rather than forcing or manipulating the user into a certain decision, an AI system should be developed in a way that would allow it to inform the user regarding the options available, thereby enhancing rather than hindering the user's autonomy. AI systems should not impinge on collective and individual self-determination and the processes of democracy.

A2.3 Privacy

Developers should try to ensure that different AI applications—including both robots and online softbots—will not needlessly infringe on people's privacy or

 | DOI:10.1163/9789004682900_028

make use of personal data without consent. This requires paying considerable attention to data protection and security. Additionally, users should have a reasonable degree of control over how their personal data are acquired, used, and stored. The development and use of AI should also be sensitive to people's personal identity, including one's appearance, voice, and other individual features that could be used for undesirable purposes (e.g., manipulation or deception).

A2.4 Responsibility

Developers should strive to create AI systems in a way that does not diminish human responsibility for the actions taken by the system. Although AI systems are becoming increasingly autonomous, the responsibility for their actions should always rest with human beings. Systems that have the potential to create so-called "responsibility gaps" either should require human input for any morally or legally significant decisions or should not be developed in the first place. The attribution of responsibility to AI systems is largely recognized as dangerous and is not in compliance with existing international and domestic laws. AI systems should also be developed in a way that will not needlessly obscure the attribution of responsibility to different human stakeholders and that will, if possible, clarify it instead.

A2.5 Transparency and Explainability

Whenever possible, the inputs and outputs of AI systems should be made transparent and traceable in order to ensure high explainability of AI decision making. Knowing how a system arrived at its decision is the key to diagnosing faulty decisions and investigating accidents. It is also important to enable the public to understand why specific AI decisions are made (especially sensitive ones, such as those concerning employment or medical treatment), how AI systems operate in general, and their limitations. When transparent AI is not possible, developers should be aware of potential hazards (e.g., machine bias in AI systems based on deep learning) and take them into consideration.

A2.6 Fairness, Equity, and Non-discrimination

Developers should strive to create AI systems that function fairly and are free of bias. The development and use of AI systems should foster social equity, solidarity, and human rights rather than being detrimental to them. This requires paying close attention to the impact of different AI applications on various areas of human activity and the job market in order to facilitate fair distribution of benefits attained through the use of AI. It also requires attention to the applications' impact on different groups of people while giving fair consideration to the interests of all parties affected. AI systems should not perpetuate or exacerbate already existing social biases, prejudices, and stereotypes.

A2.7 Diversity and Inclusion

AI development and use should be an inclusive and diverse undertaking, sensitive to cultural, social, and other differences relevant to AI applications. In the development process, the impact of AI systems on vulnerable groups should receive particular consideration. Additionally, it is important to pay close attention to how AI is used and perceived in different cultures and societies, and to how various ways of developing it would affect different groups of people. AI development should be especially sensitive to the needs of disadvantaged and marginalized groups, as well as to those of developing countries, so as to reduce rather than increase the already existing disparities.

A2.8 Integration and Collaboration

Interconnectivity and interoperability of AI systems, as well as international collaboration, communication, and exchange of information, should be promoted in order to enhance progress in the development and use of AI systems across the globe. International collaboration and integration of AI systems serve to achieve the goals of AI at the global level, promote trust and openness among researchers and developers, and provide a more efficient way to solve the many problems related to AI development. Establishing global AI governance may help in achieving these goals and in preventing so-called "ethics washing."

A2.9 Caution

AI systems should be developed with a great degree of caution and prudence to ensure their safe functioning. Developers should attempt to anticipate the risks, loopholes, and uncertainties associated with AI systems so as to minimize the likelihood of unintended negative outcomes. It is particularly important to bear in mind the possibility of dual use, to consider the long-term effects of AI systems (both inside and outside their immediate domains of application), and to find sustainable solutions to related problems. AI systems should be subjected to strict testing, standardization, and regulation.

A2.10 Security and Robustness

AI systems should be developed to be secure and reliable. To the extent possible, they should be protected from accidents, misuse, access by unauthorized third parties, to prevent hacking, data leaks, or other forms of attacks. Although the systems should normally perform their intended functions reliably and accurately, they should also come with safeguards against misuse, abuse, and malfunction.

APPENDIX 3

Guidelines for Improvement of Lawyers' Qualifications

Julija Kiršienė, Edita Gruodytė, Aušrinė Pasvenskienė and Paulius Astromskis

1. Technology is a permanent structural change, leading to unprecedented legal challenges.
2. The practice of law will require fewer general support staff members, junior lawyers, and generalists, and more lawyers with a new generation of interdisciplinary legal training, technology-related skills and knowledge. The new generation is also likely to bring more hybrid professions.
3. Entrepreneurial spirit, curiosity, creativity, and strategic thinking skills should assume far more significance in the education and recruitment of future lawyers.
4. Other skills and areas of knowledge likely to be of increasing importance for the graduate of the future include technology; practice-related skills (e.g., collaboration, advocacy, and negotiation); business skills such as basic accounting and finance; project management; international and cross-border law; interdisciplinary experience; resilience, flexibility, and ability to adapt to change.
5. Law schools may be able to best improve their curriculum to prepare law students for today's practice environment by including more diverse experiential learning; preparing students for transactional practice; focusing on the business side of law; exposing students to legal processes and case management requirements; emphasizing interpersonal and advocacy skills; and requiring proficiency with legal technologies.
6. Law schools need to expand the mandatory curriculum beyond fields of substantive law by offering an additional course introducing case management processes and legal technology.
7. More specific legal technology skills (such as database management, statistics, analytics, and digital communications) can be taught in electives and clinics throughout the course of the law degree.
8. Executive education programs can further foster ongoing learning by focusing on holistic legal project management, as well as on legal technology literacy.

 | DOI:10.1163/9789004682900_029

9. When modeling the optimal law and technology program, the variables of (a) complexity of technological progress, (b) knowledge and skills, (c) student benefits, and (d) teachers and students should be within the main scope of inquiry.
10. Identifying the gaps in current legal education, methods of infusing technology-related outcomes throughout the curriculum, and disseminating best practices and optimal architecture for law and technologies study programs, among other issues, form an important interdisciplinary research agenda for legal education's future.
11. Comprehensive national and institutional strategies and policies addressing the complexity of various opportunities and challenges that digital technologies bring to education must be in place.
12. More complex digital technologies, such as AI-powered tools, require special attention, and their potential together with possible risks should be addressed within national and institutional strategies and policies on digital technologies in education.
13. Collaboration among various stakeholders (the state, education institutions, teachers, students, parents, businesses) is crucial to recognize the needs and interests digital technologies must adhere to and help to achieve.
14. Skilled and confident teachers should be a priority; digital technologies must serve teachers and should not burden them in the exercise of their educational mission.
15. Digital technologies should be used to foster quality in teaching and learning.
16. The use of digital technologies for teaching and learning should complement the acquisition of other necessary and uniquely human skills.
17. Teaching and learning of digital technologies should continue through all phases of life.
18. Instruction in the effective and responsible use of digital technologies must form a part of education.
19. The possible effects of digital technology on learners' fundamental rights must be understood, evaluated, and recognized at all stages.
20. In view of the continuous changes in digital technologies, constant monitoring and evaluation of their application in and for education must be ensured.

Index

Printed in the United States
by Baker & Taylor Publisher Services